# MYTH, LITERATURE, AND THE UNCONSCIOUS

# MYTH, LITERATURE, AND THE UNCONSCIOUS

*Edited by*

*Leon Burnett, Sanja Bahun, and Roderick Main*

Routledge
Taylor & Francis Group
LONDON AND NEW YORK

First published 2013 by
Karnac Books Ltd.

Published 2018 by Routledge
2 Park Square, Milton Park, Abingdon, Oxon OX14 4RN
711 Third Avenue, New York, NY 10017, USA

*Routledge is an imprint of the Taylor & Francis Group, an informa business*



British Library Cataloguing in Publication Data

A C.I.P. for this book is available from the British Library

ISBN-13: 9781782200024 (pbk)

Typeset by V Publishing Solutions Pvt Ltd., Chennai, India

# *CONTENTS*

## PART II: OEDIPUS RECONSIDERED



## PART III: THEORISING MYTH AND THE UNCONSCIOUS



## PART IV: READINGS IN MYTH AND THE IMAGINARY

# *ABOUT THE EDITORS AND CONTRIBUTORS*

**Sanja Bahun**, PhD, is Senior Lecturer in the Department of Literature, Film, and Theatre Studies, University of Essex. She has authored *Modernism and Melancholia: Writing as Countermourning* (2013) and edited *Violence and Gender in the Globalized World: The Intimate and the Extimate* (2008), *From Word to Canvas: Appropriations of Myth in Women's Aesthetic Production* (2009), *Myth and Violence in the Contemporary Female Text: New Cassandras* (2011), and *Language, Ideology, and the Human: New Interventions* (2012).

**Saugata Bhaduri**, PhD, is Professor and Chairperson at the Centre for English Studies, Jawaharlal Nehru University, New Delhi, India. His diverse areas of research interest include contemporary literary and cultural theory, Indian and Western philosophy, folklore and popular culture studies, and translation and comparative literature studies. Some of his recent books are *Literary Theory: An Introductory Reader* (2010), *Perspectives on Comparative Literature in the Age of Globalization* (2010), *Translating Power* (2008), *Negotiating "Glocalization"* (2008), and *Les Yogasutras de Patanjali* (2008).

**Paul Bishop**, PhD, is Professor of German at the University of Glasgow. He is the author of various works on German and European literature and thought, including *The Dionysian Self* (1995), *Synchronicity and Intellectual Intuition* (2000), and *Analytical Psychology & German Classical Aesthetics* (2007–2008), and editor of *Jung in Contexts* (1999) and *The Archaic* (2012).

**Leon Burnett**, PhD, is Reader in Literature and Director of the Centre for Myth Studies at the University of Essex. He has edited *F. M. Dostoevsky (1821–1881): A Centenary Collection* (1981), *Word in Time: Poetry, Narrative, Translation* (1997), and *The Art of Accommodation: Literary Translation in Russia* (2013). From 1992 to 2000 he edited *New Comparison: A Journal of Comparative and General Literary Studies.*

**Paul Cantz**, PsyD, ABPP, is Clinical Assistant Professor of Psychology in the Department of Psychiatry at the University of Illinois at Chicago (UIC) College of Medicine and Associate Director of Training/Assistant Professor at the Adler School of Professional Psychology, Chicago, IL. His most recent publications include "Cross cultural reflections on the feminine 'Other': Hebraism and Hellenism redux" in: *Pastoral Psychology* (2013) and "A psychodynamic inquiry into the spiritually-evocative potential of music" in: *International Forum of Psychoanalysis* (2013).

**Lyndon Davies** is a poet, reviewer and essayist living in Powys, UK. He has published two collections of poetry, *Hyphasis* (2006) and *Shield* (2010). He co-runs the Glasfryn Seminars, a series of literary discussion groups, and a yearly festival of innovative poetry, The Hay Poetry Jamboree.

**Roderick Main**, PhD, is Professor in the Centre for Psychoanalytic Studies, University of Essex. He is the author of *The Rupture of Time: Synchronicity and Jung's Critique of Modern Western Culture* (2004) and *Revelations of Chance: Synchronicity as Spiritual Experience* (2007) and the editor of *Jung on Synchronicity and the Paranormal* (1997).

**Eric Rhode** is a child psychotherapist, independent scholar, and former broadcaster on film and the arts. He is the author of *Tower of Babel* (1967), *A History of the Cinema from Its Origins to 1970* (1976), *On Birth & Madness* (1987), *The Generations of Adam* (1990), *Psychotic Metaphysics* (1994), *On Hallucination, Intuition, and the Becoming of "O"* (1998), *Plato's Silence* (2003), *Notes on the Aniconic* (2003), and *Axis Mundi* (2008).

**Robert Segal**, PhD, is Sixth Century Chair in Religious Studies at the University of Aberdeen. He is the author of *The Poimandres as*

*Myth: Scholarly Theory and Gnostic Meaning* (1986), *Joseph Campbell: An Introduction* (1987, 1990, 1997), *Religion and the Social Sciences: Essays on the Confrontation* (1989), *Explaining and Interpreting Religion: Essays on the Issue* (1992), *Theorizing about Myth* (1999), and *Myth: A Very Short Introduction* (2004), and the editor of *The Gnostic Jung* (1992), *Jung on Mythology* (1998), *The Myth and Ritual Theory* (1998), *Hero Myths* (2000), *The Blackwell Companion to the Study of Religion* (2006), *Myth: Critical Concepts* (2007), and *The Hero's Quest* (co-edited, 2013).

**Angie Voela**, PhD, is Senior Lecturer (Associate Professor) of Psychosocial Studies in the School of Law and Social Sciences, University of East London. Her recent publications include "In the Name of the Father—or not: individual and society in popular culture, Deleuzian theory, and Lacanian psychoanalysis" in: *Psychoanalysis, Culture and Society* (2011) and "Heterotopia revisited: Foucault and Lacan on feminine subjectivity" in: *Subjectivity* (2010).

**Janet A. Walker**, PhD, is Professor of Comparative Literature at Rutgers University, US. She is the author of *The Japanese Novel of the Meiji Period and the Ideal of Individualism* (1979). Her recent publications include "Van Gogh, collector of 'Japan'" in: *The Comparatist* (2008) and "Reading the postcolonial diasporic novel as picaresque: Bharati Mukherjee's *Jasmine* and Radhika Jha's *Smell*" in: *Home and the World: South Asia in Transition* (2006).

**Steven F. Walker**, PhD, is Professor of Comparative Literature at Rutgers University, US. He is the author of *Jung and the Jungians on Myth* (1995, 2002), *A Cure for Love: a Generic Study of the Pastoral Idyll* (1987), *Theocritus* (1980), and *Midlife Transformation in Modern Literature and Film: Jungian and Eriksonian Perspectives* (2012). His other recent publications include "Borderline personality disorder and the enigma of *Tartuffe*" in: *Quadrant* (2010) and "Nabokov's *Lolita* and Goethe's *Faust*: the ghost in the novel" in: *Comparative Literature Studies* (2009).

**Jason Whittaker**, PhD, is Professor of Blake Studies and Head of the Department of Writing at University College Falmouth. He is the co-author of *Radical Blake: Influence and Afterlife from 1827* (with Shirley Dent, 2002) and *William Blake and the Digital Humanities* (with Roger Whitson, 2013), and the editor of *Blake, Modernity and Popular Culture* (2007) and *Blake 2.0: William Blake and Twentieth Century Art, Music and Culture* (2012).

# INTRODUCTION

Leon Burnett

In his prefatory remarks to *Athene: Virgin and Mother in Greek Religion*, Karl Kerényi introduces a striking metaphor. He describes human beings as the fabric of the gods. The gods "exist only in the material which has been woven from human beings themselves and from their surrounding world" (Kerényi, 1978, p. 8). The material, understood as clothing, is woven from human beings, not by them. The gods themselves are impenetrable or, as we might say, in a play on words, what constitutes their divinity cannot be divined. Instead, Kerényi proposes, we are obliged to turn to the human fabric, which is "more analyzable" (ibid.).

> A Greek God comes to us in such manifold forms, from so many places, out of so many levels of past human life, that we must first of all assemble him as we would a heap of collected bones. (Kerényi, 1978, p. 8)

The investigations in this volume share a common interest in the ubiquitous body of myth—in its manifold forms and in its persistence in many cultures, including, but not limited to, the Greek. The emphasis that Kerényi places on fabric, analysis and, above all, assembly accords well with the work that appears here, written by scholars of international standing in literature and psychoanalysis and for whom text, mind, and coherence are paramount concerns. Taken together, the chapters in *Myth, Literature, and the Unconscious* position myth as an area of study in its own right, unified by a creative tension in which the interests of distinct disciplines that focus on fantasia and fable, on ritual and archetype, on quest and sacrifice, on religion and community, on nature and culture, and on attitudes to death and love, converge.

It is a futile enterprise to attempt to arrive at an exhaustive and circumscribed definition of the meaning of myth or to establish how pervasive and powerful its presence is in the contemporary world. It is as vain an endeavour as trying to pin down what time, love, or consciousness means to any one individual. Opinions differ; perspectives shift and shimmer. While inconclusive debates go on, myth continues to exercise its fascination, impose its own order, and offer a gateway to the numinous (a category in which time, love, and consciousness are all included), as it answers to an inner imperative to adapt to change and circumstance. Myth, in short, has a life of its own. It is with this life that the essays included in the book engage, each of them showing a concern to set out in appropriate terms its own carefully delineated approach to the topic in hand.

Myths are closely allied to texts and the two are often conflated, but writing about myth, the telling and retelling of what might otherwise remain unintelligible, is, as Kerényi would have us realise, an act of mythology, and is, therefore, one of the "manifold forms" by which myth is made known. The mythological text as its etymology from the Latin *textus* acknowledges, is woven, woven from material that may speak of the ineffable, but which itself is articulate, just as the accounts that we have of the Eleusinian, the Isiac, or the Orphic Mysteries give an indication of rites and practices but are not the mysteries themselves. Words, in this respect, always remain profanities. The same may be said of the representation of any mythic occurrence. When, for example, the persona in Keats's ode, viewing the depiction of a mythic scene, addresses the Grecian urn and exclaims "Thou, silent form, dost tease us out of thought / As doth eternity" (Keats, 1978, p. 373), he not only enters into a dialectic central to the essence of myth, but he also calls upon the master trope of weaving. The act of teasing signifies both vexation and pleasure in Keats's usage, for to tease is to vex as any puzzle does, but, like a puzzle, teasing so absorbs the mind that it becomes a pleasurable means of transcending the original enigma. Yet it also incorporates, metaphorically, an earlier, but now secondary, meaning of separating the fibres (of wool etc.) preparatory to spinning. If myths have the capacity to tease us out of thought, then the essays in this collection respond, in the second sense of the verb, by seeking to tease us back into thought through an examination, interrogation, and interpretation of mythological texts of all kinds that unravel the mysterious workings of the eternal verities they contain.

Keats's line ("Thou, silent form, dost tease us out of thought") alludes, of course, to the unconscious mind, an area of interest subsequently taken up and explored by psychoanalysts. A psychoanalytic approach to the unconscious (which by the twentieth century had become a noun and intermittently acquired a leading majuscule) occupies the contributors to this volume. Myth and literature have been interwoven with psychoanalysis since Sigmund Freud's celebrated use in *The Interpretation of Dreams* of Sophocles' telling of the fate of Oedipus (Freud, 1900a, pp. 261–263). This alliance is not surprising, for, like myth and literature, psychoanalysis is largely about narratives of that which cannot be approached more closely or conveyed more vividly by other means, and in psychoanalysis, as in myth and literature, the stories told are often carried by and imbued with metaphor and other tropes. In turn, psychoanalysis, in its various guises, has contributed substantially to the understanding of creative work and, in particular, literature and literary language. It also quickly demonstrated itself to be one of the most powerful tools for the interpretation of myths, and with its assumption that myths are essentially about the innermost depths of the human mind gave fresh impetus and urgency to the contemporary study of these ancient tales. If, in the heady early days of psychoanalytic discovery, there was a tendency to use theories of the unconscious as master narratives into which the exotic content of myths could be translated without remainder and thereby domesticated for the modern mind, recent theorising is more likely to recognise an analogical relationship and reciprocal influence between the two disciplines, with psychoanalysis readier to learn from, as well as to interpret myths and their literary treatments (Sels, 2011). Indeed, this was implicit in the originative approaches of both Freud and Carl Gustav Jung, each of whom, in candid moments, acknowledged that psychoanalysis could not subsume myth and may even itself be a form of mythology. Wrote Freud in 1933: "The theory of the instincts is so to say our mythology. Instincts are mythical entities magnificent in their indefiniteness" (Freud, 1933a, p. 95). Wrote Jung in 1940: "Even the best attempts at explanation are only more or less successful translations into another metaphorical language ... The most we can do is to *dream the myth onwards* and give it a modern dress" (Jung, 1940, par. 271).

Anthony Stevens, at the start of *Ariadne's Clue*, refers to the "vast array of cultural information that anthropology, history, and psychology have amassed" from the study of symbols (Stevens, 1998, p. 3). Indebted to the pioneering work of Freud in uncovering the pathological relationship between myths and dreams and of Jung in exposing the role of myth in understanding the archetypal basis of the collective unconscious, later researchers into the unconscious have taken the fundamental insights of the founding fathers of psychoanalysis in different, and sometimes contrary, directions (see, e.g., Merkur, 2005; Walker, 1995). The title of Stevens' book, as he explains, is drawn from the Greek myth concerning the great labyrinth at Knossos, the site of Ariadne's extreme distress and her timely rescue by Theseus, who was aided by a clew, or ball of thread (Stevens, 1998, p. 3). Theseus's "daring expedition", Stevens remarks, "resembles the journey of other heroes such as Orpheus and Aeneas into the Underworld, the realm of dead ancestors and the unconscious" (ibid., p. 4). Already, we can see in this brief comment, how individual adventures (or "mythologems" as Kerényi preferred to call them) tend to cohere in mythology as their common elements are perceived and aggregated.

Although Theseus, Orpheus, and Aeneas all belong to Greco-Roman mythology, it is possible to find the same symbols and structures in evidence in other cultures. Indeed, that is the next step that Stevens takes in noting how weaving has "acquired world-wide religious and ritual significance". In the Upanishads, he observes,

> The thread (*sutra*) is described as linking "this world to the other world and all beings". The thread is both *atman* (self) and *prana* (breath) and is linked to the central point in the cosmos, the sun. It is written that the thread must "in all things be followed back to its source" .... The thread, therefore, may be understood as an archetypal symbol of the life principle stretching through time as a means of conscious orientation and a guide to understanding. (Stevens, 1998, p. 4)

There are links within myths, links across myths, and links that comparative mythology and interdisciplinary scholarship establish. These are the threads that clothe the gods and thus make the invisible visible. The threads are woven from the ideas, the images, and the words of human beings and from the external world that surrounds them and composes their souls—and the world soul, the *anima mundi*.

Myth, in this sense, accounts for the world, but equally the world in its own right is called to account for myth. Its account is a matter of articulation, establishing the kind of assembly and coherence which Heraclitus referred to as the logos—the unifying principle. This unifying principle, however, when understood as the law of transformation is also what defines mythos. Mythos and logos come together in "mythology", a word denoting a body of myths but also a study of myths. The chapters in this book belong in the latter category. If the god at the centre of the myth is likened to a heap of bones, as noted earlier in this introduction, then the essays in *Myth, Literature, and the Unconscious* may be said to be engaged in the scholarly exposition of the skeletal items, which have been collected, sorted, assembled, and finally clothed.

The remainder of this introduction offers a summary of the chapters and a rationale for the organisation of the work into five parts.

The first part consists of two wide-ranging chapters that set the context for the whole collection in their breadth of reference and historical scope. Each of these chapters argues strongly for the cross-temporal relevance of myth and mythic stories, and charts their continuous interaction with the realms of the intrasubjective (psychic) and the intersubjective (group behaviour).

In "Apocalypse, transformation, and scapegoating: moving myth into the twenty-first century", Steven Walker offers a detailed examination of myths that involve apocalypse and scapegoats, from their ancient sources to their socio-political relevance in our time. He observes that, for better and for worse, myth has been a powerful force for change in the past and will continue to be so in the future. He contends that intellectuals need to grapple with the emotional force of myth, and also to contextualize it in terms of its intrapsychic impact as well as its social force of persuasion. Walker notes that myths involving apocalypse and scapegoating are among those that are potentially the most dangerous in our time, and dealing with them judiciously involves knowing how to submit to their archetypal emotional force before moving on to rational analysis. The chapter uses the framework of Jungian depth psychology to show how in a diverse range of texts—from Peter Weir's film *The Last Wave* to the *Bhagavad Gita* to Robert Louis Stevenson's *Dr. Jekyll and Mr. Hyde*—the themes of apocalypse and scapegoating can be contextualised in terms of the need for radical personal transformation.

Jason Whittaker's "The divine image: remaking Blake's myths" reviews the influence of William Blake's exercise in personal mythography from the visionary poet's rediscovery by the Pre-Raphaelites to his more extensive rehabilitation in the twentieth century when his mythmaking was established as a credible alternative to inherited orders of thought. The chapter looks at four literary-artistic figures who used Blake's mythic writings as a starting point for their own probing of social and psychological conditions. The poet W. B. Yeats and the artist Austin Osman Spare are shown to be interested in occult applications of Blake, often against the original artist's explicit intentions, the former seeking a theosophical account of the universe, the latter exploring practical applications of psychomancy. It is argued that some of their insights were shared by Angela Carter and J. G. Ballard, though the often nightmarish universes that the writings of these two invoke are motivated by a different impetus, namely, Blake's concepts of energy and his non-linear imagination. The chapter concludes by focusing on Blake's influence as a practice rather than a set of texts or allusions, whereby the artist seeks ways to view this world from multiple perspectives rather than a single vision.

Part II presents a series of three essays that prompt a revaluation of the centrality of the Oedipus myth. By focusing on what is arguably one of the most widely discussed, most frequently replicated, and most fervently engaged myths in our cultural history, this part is emblematic of a central objective of the volume: it exemplifies the study, and underlines the very necessity, of the interlinked consideration of literature, myth, and the unconscious.

Saugata Bhaduri's "The Yayāti complex: a contra-oedipal take on myth and the unconscious" juxtaposes the classical Greek account of Oedipus and its Freudian interpretation with the "reverse" mythic narrative of Yayāti and postulations about the unconscious found in classical Indian sources. Bhaduri argues that the well-known classical Indian myth of Yayāti (as originally narrated in the *Mahābhārata* and followed up in other sources like the *Bhāgavata-purāṇa*, *Viṣṇu-purāṇa* and *Harivamśa*) provides an interesting counterpoint to the Oedipus myth. Unlike the latter, where the son has to kill the father in a foretold game of contested sexuality, Yayāti's is the reverse story of a son's sacrifice of his own youth and sexual prowess for his father. Bearing in mind the connection established in psychoanalysis between the Oedipus myth and the unconscious, this chapter reads the reverse myth of Yayāti and the related postulations on the unconscious in classical Indian literary and philosophical sources to ask whether the relationship between mythology and the unconscious can be otherwise than oedipal—whether, in fact, a case may be made for a Yayāti complex.

Paul Cantz's chapter, "The slaughter of Isaac: oedipal themes in the Akedah narrative revisited", addresses the complementary relationship between the Oedipus myth and the mythic story of the binding of Isaac in Genesis 22 (the "Akedah"). It has been suggested in the critical literature that the Biblical account of the binding of Isaac represents the Jewish adaptation of the Oedipus myth, with some authors maintaining that the Biblical narrative communicates a culturally based message about psycho-moral evolution of our instinctual drives. By taking into account the counter-scriptural rabbinic traditions that emphasise the actual slaughter and subsequent resurrection of Isaac at the hands of Abraham, this chapter demonstrates the complementary relationship that these two cultural legends share. Here, the ancient Greek mythological-literary accounts of Oedipus and the texts of the counter-scriptural rabbinic traditions highlight the uncomfortably stubborn schematics of our instinctual/archetypical heritage, while the hopeful Biblical narrative reveals the potential for instinctual transcendence. To support this hypothesis, psychoanalytical, anthropological, archaeological, artistic, and theological elements of the stories, as well as their practical use, are all considered.

Angie Voela's chapter has Oedipus meet Ahab in popular culture, exploring through these mythic templates the notions of fate, human agency, event, and truth. "From Oedipus to Ahab (and back): myth and psychoanalysis in science fiction" offers a reading of the popular novel and television series *Flashforward*, in which an unpredictable complication in a physics experiment produces a glimpse of the future for millions of people and raises questions about the limits of scientific knowledge, predetermination, and free will, the human ability to alter the future, and the extent to which fate is ineluctable. Two overt references are made, one to the ancient Greek myth of Oedipus, and the other to Captain Ahab, the monomaniacal protagonist of Herman Melville's *Moby-Dick*. Where Oedipus meets Ahab, Freudian and

Lacanian psychoanalysis meet Deleuze and Guattari, for whom Captain Ahab stands as the antipode of the tired psychoanalytic figure. This chapter explores the limits of the myth of Oedipus and the range of its metamorphoses that strengthen or weaken its explanatory value in contemporary theory and culture by focusing on the notions of fate, human agency, event, and truth as represented in popular culture. The paper revisits both the Deleuzian arguments for dismissing Oedipus, and the attempts in the Freudian field, by Žižek, to undermine the Deleuzian argument and, by Flieger, to modernise Oedipus by transforming him into a contemporary "Argonaut".

The three chapters in the third part of the volume focus on the relationship between myth and psychoanalysis / depth psychology. The first of these looks at how Freudian and Jungian approaches to myth, despite their important differences, are even more strikingly similar in the way they both seek to differentiate themselves from nineteenth-century approaches; the second, employing findings in object relations theory and anthropology, examines the mythic and psychoanalytic importance of the equation of nourishment, dreaming, and visionary thought; and the third presents a textual and contextual analysis of Jung's writings on synchronicity in order to demonstrate how they support the author's mythopoeic thinking in his attempt to "re-enchant" the modern world.

Robert Segal's "Freudian and Jungian approaches to myth: the similarities" argues that the theories of both Freud and Jung epitomise twentieth-century approaches to myth in denying that myths are the now superseded primitive counterpart to science. For both psychologists, myths are neither literally nor allegorically about the external world, which they do not help either to explain or to manipulate, but are really about the unconscious mind, which they help to encounter. While Freud and Jung may disagree in their particular models of the unconscious mind, they are alike in interpreting myths psychologically, in being primarily concerned to distinguish their approaches from those of such representative nineteenth-century theorists as the "nature mythologists" Edward Tylor and James Frazer, and in viewing myths, whether positively or negatively valued, as compatible with science.

Eric Rhode advances the claim that there is a strong component of what could be called "concrete thought", or what Wilfred Bion has termed "beta thinking", in mythopoeia, similar to that of dream or poetry. "The boy who had dreams in his mouth" focuses on one of Jean Piaget's patients, a certain child, a poet in the making, who claimed that he dreamt in his mouth. With reference to anthropological research and drawing on psychoanalytic theory, the chapter explores the concrete equation of nourishment and dreaming, and of mouth and certain mouth-like apertures such as mountain caves that have been believed to be propitious to visionary thought.

In "Myth, synchronicity, and re-enchantment", Roderick Main proposes that Jung's writings on myth and mythopoeia can be seen as part of an attempt to re-enchant the modern world, but that the success of his attempt was limited so long as he perceived myth solely in terms of the projection of intrapsychic, albeit archetypal, contents. Yet, as Main observes, with the theory of synchronicity, developed late in his life, Jung felt able to postulate a parallelism and acausal connectedness between inner and outer events that allowed him to find mythic motifs not only in the mind but also in external situations and events. The chapter examines the implications of synchronicity for Jung's theory of myth and his interest in mythopoeia, and their joint relationship with Jung's overarching project of re-enchantment.

As a complement to Part III, the two chapters in Part IV focus on the relationship between literature and myth, and provide detailed analyses of specific literary treatments of mythic motifs: a Japanese gothic story by Akinari Ueda as a depiction of the Jungian process of encountering the world of the spirits and the appeal of the sphinx for Théophile Gautier, serving as a symbol for what is most unfathomable or inexpressible in the human psyche.

In "The confrontation with the anima in Akinari Ueda's story 'Jasei no in' ('The lust of the serpent', 1776)", Janet A. Walker focuses on Akinari Ueda's famous Gothic story "The lust of the serpent" (*Tales of Moonlight and Rain*, 1776). In this reading, the orientation of Ueda's story is seen as derived from an expression of the fear, similar to that noted by Jung in reference to "modern European man", that modern, rational Japanese man was losing contact with "the world of the spirits". The story is interpreted as a depiction of a male encounter with this world of the spirits, in the form of a serpent-woman, and of an objectivisation of the anima that finally enables him to attain to self-culture. While the author firmly situates the story in an East Asian philosophical-mythological, psychological, and literary context, she also argues that the story shares with the Jungian, "Western", project a sense of the importance of separating the inner and outer worlds for the psychic harmony of the individual and of society as a whole.

Leon Burnett discusses the hybrid nature of the sphinx: in form part-human, part-beast; in provenance part-Egyptian, part-Greek; and in essence part-knowable (as riddle) and part-unknowable (as enigma). "Sorrow and surprise: a reading of Théophile Gautier's sphinx complex" explores the appeal of the mythological creature for the French poet, prose-writer, and art critic, who occupies a seminal position in modern figurations of the sphinx as a mythical correlative for what is most unfathomable in the human psyche. Following a brief survey of representations of the sphinx in the French author's writing, the chapter offers a detailed reading of Gautier's review of paintings by Théodore Chassériau, which belong to the artist's "Greco-Asiatic cycle", in order to demonstrate the pervasive presence of a well-defined "sphinx complex" that informed the writer's aesthetic stance.

While engaging all three facets of the volume, the discussions in the previous two parts are governed in the main by psychoanalysis and literature, respectively. Part V foregrounds myth. To this end, the concluding part of the volume takes a single—paradigmatic—myth, and offers, in its two chapters, radically contrasting accounts of the modern reception of Orpheus. Illuminating one of the most influential and most unsettling myths about creativity, this part indirectly summons all the major themes and implications of the volume to underscore the openness and cross-historical productivity of myth.

"From the archaic into the aesthetic: myth and literature in the 'Orphic' Goethe" examines the intellectual background to Goethe's late poem, "Primal words. Orphic", in the light of his involvement with the early nineteenth-century debate about myth and, in particular, ancient Orphic teaching. As Paul Bishop points out, Goethe's interest in neo-Platonism is well documented, particularly as mediated through the work of Plotinus. At first glance, his poem looks like a series of neo-Platonic initiatory invocations, leading the reader from a daimonic world, via a process of transformation, to a loving encounter with the ineffable One, but, as Goethe's subsequent notes on the poem make clear, this initiation can also be understood in a psychological and existential sense. Bishop demonstrates how, as a consequence, the poem takes us beyond the neo-Platonic framework to a consideration of the dialectical relation between freedom and necessity and of the possibility of transcending time and space.

Lyndon Davies asks, in "Orpheus. Eurydice. Blanchot: some thoughts on the nature of myth and literature", what it is about the myth of

Orpheus that makes it still resonate and impact on our understanding of the unconscious and on creativity. The chapter acknowledges Orpheus as the archetypal poet (or artist or musician), a celebrant and a mediator, but also as the one who breaks the bonds and breaches the limits. As Davies states, the myth of Orpheus and Eurydice is a staple of Western European culture, a thematic and symbolic resource for writers, craftspeople, and artists in every age and genre. Destruction, pain, and loss are interwoven with charm, potency, and sensuous delight in this mythic figure. The final chapter of the collection considers what it is it about this myth that makes it so enduringly appealing, constantly renewing our understanding of the unconscious and of creativity. It probes the implications of Maurice Blanchot's extraordinary essay "The Gaze of Orpheus", which claims that Orpheus risks everything that is sacred to his art for an outcome that is beyond his comprehension. This essay, the author argues, is about writing, but it is also about the very nature of myth and literature, and the inextricable link between these two and the unconscious.

## References

Freud, S. (1900a). *The Interpretation of Dreams. S. E. 4, 5.* London: Hogarth.

Freud, S. (1933a). *New Introductory Lectures on Psycho-Analysis. S. E.* 22: 1–182. London: Hogarth.

Jung, C. G. (1940). The psychology of the child archetype. In: *C. W., 9i,* (2nd ed.): pp. 149–181/pars. 259–305. London: Routledge & Kegan Paul, 1968.

Keats, J. (1978). *The Poems of John Keats.* Jack Stillinger (Ed.). London: Heinemann.

Kerényi, K. (1978). *Athene: Virgin and Mother in Greek Religion.* Murray Stein (Trans.). Woodstock, CN: Spring.

Merkur, D. (2005). *Psychoanalytic Approaches to Myth: Freud and the Freudians.* New York: Routledge.

Sels, N. (2011). Myth, mind and metaphor: on the relation of mythology and psychoanalysis. *S: Journal of the Jan van Eyck Circle for Lacanian Ideology Critique,* 4: 56–70.

Stevens, A. (1998). *Ariadne's Clue: The Symbols of Humankind.* Princeton, NJ: Princeton University Press.

Walker, S. (1995). *Jung and the Jungians on Myth: An Introduction.* New York: Garland.

# PART I

## MYTH IN THE MODERN WORLD

CHAPTER ONE

# Apocalypse, transformation, and scapegoating: moving myth into the twenty-first century

*Steven F. Walker*

"Emotion" is a word that tends to put intellectuals off. However, to deal intellectually with myths one must also engage with their emotional effect—not just on the mind of the masses, but on one's own highly educated mind. In Jungian terms, whenever an archetype or archetypal pattern is constellated—whenever it is activated in the unconscious—the conscious response to it involves strong emotion. To sidestep this emotional response is to short-circuit the process of coming to terms adequately with the power of the myth. Unfortunately, it is at the moment of emotional response that intellectuals tend to sidestep the emotional response in favour of a mainly rational and even hyper-rational conceptual discourse. That is, I believe, a mistake, because, although emotional response can lead to emotional thinking, emotional thinking is a necessary step in the direction of rational thinking, at least in regard to the analysis and understanding of powerful myths. Emotional thinking, like emotion itself, may be confusing and disturbing to the rational mind, but it provides access to unconscious material that the rational mind can then assimilate and analyse.

The myth of the Apocalypse is a case in point: a magnificent evocation of cosmic destruction leading to world renewal, whose emotional power possessed the mind of John of Patmos completely and, as we shall see, wound up half-possessing the mind of D. H. Lawrence almost two thousand years later. Edward F. Edinger has argued in his wonderful book *Archetype of the Apocalypse* (1999) that the apocalypse myth represents an archetypal power at work in the depths of the individual psyche that also has a world-historical dimension, expressing itself not only in terms of an ordeal of inner psychological evolution and change but also in the bloody political and social antagonisms that continue to afflict the modern world. In my opinion, however, coming to terms with the power of this myth involves first submitting to its emotional power, and only then divesting it of its enchanting and alluring cosmic, or theological, or world-historical, dimensions in order to reconfigure its significance as the projection of archetypal contents of the psyche onto the screen of the world. Thus I cannot follow Edinger in ascribing to the archetype of the apocalypse, powerful as it is in terms of the fate of the individual, any power whatsoever over the fate of the world. More generally, attributing to the collective unconscious any type of world-historical agency that in the past was attributed to the gods, to God, or to the dialectic, is not a step I am willing to take.

But, assuming that the myth of the apocalypse represents a dimension of the human potential inscribed in the archetypal depths of the psyche, what human potential does the myth of the apocalypse have as its ultimate referent? I shall argue that it is the potential for psychic transformation. The final scene of Peter Weir's 1977 film *The Last Wave* provides a good example of the inner workings of this archetype. In the course of the film the Sydney corporate tax lawyer David Burton (Richard Chamberlain) has been drawn inexorably into the world of Australian aborigine tribal culture, and has left his family and career behind in order to discover for himself who he really is. He eventually finds his new identity expressed in terms of a transformational image of a tribal shaman figure. His midlife spiritual initiation drama ends as he struggles to emerge from the anguish of initiatory transformation in the darkness of the Sydney sewer system into the early morning light of a nearby beach. In terms of the film's apocalyptic theme, what David sees rushing towards him is the "last wave" that he has been led to imagine will destroy the world, or at least the Aussie world as he knows it, a familiar world of barbies and wine and corporate comfort. But that is not what actually happens next. After David, kneeling in the gentle surf, washes his eyes—cleans the doors of perception—with the salt water of purification, he looks out, and the camera focuses on a beautiful, but deliberately unrealistic image of a huge wave about to engulf him. At that moment David looks down and closes his eyes. At the end of a film that up to this point has catered to the popular audience's taste for apocalyptic fantasies, the director has given the intellectual part of his audience a point to ponder: that the Last Wave may not be a cosmic happening, but rather a powerful intrapsychic fantasy. David Burton sees the Wave inside himself, not outside himself. The suggestion is clearly made that it is he who is transformed, not the world.

So one way to think rationally about an inner experience of the myth of apocalypse is to categorise it in Jungian terms as the result of the activation of what Jung called the archetype of rebirth, the archetype that represents the human potential for inner transformation (see Jung, 1970, pp. 45–81). In the interests of rational as opposed to emotional thinking, let us first strip the myth of apocalypse of any grandiose cosmic significance. Looked at rationally and psychologically, the myth of apocalypse does not really concern world destruction and renewal but, as St. Paul put it, the renewal of our minds.

That is perhaps why D. H. Lawrence, dying of tuberculosis, became obsessed with the *Apocalypse* of John of Patmos, a text that had been the occasion for innumerable emotional rants in the colliers' non-conformist chapel services of his childhood. It was, at the beginning and then at the end of his life, a text he loved to hate. Lawrence's last book, also entitled *Apocalypse*, constituted a savage attack on John of Patmos and later Patmosians, but it was also a paean to the emotional impact on him of the cosmic apocalyptic vision of the New Testament text, whose power as a myth, he believed, stemmed from its ultimate origin in Chaldean star worship and pagan initiation rituals. "I would like", he wrote, "to know the stars again as the Chaldeans knew them.... And in my Mesopotamian self I long for the sun again ... But our experience of the sun is dead, we are cut off" (Lawrence, 1999, p. 51).

Lawrence's primitivist nostalgia for Etruscan, Chaldean and Greco-Roman polytheistic cultures' sense of connection with the cosmos takes us back to William Wordsworth's savage sigh:

> Great God! I'd rather be
> A Pagan suckled in a creed outworn;
> So might I, standing on this pleasant lea
> Have glimpses that would make me less forlorn;

> Have sight of Proteus rising from the sea;
> Or hear old Triton blow his wreathèd horn.
> (Wordsworth, 2008, p. 270)

Like Wordsworth, Lawrence realised—or half realised—that the vision of what he wanted to see out there in the cosmos would be the result of a process of what Jungians call a "projection" of archetypal material from the psyche onto the outside world. "I would like," wrote Lawrence, "to put my ego into the sun, and my personality into the moon, and my character into the planets" (Lawrence, 1999, p. 51). Although it was impossible for Lawrence to become a Chaldean—just as it was impossible for Wordsworth to time-travel and become "a Pagan suckled in a creed outworn"—there still remained for him the possibility of the release of his imagination triggered by the renewal of his love-hate relationship with the myth text of John of Patmos' *Apocalypse*, and his obsessive fascination with it—his emotional response to the power of the myth—became the support for an inner vision that helped to satisfy the longings of his soul. But longings for what? On this point Lawrence is perhaps not entirely lucid; in my opinion, he remained stuck to some degree in emotional thinking. Having experienced the emotional impact of the apocalypse myth, he expressed his sense of fascination and wonder in compelling poetic language, but his rational mind remains somewhat subordinated to the emotion generated by contact with an archetypal dimension of the psyche that C. G. Jung called the archetype of rebirth. His regressive nostalgia for a Chaldean—or Etruscan, or Greco-Roman—Golden Age where culture and cosmos were connected—where we were not "cut off" (ibid.) from the sun—conceals a longing on his part for self-transformation, that was probably stimulated by the contemplation of his imminent death from tuberculosis. He may not be able to become a pagan or a Chaldean, but he can become—however partially and reluctantly—a Patmosian, since the Apocalypse of St. John of Patmos was indeed a significant part of the "creed" in which as a child he was "suckled". However "outworn" this creed of his childhood non-conformist chapels may appear to him now, through it he is able imaginatively to re-experience the power of the apocalyptic myth, but this time with all his adult critical faculties on the alert. There remained only for him to take the last step: to achieve intellectual clarity on the issue of the ultimate referent of his emotional fascination with apocalypse myth, that is, to discern behind the emotional lure of the cosmic myth the personal referent of a glimpse into an inner process of rebirth and transformation.

Recognising the inner personal referent of a myth that presents itself as a powerful vision of world destruction and regeneration is not an easy enterprise. Jung himself first toyed with the idea that his thrice-repeated dream in April, May and June of 1914 of a devastating cold wave that swept through north-eastern France might have been a premonitory dream predicting the onset of World War I (although I don't think you had to be much of a prophet in the spring of 1914 to foresee the likelihood of war). Only with the third insistent occurrence of the dream did the personal nature of the vision become clear to him. As he recounts in his autobiography *Memories, Dreams, Reflections*, "there stood a leaf-bearing tree, but without any fruit (my tree of life, I thought), whose leaves had been transformed by the effects of the frost into sweet grapes full of healing juices. I plucked the grapes and gave them to a large, waiting crowd" (Jung, 1963, p. 176). So a dream that Jung was initially inclined to interpret as prophetic of apocalyptic world events ultimately pointed towards the theme of personal transformation. In this personal context then, his dream was prophetic: Jung's own midlife transformation did indeed lead to his coming into his own as an innovative psychologist, whose therapeutic work and writings would help many people.

For another example of how a text can subtly contextualise an apocalyptic cosmic vision in terms of personal transformation, we now turn to the opening of the *Bhagavad Gita*, where the prince and warrior Arjuna is described as almost having a complete nervous breakdown just before the great battle of Kurukshetra is about to begin. This personal crisis leads to his charioteer and spiritual mentor Krishna expounding over the first ten of the eighteen chapters of the *Gita* a new and original doctrine showing how the spiritual warrior, the yogi, should act with full mental equilibrium, having renounced any expectation of personal rewards for the results of his actions. Arjuna listens carefully, but it is clear that philosophical enlightenment is not enough for him; his unsettled and precarious state of mind also requires the healing emotional stimulus of an apocalyptic vision in order to complete his transformation from disheartened hero into spiritual warrior and yogi.

Arjuna's apocalyptic vision will be the substance of book eleven of the *Gita*, and I will argue that it falls—significantly—into two separate parts. The first part satisfies Arjuna's request to Krishna to reveal to him his cosmic form as lord of the universe (cf. the figure of Christ as Pantokrator in John of Patmos). Krishna agrees to give him "divine sight" in order for him to be able to see "the entire universe ... centered here in this body of mine", which is all that Arjuna had asked for. Krishna then adds—significantly—that he will also show Arjuna "whatever else you desire to see" (van Buitenen, 1981, p. 113).

So Arjuna's apocalyptic vision falls into two distinct parts: the first, in which Krishna reveals to Arjuna his cosmic form, and the second, in which Arjuna will see "whatever else" (yac cânyad)—as yet unspecified—he might wish to see in addition. The first part of the vision is narrated in the epic third person, and recounts how Arjuna saw the whole universe centred in Krishna, and how he was stunned by the emotional impact of this numinous vision. But then something curious happens: Arjuna "folded his hands" (krtânjalir) and "bowed his head" (pranamya shirasâ) as the second part of the vision begins (van Buitenen, 1981, p. 113). At this juncture I would argue that Arjuna can no longer be imagined as looking outwards towards the transformed figure of Krishna, but rather as looking inwards into his own mind (cf. David Burton at the end of *The Last Wave*), where he experiences a very different kind of vision of Krishna. Appropriately, the narrative of the *Gita* switches from third to first person narration, and it is Arjuna himself who describes, his head bowed down, what he sees with his inner eye. What he now sees as an inner vision presumably represents everything he personally wanted to see; it is the part of the vision that is designated as what refers to him personally; it is the part of the vision that corresponds to his deepest inner need. It is "what *he* wants to see".

And what Arjuna "wants to see" is downright horrific! It is a grotesque nightmare vision of Krishna as a bloodthirsty ogre with flaming mouths and dreadful tusks, who devours all of Arjuna's foes, including his revered teachers who have chosen to fight on the opposite side. Horrific details accumulate, such as "there are some who are dangling between your teeth, / Their heads already crushed to bits" (van Buitenen, 1981, p. 115). It has turned out that what Arjuna most wanted and most needed to see was a vision of his friend and mentor Krishna as the Flaming Mouths of Death and Universal Destruction, as the Divine Slayer of all those Arjuna had hesitated to kill not long before. No doubt, this vision quickly frightens him, and soon he is begging Krishna to revert to his more comforting god-like form. But the apocalyptic vision has provided him with the healing symbol he needs for his transformation. It has displaced Arjuna's warrior mission from the personal onto the archetypal plane; the eventual death of his enemies is no longer envisaged as solely the result of his own personal agency; it is Krishna, the embodiment of cosmic death and destruction, who will ultimately slay them. From now on Arjuna's initiatory ordeal is essentially over, as he has been transformed into a spiritual warrior and yogi, who can return to the battlefield and kill his enemies, even if they happen to be his revered elders and teachers, but without being motivated by ambition and the desire to reap the personal rewards of victory. Even so, the choice to fight or not to fight is ultimately left up to him, as Krishna indicates clearly at the end of the *Gita*: "Reflect upon this knowledge I have propounded to you, this mystery of mysteries, in its entirety, and then do as you are pleased to do" (van Buitenen, 1981, p. 143). Arjuna has been radically transformed from a conscience-stricken warrior to a spiritually enlightened warrior yogi, not only through Krishna's spiritual teachings, but also through an apocalyptic vision that enabled him to come to terms with his own worst fears. That is why Krishna now believes that he is able to make a rational decision as to whether fighting or refraining from battle is the better course of action for him.

The myth of apocalypse, of world destruction and renewal, with its inner link to the archetypal process of individual transformation, is of particular relevance to the concerns of our own time. For the French scholar Bruno Etienne, it is a myth that has attained new power in our world because of "les amants de l'apocalypse" ("the lovers of the apocalypse")—because of the men, especially young men (but also some young women), who have fallen in love with the myth of apocalypse, and pose an ever present danger to our world's welfare and security (see Etienne, 2002). Understanding the depth of their passion and the way that their archetypal needs are being exploited by politicians is a necessity for intellectuals today. For, as long as this archetypal need for rebirth and transformation is cynically manipulated by self-serving politicians and psychopathic leaders, there will always be a constantly renewed source of potential young terrorists in love with the myth of apocalypse. This is so because the myth of world destruction and renewal that possesses them is the expression of their own unconscious need for radical personal transformation. Even if the so-called war on terror is a case of the cure being possibly worse than the disease, the need to manage intelligently the appeal of terrorism will always be with us.

Uninitiated youth will tear our civilisation down—the civilisation that has failed them in a crucial way. We will have to take their intense needs for inner self-transformation seriously, since what does not get resolved in the inner world of the psyche will find a way of projecting itself onto the outer world.

Sigmund Freud got it right a long time ago: for young people trying to enter the stage of young adulthood, "love and work" are the primary goals. We should be very clear that depriving the young of any hope of reaching these two goals may well have "apocalyptic" consequences. When no civilised initiatory challenge is given to them, when no sane mentorship occurs, then disaster is in the offing. In a fairly recent *New Yorker* article entitled "The Kingdom of Silence", Lawrence Wright describes how he was on assignment teaching young Saudi journalists more about the craft of their trade. In the process he learned a lot about the situation of young people in Saudi Arabia, and in particular how the young men and women were increasingly forbidden almost all forms of contact and conversation by the ever-increasing power of Wahabi Islamic fundamentalists in their country. This has meant that young Saudi men's knowledge of women their own age is gained mainly from internet pornography—so much for "love". Add to this their generalised unemployment—so much for "work"—and you have the recipe for another 9/11: young men throwing themselves into the arms of death, expecting that seconds afterwards their need for social recognition and sexual love will be satisfied in paradise. This is the type of emotional—and magical—thinking we do not want to encourage—to say the least!

Terrorism is certainly a complex phenomenon, and no one solution is likely to work, especially since, as has frequently been noted, one person's "terrorist" is often another person's "freedom fighter". But neglecting the basic archetypal need for radical personal transformation among the young is certainly one road to Armageddon. Meeting those archetypal needs in a civilised way means, first of all, taking these needs very seriously. Along with dealing intelligently and seriously with global warming, dealing intelligently and seriously with uninitiated young people—jobless and loveless—ought to be at the top of our social and political agenda. But so far the latter seems to be not much on the agenda at all.

Another example of a modern problem where focusing on its archetypal dimension can alert us to dangers, that otherwise might not be foreseen, is scapegoating. The Holocaust, death camps, gulags, torture prisons and killing fields are reminders that the scapegoating process has been a notable feature of the barbarism of the last one hundred years. Yet, in stark contrast to the scapegoating ritual of the ancient Hebrews, scapegoating in modern times has been a thoroughly unconscious activity. The original scapegoating process as described in the book of *Leviticus* (16.20–22) as part of the Day of Atonement was a carefully scripted ritual, in the course of which a goat was symbolically made to bear the weight of the sins of the people, and then driven out into the wilderness. What an admirably civilised ritual it was! Nobody was hurt—even the goat wasn't hurt, since goats easily survive in the wilderness—and by the end of the ritual the people feel free from collective anxiety and guilt for another year.

By contrast with the consciously scripted Hebrew scapegoat ritual and its mythic subtext, the modern unconscious process of scapegoating has caused more human misery than one can even begin to tally up. It is not too late, however, to see into the unconscious and indeed archetypal dimensions of the scapegoating myth, and to find better ways of handling our nagging sense that we have done the things we ought not to have done, and have not done the things we ought to have done. René Girard and Jung will help us in this project, by providing us with some useful insights, especially so if we tweak their theories a little.

Girard's anatomy of the scapegoat (as in *Le bouc émissaire*, 1982) insists that the scapegoat is always innocent—always—of the accusations made against it. There are, he maintains, no exceptions to this rule. Scapegoats and scapegoated groups are never guilty. They may not be innocent in all respects (what human being is?), but as regards the charges laid against them, they are always completely innocent. However, adds Girard, when we look into the mythology created by human cultures over the ages, we discover to our dismay that the tales always come out on the side of the scapegoaters.

In specifically Jungian terms, the myth of the scapegoat may be said to involve shadow projection. Projection of the shadow (the repressed contents of the unconscious) occurs when an individual or a group projects something they feel dimly disturbed about—some half-conscious or even totally unconscious source of anxiety—onto another individual or group. Having thus shifted the burden of guilt onto someone outside—having projected, for example, some of their sense of moral inferiority onto the outside, onto the accused scapegoat—the individual or the group can heave a sigh of relief, and feel righteous, even self-righteous, and blissfully free from the nagging sense of guilt that had plagued them.

If the process of scapegoating simply stopped with shadow projection, no great harm would have been done. But it does not stop there. Scapegoating leads to the isolating of the scapegoat, and then to its exile—or incarceration—or execution. It can be a very nasty process, and shadow projection—which produces at the most irritation or anger—is not enough by itself to account for its ultimate horrors. Jung did not speak much of the scapegoat myth, but in his *Answer to Job* he interprets Yahweh's allowing his faithful servant Job to suffer every horror short of death as a sign of Job's being scapegoated. For Jung, Yahweh is woefully unconscious of himself, and is only dimly aware that he has moral doubts about himself—doubts about his ultimate goodness especially, and it is Job who must pay the price for the deity's unconscious self-doubt. Up to this point Girard's theory also works well: Job is in this respect quite innocent, in that he is anything but a doubter; his faith in Yahweh—his loyalty to Yahweh—is, in fact, exemplary.

But I think something more significant is involved than what Jung proposed. The key lies in the opening scene, when Job makes sacrifice in case any of his children would have "cursed God in their hearts" (Mitchell, 1987, p. 5). Thus this splendid mythic text suggests that it is this fear of being hated and cursed that constitutes Yahweh's secret anxiety, and what he allows Satan to put Job through is explicitly designed, in the terms of the bet that the two divine antagonistic beings make with each other, to see whether Job, if pushed far enough, will curse him in his heart. But, in spite of atrocious suffering, Job refuses to curse God in his heart, and so is revealed as the ultimately innocent scapegoat.

So the myth of Job reveals a dimension of scapegoating that cannot be accounted for by shadow projection alone. In the divine drama represented in the myth, what is projected onto Job—what he seems to be latently suspected of, if not directly accused of—is what, for Yahweh, is the ultimate evil. If Job were to "curse God in his heart", this would be tantamount to dissolving the sacred covenant of the bond that joins man and God—the ultimate betrayal from Yahweh's standpoint. That suggests that, not only is shadow projection involved in scapegoating, but something even more disturbing—the projection of the very archetype of evil. It is because the scapegoat is loaded with the weight of the burden of the projection of ultimate evil that the treatment of the scapegoat is often so vicious and murderous. Shadow projection may produce irritation, aggravation, and even hatred towards the one saddled with the projection; but in the case of scapegoating, the additional projection of the archetype of evil leads the scapegoaters to scream for the scapegoat's blood.

An example of the significant difference between personal shadow projection and archetypal scapegoating may be found in a text that presents a classic pre-Jungian anatomy of the shadow: Robert Louis Stevenson's *The Strange Case of Dr. Jekyll and Mr. Hyde*. In one of its most dramatic scenes, Mr. Enfield, the sophisticated London man-about-town and bosom friend of the lawyer Utterson, is describing to his friend how he was "coming home ... about three o'clock of a black winter morning" when he witnessed a peculiar event in the hitherto totally deserted streets: a smallish man (later revealed to be Mr. Hyde) was trudging along, when he collided with a girl "of eight or ten", "who was running as hard as she was able down a cross street". "And then", recounts Mr. Enfield, "came the horrible part of the thing: for the man trampled calmly over the child's body and left her screaming on the ground". A small crowd of people rush out of the neighbouring buildings, including the girl's own family and a doctor. But notice that the girl is basically unhurt—frightened, but unhurt. As Enfield tells the story, "the child was not much the worse, more frightened, according to the Sawbones; and there you might have supposed would be an end to it" (Stevenson, 1999, pp. 33–34). But this is not the end of the matter: the process of scapegoating Mr. Hyde has just got under way, and the near equivalent of a lynching mob begins to coalesce around him, all of whose members, including Mr. Enfield and the normally unemotional doctor, begin to loathe Hyde's very sight. Soon they are threatening Hyde with a public scandal if he does not hand over a large sum of money to the girl's parents. Although Mr. Hyde has not hurt or even intended to hurt the girl, he is treated by the crowd like an immoral monster. In other words, the projection onto Hyde of the archetype of evil has put the crowd into a scapegoating frenzy. But a cool and rational analysis of what Hyde has actually done—accidentally having run into a girl who had rushed across his path—as opposed to what he seems to have been accused of doing—deliberately harming an innocent child—would surely result in a verdict of non-guilty.

Scapegoating begins as an unconscious process; if people were aware of their first inner movements in that direction, they would not continue it, because the beginning of the scapegoating process would offend their most basic sense of morality: it is not right to accuse people falsely. So—to continue with Stevenson's scene—what was possibly going on in the unconscious of the veritable lynch mob that constituted itself around the figure of Mr. Hyde? Stevenson, an unconventional and somewhat Bohemian figure, yet also aspiring for the Victorian respectability of a successful writer, gives us a clue now and again. For instance: what in the world is an eight or ten year old girl doing rushing down a cross street in the wee hours of the morning? We can easily guess the reason why Hyde (and, for that matter, Enfield) are out and about, returning home long after most of the world has gone to bed; we guess at their pursuit of secret pleasures and at the double life of otherwise respectable Victorian gentlemen. But the little girl—why is she out and about? What is she running from? She could be a thief, or a child worker forced to put in inhumanly long hours in some workshop or factory, or a child prostitute trying to get home safely. One way or another, she could be part of a Victorian world of oppressed and abused children, with which her parents and the members of the crowd are in total collusion. Consequently, as a means of assuaging their feelings of collective guilt, they are quite ready to cooperate with extorting funds from the somewhat well-to-do Mr. Hyde caught in an embarrassing situation. A glimpse into Victorian moral hypocrisy is there for those readers who are willing to speculate concerning what might lurk behind the veil of the public outrage. The crowd's sudden willingness to move things into the dark zone of scapegoating is the nasty result of the dis-ease and the guilt of living in a world, and of being in collusion with a world, in which children are mercilessly exploited in a variety of ways. Blaming Mr. Hyde for his allegedly brutal treatment of a child—when he has simply been the co-victim of a kind of pedestrian traffic accident—eases their conscience; for them it is too good an opportunity for scapegoating to miss.

The tragic annals of scapegoating persecution are part of the kind of history we certainly hope we are not doomed to repeat through ignorance of the nature and the power of the scapegoating myth. Of course, as with the archetypal need for radical individual transformation, cynical politicians and psychopathic leaders willing to exploit this ignorance are not lacking. That is why the ignorance must go. If large numbers of people do not become alert to the dangers and the immorality of the scapegoating process, humanity will continue on with its sorry tendency to do with its left hand what the right hand does not even comprehend in the slightest. So it is of crucial importance that scapegoating's earliest manifestations in shadow anxiety and projection be recognised as soon as possible. For, once the archetype of evil is projected, once the archetypal force of the myth is fully constellated, resistance based on rational analysis becomes more and more difficult, and emotional thinking tends to carry the day.

Recent examples are not lacking. For instance, what are we to make of Operation Shock and Awe and the pyrotechnic display of state-of-the-art weaponry in Baghdad in 2003? There was clearly shadow projection, to begin with: who had the real weapons of mass destruction, if not the USA? The innocent scapegoat would be—of all people—Saddam Hussein, a totally nasty dictator, no doubt, but on this one count totally innocent, since the fact was that he had no weapons of mass destruction at all, although he foolishly failed to admit this publicly. What might require more intensive analysis is the effect on the American citizenry, as upright and moral as any other in the world, of their knowledge of their own government's stockpiling of WMDs for several decades, thus putting themselves and the rest of the world at risk of Armageddon. Not that this anxiety was talked about much in America—keeping it unconscious may be part of the problem. But this circumstance must have made it an even heavier burden for the American public to bear, and an even greater unconscious source of guilt and anxiety.

Here is another example: the so-called War on Drugs. I have written about this as an instance of scapegoating at greater length in the second edition of my book *Jung and the Jungians on Myth* (Walker, 2002, pp. 165–168), but I will summarise the argument briefly. The outrageously severe sentencing of large numbers of especially minority young men for the crime of drug dealing and distribution smacks of scapegoating; with such an incredibly large percentage of the American population being put behind bars, it also suggests a gulag mentality. Nonetheless these drug offences are crimes only when defined as such by the laws, and there are many reasonable people across the political spectrum in America and abroad, who have urged, and are urging now, the decriminalisation of many drug-related offenses. Should their views prevail, then the terrible irony will be that some long term inmates of the prison system will eventually be declared innocent of their crimes, since the acts that got them into prison in the first place will have been no longer legally defined as such—although their newly acquired innocence will have happened too late to have spared them years of suffering.

Therefore, one issue that needs to be examined carefully is the question of what is the nature of the shadow projection that is going on with this prosecution of a War on Drugs. Consider the possibility that drug dealers bear the projection of the shadow side of business and corporate power, in that they, like many legitimate business people, are ruthlessly out for profit, even at the expense of community welfare. Drug dealers are not all nice people, of course, but neither are many legitimate business people and corporate leaders. It is unfair to punish the first for the sins of the second. It is really that simple—or would be, if the archetype of evil had not been projected, to the point where it is often hard, even among enlightened intellectuals, to have a rational conversation about the issue. Let us hope that, in this case as in others, rational thinking will eventually prevail over emotional thinking.

## *References*

Edinger, E. F. (1999). *Archetype and Apocalypse: Divine Vengeance, Terrorism, and the End of the World*. G. R. Elder (Ed.). Chicago, IL: Open Court.

Etienne, B. (2002). *Les amants de l'Apocalypse: pour comprendre le 11 Septembre*. Paris: Éditions de l'Aube.

Girard, R. (1986). *Le bouc émissaire*. Paris: Livre de Poche.

Jung, C. G. (1963). *Memories, Dreams, Reflections*. A. Jaffé (Ed.). R. and C. Winston (Trans.). New York: Vintage.

Jung, C. G. (1970). *Four Archetypes*. R. F. C. Hull (Trans.). Princeton: Princeton University Press.

Jung, C. G. (2002). *Answer to Job*. R. F. C. Hull (Trans.). Princeton: Princeton University Press.

*The Last Wave*. (1977). P. Weir (Dir.). Richard Chamberlain, Olivia Hamnett, et al. (Feat.). Ayer Productions, Australia. DVD. New York: The Criterion Collection, 2001.

Lawrence, D. H. (1995). *Apocalypse*. London: Penguin Books.

Mitchell, S. (Trans.) (1987). *The Book of Job*. New York: Harper Perennial.

Stevenson, R. L. (1999). *The Strange Case of Dr. Jekyll and Mr. Hyde*. M. Danahay (Ed.). Peterborough, ON: Broadview.

van Buitenen, J. A. B. (Ed. and Trans.) (1981). *The Bhagavadgita in the Mahabharata: A Bilingual Edition*. Chicago: University of Chicago Press.

Walker, S. F. (2002). *Jung and the Jungians on Myth: An Introduction*. New York: Routledge.

Wordsworth, W. (2008). *The Major Works*. S. Gill (Ed.). Oxford: Oxford University Press.

Wright, L. (2004). The Kingdom of Silence. *The New Yorker*, 5 January 2004.

CHAPTER TWO

# The divine image: remaking Blake's myths

*Jason Whittaker*

> I must Create a System, or be enslav'd by another Mans
> I will not Reason & Compare: my business is to Create
>
> —*Jerusalem* 10.20–21; Erdman, 1988, p. 153

These words of Los, taken from William Blake's last great epic poem, *Jerusalem: The Emanation of the Giant Albion*, are an important stimulus for Blake's influence on subsequent generations of writers and artists. Tony Tanner, in *City of Words* (1971), suggested these lines served as the rubric for an entire span of post-war writers and poets including Allen Ginsberg, Thomas Pynchon and Kurt Vonnegut, all of whom were concerned to create rather than "Reason & Compare". Although the vogue for psychoanalytic interpretations of Blake has not flourished since its most fertile period between June Singer's *The Unholy Bible: A Psychological Interpretation of William Blake* published in 1973 and Diana Hume George's 1980 book *Blake and Freud*, Blake as an artist of the unconscious has recently started to attract considerably more interest via phenomenological and postmodern approaches, for example in the work of Mary Lynn Johnson, Peter Otto, and Laura Quinney. In *William Blake on Self and Soul*, Quinney begins with the observation that Blake was "both a political radical and a radical psychologist" (Quinney, 2009, p. xi), one whose reformulations of self and selfhood are particularly pertinent at precisely that moment when the self has been presumed to have disappeared from contemporary life. For Quinney, the legacy of empirical philosophy which other Romantics were not able to escape was the loneliness of the modern subject separated eternally from its object, its outside never quite assimilated to its inner self and thus the self "haunted" by the sense impressions that form it: "Wordsworth spelled out and bequeathed to psychoanalysis the notion of self-estrangement that is inherent in Locke's picture" (Quinney, 2009, p. 77). For Locke, rejection of innate ideas means that the self brings nothing into the world; in Blake's vision this must ultimately mean terror in the face of nature which is indifferent to the fate of the self. His answer (and one, Quinney suggests, that he shared with Neoplatonists) is to identify the self not with the ego but with the world soul, or the imagination. Blake's notion of the immortality of the soul does not imply the promise of the survival of the ego in the face of the apparent indifference of nature, but the ability of imagination to recognise the eternal now of all aspects of existence.

Blake, as Quinney is right to observe, is not entirely successful in establishing this elusive awareness, but what is important is that Blake's constant acts of imaginative system-building provide "therapeutic interventions designed to ameliorate the radical unhappiness of passivation" (Quinney, 2009, p. 99). The work of imagination, as Blake himself realised, is never complete:

> With great labour upon his anvils, & in his ladles the Ore
> He lifted, pouring it into the clay ground prepar'd with art;
> Striving with Systems to deliver Individuals from those Systems
> (*Jerusalem* 11.3–5; Erdman, 1988, p. 154)

Blake's attempt to deliver individuals from systems worked through the creation of his own mythic apparatus. In *The Sacred Wood,* T. S. Eliot remarked that Blake's supernatural "territories" and ideas illustrated the crankiness and eccentricity of his thought and that these were "not essential to [his] inspiration" (Eliot, 1924, p. 157). Over the years, I have moved from a suspicion of Eliot's remarks to a certain sympathy as I have grappled with those mythographical systems. Studies by Edward Larrissy (2006) and Steve Clark (2007) in particular emphasise that *The Sacred Wood* does not represent Eliot's fullest consideration of Blake, and that works such as *East Coker* demonstrate a much greater affinity between the two poets. However, while in his own terms Eliot may have a point insofar as Blake's myth can often appear cranky and needlessly eccentric, with regard to the reception of Blake's later work he is completely mistaken in that those ideas are essential to his inspiration. Blake is not the first writer to represent a break with the Latin tradition, but important precursors such as Bunyan can still be clearly identified within more conventional Protestant frameworks. Blake is clearly and categorically a Protestant (probably raised a Moravian according to recent research by Keri Davies, Marsha Keith Schuchard and Magnus Ankarsjö), but characters such as Los, Urizen, Enitharmon and Vala are attempts to create a new tradition that does not have simple origins in biblical typology or in other sources available at the time, such as classical mythology or the fashionable Romantic alternatives of the poetry of Ossian or Norse legends. Blake is the first writer to attempt to create a mythographical system that does not rely on an external tradition (which is by no means to say that it does not, or cannot, interface with such traditions): although Blake repeatedly refers to spiritual sources for his myths that originate outside himself, no future writer or artist could fail to recognise that the myth of the Four Zoas is thoroughly *Blakean*, in turn creating the potential for others to create their own systems.

The basis for this myth-making was identified by Blake in the earliest of his illuminated works, *All Religions are One* and *There is No Natural Religion*, as the "Poetic or Prophetic Character", what early twentieth-century critics such as S. Foster Damon (1924) and Northrop Frye (1947) were to present as synonymous in Blake with the workings of imagination.

> If it were not for the Poetic or Prophetic Character the Philosophic & Experimental would soon be at the ratio of all things, and stand still, unable to do other than repeat the same dull round over again … He who sees the Infinite in all things sees God. He who sees the Ratio only sees himself only. (*There is No Natural Religion*; Erdman, 1988, p. 3)

In *God is Not One*, Stephen Prothero takes Blake's *All Religions are One* as the starting point for the post-1960s notion that "all religions are beautiful and all are true" (Prothero, 2010, p. 1). While Prothero is right to suggest that others may invoke Blake this way, he is wrong to imply that this was Blake's own opinion. Blake himself certainly did not believe that all religions were either beautiful or true, reserving the term Druidism or natural religion for what he saw as ideologies dedicated to man's enslavement. More accurately, Blake sees a common origin for both poetry and religion: "As all men are alike (tho' infinitely various) [s]o all Religions [,] & as all similars have one source [t]he true Man is the source[,] he being the Poetic Genius" (*All Religions are One*; Erdman, 1988, p. 2). In fact, suggests Blake, and in contrast to Prothero's superficial claim, "The Religions of all Nations are derived from each Nations different reception of the Poetic Genius which is every where call'd the Spirit of Prophecy" (*All Religions are One*; Erdman, 1988, p. 1). The religious or mythic form that this poetic genius takes is infinitely various, but all such forms owe their origins to the act of imagination, a point reiterated in *The Marriage of Heaven and Hell*:

> The ancient Poets animated all sensible objects with Gods or Geniuses calling them by the names and adorning them with the properties of woods, rivers, mountains, lakes, cities, nations, and whatever their enlarged & numerous senses could perceive.
>
> And particularly they studied the genius of each city & country, placing it under its mental deity.
>
> Till a system was formed, which some took advantage of & enslav'd the vulgar by attempting to realize or abstract the mental deities from their objects: thus began Priesthood.
>
> Choosing forms of worship from poetic tales.
>
> And at length they pronounced that the Gods had orderd such things.
>
> Thus men forgot that All deities reside in the human breast.
> (*The Marriage of Heaven and Hell*, plate 11; Erdman, 1988, p. 38)

By clearly locating the source of a religious impulse in human psychology and in imagination, Blake denies a transcendental supernatural authority for systems (the activity of "Priesthood") and instead emphasises the type of divine humanism that is made most eloquently in "The Divine Image" from *Songs of Innocence*:

> And all must love the human form,
> In heathen, turk or jew.

Where Mercy, Love & Pity dwell,
There God is dwelling too (Erdman, 1988, p. 13)

"The Divine Image" is an immensely generous poem, contrasting greatly with Blake's contemporaries such as Isaac Watts, who wrote in "Praise for the Gospel":

Lord, I ascribe it to thy Grace,
And not to Chance, as others do,
That I was born of Christian Race,
And not a Heathen, or a Jew. (Cited in Lincoln, 1991, p. 159)

Such generosity is immensely important to Blake's later reception because it opens his combative and confrontational methods to those who may radically diverge from his own religious, political, and sexual principles. Blake appears to be much more concerned with praxis than dogma, and by identifying this praxis with the activity of imagination he undermines the assumption that empirical observation has access to antecedents in the real world that form the basis of our ideas through sense impressions. This assumption, most rigorously identified by Locke and then Hume as the basis of our knowledge, in turn led to the attempt, via August Comte, John Stuart Mill and the logical positivism of the Vienna Circle, to provide a coherent, reductive theory for verifying knowledge. Hume's contemporary, Thomas Reid, provided an interesting refutation of this notion by pointing out how the *sensus communis* (common sense) as a means of framing perception emphasised the active nature of imagination in organising sense impressions. By making imagination fundamental to our understanding of the world, Blake is able to ascribe it an active and positive role in the process of conceptualising reality rather than being limited to the passive reception of antecedent impressions. In Blake, "Human Imagination … is the Divine Vision" (Erdman, 1988, p. 132), and this divine vision operates constantly by creating systems that deliver individuals from systems. As Blake, through Los, delivered individuals from systems, so all who embody the poetic or prophetic character must in turn fashion their own mythic creations to further release future generations from other systems—including, if necessary, from the system devised by Blake himself.

Not that this was particularly clear in the earliest years of Blake's wider recognition, from the 1860s onwards. His popularity during the nineteenth century largely rested on his lyric poetry rather than the prophetic works in which he struggled most extensively with the philosophical problems of system-building. The first widespread selection of Blake's poetry to be published after his death appeared in the second volume of Gilchrist's famous *Life*, selected and edited rather ruthlessly by Dante Gabriel Rossetti. Subsequent editions throughout the 1870s and 1880s, notably the Aldine edition by William Michael Rossetti and the Pickering editions by Richard Herne Shepherd, expanded the scope of the poems included with the *Life*, but tended to include only short extracts of the prophetic works other than *The Book of Thel*. Even Blake's most sympathetic critic before the 1890s, Algernon Charles Swinburne, tended to consider these prophetic works largely incomprehensible, writing in *William Blake: A Critical Essay*: "Confidence in future friends, and contempt for future foes, may have induced him to leave his highest achievements impalpable and obscure" (Swinburne, 1868, p. 300).

The transformation, and one which was to have an immensely important effect on Blake scholarship in the twentieth century, came with publication of the three-volume *The Works of William Blake: Poetic, Symbolic, and Critical*, edited by W. B. Yeats and Edwin John Ellis and published by Bernard Quaritch in 1893. Yeats and Ellis's influence owed little to their editorial work, the poorly reproduced illustrations of the illuminated books only being surpassed by the clumsy rewriting of *Vala*. As Deborah Dorfman observes, their three-volume edition of Blake is "one of the most idiosyncratic and poorly put-together among literary critiques ... albeit brilliant and revolutionary" (Dorfman, 1969, p. 192). In terms of their editorial work, although they had a role to play in bringing various neglected texts of Blake's into the public domain (most notably *Vala* itself), the most significant consequence of their mangling was to prompt further, more scholarly editions, notably those of John Sampson in 1905 and the authoritative Geoffrey Keynes edition in 1925. More important was the critical assumptions that changed after Yeats and Ellis gave an account of their symbolic system. As Bentley notes, "Ellis & Yeats were clearly learned about occult mysteries and secret societies, but their enthusiasm outran their knowledge, and their works should not be approached without a carefully digested understanding of the less speculative if less inspired Blake books" (Ellis & Yeats, 1977, p. 30). Despite, or even because of, this enthusiasm, however, Larrissy is still able to remark that it "is not an exaggeration to say that Yeats was one of the first serious scholars of Blake" (Larissy, 2006, p. 37), and Dorfman agrees that, whatever their other failings, Ellis and Yeats at last laid to rest any serious notion that Blake's ideas were mad rather than simply difficult.

Yeats's most sympathetic recent critic, Arianna Antonielli, notes that one of the consequences of Yeats's deep engagement with Blake was that, while he may not really have understood *Blake* that well at all it inspired him to return to writing with a "new *furor poeticus*" and also to systematise his own thought for the first time (Antonielli, 2008, p. 12). The systems that Yeats saw in Blake were transformed, distorted even, via the lens of theosophy and the Hermetic Order of the Golden Dawn (for all that Harold Bloom argued Blake, along with Shelley and Nietzsche, counted for more than Mathers and Agrippa). For Yeats, Blake's constant four-fold systematising offered a cosmology of the imagination that stimulated Yeats, via "over-schematized and needlessly complex" concordances (Masterson & O'Shea, 1985, p. 64), to create his own poetic theory of correspondences. Elsewhere, I have defined this process of creative collaboration with regard to Blake's work as "zoamorphosis" (after the four, warring zoas in Blake's mythic giant, Albion), a process that "embodies Blake's sense of conflict-based collaboration: a collaboration that enables the transformation of the past due to disagreement" (Whitson & Whittaker, 2012, p. 7). Because Blake invites contrary readings, the mutations that occur within the transmission of his art and poetry through such misreadings almost inevitably tell us more about the poet, writer, or artist transmitting Blake than they do about the original. For more assiduous and careful critics who followed Yeats, beginning with S. Foster Damon and reaching an important fruition with Northrop Frye, the determination to treat Blake's systems seriously resulted in valuable insights as to how Blake's four zoas could explain aspects of human psychology, socio-political interactions or religious philosophy. The early success of this recuperation of Blake as a systematic thinker accounts in part for the grouchy assessment of Eliot in *The Sacred Wood*. It was not really until the 1980s and 1990s that a serious reappraisal of Blake as a comprehensive system-builder underwent any form of thorough deconstruction, notably in Leopold Damrosch's *Symbol and Truth in Blake's Myth* (1980), in which Damrosch demonstrated how Blake's thought was often shot through with contradictions which could not be satisfactorily explained by Blake's critics. My own favourite (and a much more humble exercise than Damrosch's rather antagonistic and sometimes self-glorying attack) is Morris Eaves's 1995 essay, "On Blakes we want and Blakes we don't", in which he admits his own failures to comprehend the potential totality of explanation for which he finds constant allusions in Blake ("Mark well my words! they are of your eternal Salvation", *Milton* 2.25; Erdman, 1998, p. 96). As Eaves observes, systematic clarity is something he finds more in the great critics of Blake, such as Frye, than in Blake himself.

Yeats's account embodies, then, a particular approach to Blake's myth-making that was well-established in the twentieth century as a perfectly authoritative critical model. Blake's system could often be fractured or apparently incomprehensible, in particular as he struggled with the "rough basement" and "stubborn structure of Language" (*Jerusalem* 36.58–9; Erdman, 1988, p. 182). With careful reading and appropriate hermeneutic activity, however, the potential of uncovering that system as a comprehensive totality remained a valid and worthwhile objective to the student of Blake. However, a near contemporary of Yeats used Blake in a very different way, one which for me has provided a much more fruitful way into the Romantic poet and artist's myth-making.

Austin Osman Spare was an occult artist and writer who, after studying at the Slade and making a name for himself as a precociously talented draughtsman (for which skills he was employed as a war artist during the First World War), became loosely involved with Aleister Crowley, theosophy and the Hermetic Order of the Golden Dawn (Grant, 1975, pp. 8–25). He knew Yeats, having worked with him on the magazine *Form*, but it was through a more private sphere of practice that he proved himself a much more interesting, if ultimately minor, innovator. In his earliest works such as *Earth Inferno* (1905) and *A Book of Satyrs* (1907), Spare demonstrated a style that owed much to Aubrey Beardsley and decadent art, but when he began work on *The Book of Pleasure (Self-Love): The Psychology of Ecstasy* in 1909, publishing it finally in 1913, he began to combine magic and art in a process which he referred to as sigilisation: the artist, by investing an abstract symbol, the sigil, with a particular desire that is focused on via sexual techniques, then deliberately repressing and forgetting that meaning so as to drive it into the subconscious, thus allows the desire to complete its own untrammelled activity. Spare's rather makeshift understanding of psychoanalysis was interesting in that like the Surrealists he was deliberately exploring ways of enabling unconscious activity to enter into daily life (and, like them, he employed automatic art and collage), a process that various contemporaries considered as placing his art on a par with that of Blake's.

Although Spare shared with Blake an interest in the human body, his own depictions were closer to the art of Auguste Rodin than neoclassical idealism. It is in his writing, however, that Spare demonstrates himself to be one of the most Blakean of the early twentieth-century figures. In *The Focus of Life* (1921), for example, he depicts a psychomachy of three vaguely identified beings or forces—Zos, Kia and Ikkah—the conflicts of which are commented upon ironically by Aâos and his sister Tzulah, emanations of the artist that are particularly reminiscent of the prophet Los and Enitharmion. Near the beginning of *The Focus of Life*, Aâos addresses his sister thus:

> I bring a sword that contains its own medicine: The sour milk that cureth the body. Prepare to meet God, the omnifarious believing,—Thyself the living truth. Die not to spare, but that the world may perish. Nature is more atrocious. Learning all things from Thee in the most sinister way for representation: from thy thought to become thereafter. Having suffered pleasure and pain, gladly dost thou deny the things of existence for freedom of desire—from this sorry mess of inequality—once so desired. And is fear of desire. The addition of the "I" of a greater illusion. Desire is the conception I and induces Thou. (Spare, 1993, p. 7)

Probably the strongest connection between Spare and Blake lies, then, in his creation of a personal mythology, what he sometimes referred to as "witchcraft", which saw godhead as an emanation of inner psychic energy expressed in art. There are important differences between the two, of course, not least the fact that Spare saw his spiritual ideas as a product of witchcraft and occult practices, while Blake believed that Christianity was the basis of his visions. Likewise, whereas Blake's later poetry seeks annihilation of the self, Spare is always concerned to find fulfilment of that self. Yet while some of these differences are fundamental, others are more apparent and superficial, as in the rejection of both artists of conventional notions of the ego even if they locate a stronger source of the self elsewhere.

The important distinction between Spare and Yeats, however, lies in Spare's completely different approach to systematisation. While Yeats sought careful analogies and correspondences that had a long tradition in western occult practices through to the Cabbalism of Mathers and the ritual magic of the Golden Dawn, Spare represented a fundamental break with such traditions: here, quite literally, was one who had to create his own systems or be enslaved by another's. As such, Spare has frequently been claimed as one of the progenitors of chaos magic, his significant contribution being that once a method of practice had been established (the process of sigilisation), he did not propose any conscious formalisation of the mythopoetic outcomes of that method. For Spare, the products of his mythology were Aâos and the Kia, just as for Blake they had been the Four Zoas, and for other practitioners they would take other forms not necessarily mythological at all but embodied in particular manifestations of the artist's will. Yeats provided an important link between Blake and Spare as he provided the text of *The Four Zoas*, which appeared to have had a profound effect on Spare's writing style at the very least. More than this, however, Spare revelled in an un-systematic application of Blake's artistry: what for nineteenth-century critics had been obscure failings to be ignored or, as with Yeats, a challenge to be resolved, instead became a loose, liberating artistic practice. If Blake sometimes failed to incorporate all elements of his system into a coherent structure, or changed his mind (which does indeed appear to be the case following his failure to complete *The Four Zoas*, after which Los especially comes to dominate Blake's mythic thought), this seems to be of little concern to Spare. What matters is what works in a particular instance and a particular time.

Although they were connected by a shared interest in what may be termed occultism, Yeats and Spare then took very different lessons from Blake's mythmaking. However, it is quite clear that in each instance what Blake's mythography did offer each of them was the example of how to create a new system. In the three-volume *Works* as well as much of *A Vision*, Yeats still offers some connection to theosophy and what he considers a perennial philosophy: in practice, however, Blake is as liberating for Yeats as he is for poets such as Ginsberg and novelists such as Joyce Cary in *The Horse's Mouth*, offering a precursor and antecedent that justifies a break with tradition. Blake may have failed during his lifetime in terms of communicating his mythic structures to contemporaries, but the fact that a record of that attempt survived means that later writers will not have to explain their own attempts to stand outside conventional patterns of hermeneutic procedure.

Following the Second World War, and particularly after the 1960s, the notion that any such system-building may require an explanation is itself ameliorated. Much of this, of course, is due to the final acceptance of that great Modernist experiment of the early twentieth century that had swept aside so many historical conventions in art as in other subjects. Unsurprisingly it is during this period that Blake becomes more fashionable than ever before, although two examples from the 1970s will suffice to demonstrate some of the ways in which Blake's systems are employed. Of the examples to be considered here, both take *Milton a Poem* as their exemplary text, but how they deal with that epic poem differs considerably. The first of these, *The Passion of New Eve* (1977), is the result of a wide-ranging interest in Blake on the part of Angela Carter, while J. G. Ballard's *The Unlimited Dream Company* (1979) is a more concentrated reading of that poem.

Carter's interest in Blake was extensive and frequently antagonistic. As she wrote in 1991, "When I was a girl, I thought that everything Blake said was holy, but now I am older and have seen more of life, I treat his aphorisms with the affectionate scepticism appropriate to the exhortations of a man who claimed to have seen a fairy's funeral" (Carter, 1991, p. x). As Christopher Ranger observes, the apparent flippancy of this remark should not detract from the fact that Carter's relationship with Blake became more useful as it moved from daughter and father figure to that with another fellow traveller (2007, p. 140), and there was more than a little self-irony in the fact that while she may never have claimed to have seen a fairy funeral (and certainly understood how Blake's laconic references to such events often worked), by the time of her death she had become a notable editor of various collections of fairy tales as well as reworking them in her own books, most notably *The Bloody Chamber* (1979). She frequently alluded to Blake, with *The Passion of New Eve*, written not long before she began work on *The Sadeian Woman* (1979), offering her most sustained example of a critique of Blake.

Set in a post-apocalyptic New York, *The Passion of New Eve* introduces Evelyn, a dissolute Englishman, who lives as a pimp on the earnings of the black dancer Leilah. After he abandons her to travel across a disintegrating United States, he is captured in Beulah, "a place where contrarieties exist together" (Carter, 1977, p. 48) and converted into a conventionally beautiful woman, the new Eve of the title. Having escaped from Mother, the matriarch who engineers this sex change, Eve is unfortunate enough to be caught by the misogynistic Zero the poet and thus becomes embroiled in his war with the transsexual Tristessa. While the violence of the novel owes perhaps more to de Sade (as in her earlier *The Infernal Desire Machines of Doctor Hoffman*, 1972), the contrarian Blake of *The Marriage of Heaven and Hell* also has an important role to play, offering Carter a position from which to attack the sediment of Blake's later vision. His ideal of Beulah, for example, is pleasant but inferior to the more masculine paradise of Eden:

> There is a place where Contrarieties are equally True
> This place is called Beulah, It is a pleasant lovely Shadow
> Where no dispute can come. Because of those who Sleep.
> Into this place the Sons & Daughters of Ololon descended
> With solemn mourning into Beulahs moony shades & hills
> Weeping for Milton: mute wonder held the Daughters
>    of Beulah
> Enrapturd with affection sweet and mild benevolence
> Beulah is evermore Created around Eternity; appearing
> To the Inhabitants of Eden, around them on all sides.
> But Beulah to its Inhabitants appears within each district
> As the beloved infant in his mothers bosom round incircled
> With arms of love & pity & sweet compassion. But to
> The Sons of Eden the moony habitations of Beulah,
> Are from Great Eternity a mild & pleasant Rest.
> (*Milton* 30.1–14; Erdman, 1988, p. 129)

Carter rejects this vision as one where women are "ensnared" in marriage, or legalised prostitution as she refers to it in *The Sadeian Woman*. Likewise, it is tempting to see Zero the Poet as an ironic inversion of Los the Prophet, and in the figure of Mother Carter takes a great deal of pleasure in reversing the status of Blake's dangerous zoa, Vala:

> And now Mother was armed. The monstrous being brandished an obsidian knife as black as she was. I found it very difficult to see, in that abattoir light, and remember, now, an atmosphere rather than an event—a lowering sense of antique ritual; of the presence, also, of stern adults who knew what was best for me better than I did

> myself; the full panoply of human sacrifice, in fact. Yet a perfect twentieth-century enamelled trolley stood beside Mother, containing a covered tray which, hopefully, held syringes with anaesthetics inside them. (Carter, 1977, p. 70)

Carter, more clearly than any of the writers considered here, inverts Blake's system. The whore, Rahab, becomes one of the models for her imposing Mother (though Carter avoids creating her own uncritical, apocalyptic vision of womanhood via some carefully contrived bathos), and the "lineaments of Gratified desire" that Blake sought in wives as well as such whores (Erdman, 1988, p. 474) is rightly subjected to scrutiny as the same dull round of barely concealed misogyny that has afflicted plenty of radical male writers. Yet, despite this conflict and contest, that very scrutiny itself sends us back to Blake: "Every thing that lives is holy" is a phrase that is repeated in both *The Marriage of Heaven and Hell* (plate 25; Erdman, 1988, p. 45) and *Visions of the Daughters of Albion* (8.10; Erdman, 1988, p. 51). Adrienne Rich (1995, p. 45) observed that throughout her career Carter returned to stories of the past to challenge precisely those assumptions that appear natural and thus invisible. Yet if Blake could all too easily fall into those assumptions, particularly in his later works, concerning the all-too-inevitable subservience of the female to the male, the early visionary who had known and admired the work of Mary Wollstonecraft certainly had more in common with the twentieth-century feminist, while the poet who was knowingly of the devil's party also provided her with a clear model for taking the fairy tales of the past as material for her own reconstruction work.

If Carter's attitude to Blake is clearly contrarian and confrontational, that of Ballard is much more ambivalent. Like Carter, Ballard sought to recuperate previously discredited genres in revitalised literary formats, in this case combining science fiction with surrealism in what Baudrillard considered the perfect example of hyperreality (Baudrillard, 1994, p. 123). Unlike Carter, Ballard did not display a particularly strong interest in Blake before publishing *The Unlimited Dream Company* in 1979, but in many respects this was simply a case of drawing attention to one particular aspect of the Surrealist genealogy within which Ballard saw himself, a genealogy that had been most clearly and explicitly mapped by André Breton in essays that included "Originality and Freedom" (1941) where Blake was numbered, with Novalis and

Poe, as one of the "explorers" who prepared the way for Surrealism. In *The Unlimited Dream Company*, an ironic example of visionary London fiction which transposes Blakean psychogeography to Ballard's home-suburb of Shepperton, the novel's antihero, Blake, steals a Cessna from the airport where he works as a dysfunctional cleaning attendant. Upon crashing into the suburb, his attempts to escape are foiled and, in his violent energy, he begins to convert the streets of Shepperton into a disturbing mixture of sacred and profane, mundane supermarkets juxtaposed with giant orchids and palmettos in a fashion so beloved by Breton and Ernst. The novel itself begins with the narrator speaking in prophetic mode:

> Soon there will be too many deserted towns for them to count. Along the Thames valley, all over Europe and the Americas, spreading outwards across Asia and Africa, ten thousand similar suburbs will empty as people gather to make their first man-powered flights. (Ballard, 1981, pp. 9–10)

The novel clearly draws attention to its source in *Milton*, as when Ololon recalls:

> Where once the Cherubs of Jerusalem spread to Lambeths Vale
> Milcahs Pillars shine from Harrow to Hampstead where Hoglah
> On Highgates heights magnificent Weaves over trembling Thames
> To Shooters Hill and thence to Blackheath the dark Woof! Loud
> Loud roll the Weights & Spindles over the whole Earth let down
> On all sides round to the Four Quarters of the World, eastward on
> Europe to Euphrates & Hindu, to Nile & back in Clouds
> Of Death across the Atlantic to America North & South.
> (*Milton* 35.10–17; Erdman, 1988, p. 135)

It also follows relatively closely the plot of Blake's poem. As Milton must descend into Udan-Adan to recuperate his lost female self, Ololon, engaging in a conflict with Satan at the end of the epic poem, so Blake must turn his back on the rapacious, spectral masculinity that prevents him achieving peace in these hallucinogenic final moments—for by the end of the novel it is quite clear that he has not survived the crash, engaging as he does in a final battle with the corpse of the dead pilot that is his own dead body. A number of commentators, most notably Mike Holliday (2007), have found *The Unlimited Dream Company* the least satisfying of Ballard's novels, one which appears to celebrate a kind of primeval fascism:

> Blake's personality and behaviour have strong similarities to the mind-set of fascism: for example, the megalomania, the paranoid delusions about others, the exclusion or demonization of doubters or those with alternative points of view. In particular, the fascist requires that *everything must cohere together as one*—and Alistair Cormack has pointed out that this is well described by a line written by the namesake of Ballard's protagonist, William Blake: "One command, one joy, one desire; One curse, one weight, one measure; One King, one God, one Law". (Holliday, 2007)

Holliday's quotation of *The [First] Book of Urizen* misses entirely the point that in Blake's poem it is the demiurge Urizen, not Blake, who celebrates this mythic coherence. Likewise, because he fails to see that *The Unlimited Dream Company* is a rewriting of *Milton a Poem*, he also fails to understand the source of the apparent failures of the novel. Thus Blake's inability to escape from the hell that he has created is prefigured by Albion's failure to rise at the end of the poem:

> Then Albion rose up in the Night of Beulah on his Couch
> Of dread repose seen by the visionary eye; his face is toward
> The east, toward Jerusalems Gates: groaning he sat above
> His rocks …
> His head bends over London: he sees his embodied Spectre
> Trembling before him with exceeding great trembling & fear
> He views Jerusalem & Babylon, his tears flow down
> He movd his right foot to Cornwall, his left to the Rocks
> of Bognor
> He strove to rise to walk into the Deep. But strength failing
> Forbad & down with dreadful groans he sunk upon his Couch

In moony Beulah. Los his strong Guard walks round beneath
the Moon. (*Milton* 39.32–52; Erdman, 1988, pp. 140–1)

*Milton* ends with Albion awakening, but the task of redemption—social and political, as well as spiritual—is not to be completed without much greater work. It is enough at this point that Albion has awoken to his crimes, recognised his own sins, even if he is not strong enough—yet—to confront them. Similarly with Ballard's Blake, the realisation that his attempts to absorb all others, through rape and even cannibalism, strengthen only the sick, Satanic selfhood that condemns itself to a hell by its own actions is the beginning rather than the completion of reconciliation and individuation. Holliday sees Blake as an example of a fascistic personality and believes that Ballard is condemning a proto-fascistic Romanticism on the part of William Blake, but he fails to see that *The Unlimited Dream Company* ends not with paranoia and aggression but love. Blake finally recognises that he truly is among the Reprobate rather than the Elect, that he has committed crimes and sins that require forgiveness. In recognising his guilt he is not magically released from those crimes, but he can finally move towards redemption and so reclaim his own corpse, an act of self-knowledge that directly parallels the understanding of Milton in the earlier poem:

Satan! my Spectre! I know my power thee to annihilate
And be a greater in thy place, & be thy Tabernacle
A covering for thee to do thy will, till one greater comes
And smites me as I smote thee & becomes my covering.
Such are the Laws of thy false Heavns! but Laws of Eternity
Are not such: know thou: I come to Self Annihilation
Such are the Laws of Eternity that each shall mutually
Annihilate himself for others good, as I for thee [.]
(*Milton* 38.29–36; Erdman 1988, p. 139)

This rewriting of *Milton* is significant and fully indicative of the appeal Blake has for those self-creating system-builders of the second half of the twentieth century. As Blake rewrites Milton's works to demonstrate his errors and create a new vision, one that recognises true friendship in such opposition, so Ballard, like Carter, does not draw on Blake slavishly to reason and compare but to recreate the Romantic in his own visionary universe.

In the final novel to be considered here, *The Existential Detective* (2010) by Alice Thompson, William (or "Will") Blake is the name given to the private detective in a rather grim, hard-boiled book dealing with prostitution, voyeurism and paedophilia in the Edinburgh seaside resort of Portobello. Some elements of the novel are reminiscent of Michael Dibdin's 1995 crime novel, *Dark Spectre*, and the knowing motif of naming the protagonist after Blake calls to mind Ballard's book as well as Jim Jarmusch's film, *Dead Man* (also 1995), though in this case the detective is knowingly of Blake's party unlike the innocent Johnny Depp in Jarmusch's version. Blake, the eponymous existential detective, is called in to investigate the disappearance of a young woman, Louise Verver, an amnesiac who has married into a rich family. Discovering that she had recently begun to recover certain memories before her disappearance, as well as the fact that a local prostitute has attempted to blackmail her husband, Blake's search takes him through brothels and nightclubs, leading him inevitably to perverse secrets hidden away from daily life in this small resort. At the same time, the investigation brings him once more into contact with his divorced wife, Olivia, and revives his own memories of their missing daughter.

Allusions to the poet and artist are subtle throughout the novel: "The sick rose" is cited at one point, while his ex-wife is writing a paper entitled "Innocence and experience in eighteenth-century paintings of children". Like Carter and Ballard, Thompson engages in magical-realist moments, as when Louise mysteriously turns up in a café with a copy of *Songs of Innocence and of Experience*, which Will Blake picks up to read:

> But as he read, the words kept disappearing until he was left with a blank page. He flicked through the rest of the book; all the pages were now blank. Only the title and author's name on the front remained. He staggered out of the café, leaving the book on the table, and collapsed onto the pavement outside. (Thompson, 2010, p. 54)

This section can still be read in realist mode (Blake is subject to proto-epileptic fits and this passage records his experiences of the scene), but the allusion to the Romantic is rather the repeated attempts inspired by the original William Blake to open the doors of visionary perception. As such, where Blake's presence does come alive in the novel, both as character in its pages and as a reference to the engraver and poet, is in the various sections of *The Existential Detective* that deal with desire:

> There was something about depression, he thought, that if you were lucky enough to come out the other end, made you a kind of visionary—like drugs, it was mind-altering. It seemed to give another dimension to reality, a fuller version of it, as if previously the world had seemed a theatrical stage-show of colour. It forged you.
>
> Desire returned with a vengeance, a ferocity. An abstract desire connected to pornography, rather than feeling. Most people lived life in disguise, concealing their own wants so as not to seem greedy. But we were all greedy in the end, greedy for different things. It was part of our humanity.
>
> He was powerless over his desire. He would drive down to Leith harbour where he would see the prostitutes walking up and down the streets, some looking as young as twelve in the semi-darkness, their faces always turning towards the light of a car like moths towards a flame. (Thompson, 2010, p. 44)

The William (as opposed to Will) Blake invoked here is the author of the verse, "In a wife I would desire / What in whores is always found / The lineaments of Gratified desire" (Erdman, 1988, p. 474), as well as the observer of the youthful harlots whose curse spread as a plague through London in the 1790s. Assuming that Will Blake is a comment on William, then the figure invoked in *The Existential Detective* is one both aware of the potential destructiveness as well as the brilliance of his desire, a part of humanity that if ignored or controlled leads to the callous inhumanity of the cool, intellectual villain of Thompson's novel, as well as the neglectful, dreary locale of the pub-cum-brothel, the Milton (a nod, of course, to not dissimilar themes in Blake's epic poem).

These particular examples of self-motivated system building do not, by any means, exhaust the limits of Blake's inspiration on later writers. Yeats is perhaps the odd one out in this chapter, in that his attempt to construct a coherent, even rigid, framework for Blake's ideas in order to create sense out of chaos runs counter to Spare, Carter, Ballard, and Thompson, who are more concerned with the fluid patterns of desire over order. This is not necessarily to denigrate Yeats, who provided an important link in the reappropriation of Blake as a thinker, but his

Urizenic structures were quickly recognised as systems from which individuals themselves had to be delivered. Within the other writers, and Carter is a particularly good example of this, Blake certainly does not provide a tradition of ordered concepts and mythic figures to be deployed religiously, but rather the confrontational source of imagination that rejects passivity of self in the face of an empirical world. All Blakeans are not one, but this source, generous enough to accept heathens, Turks, and Jews, as well as Christians, is what Blake considered the proper state of the divine image.

## *References*

Ankarsjö, M. (2009). *William Blake and Religion: A New Critical View*. Jefferson, NC: McFarland.

Antonielli, A. (2008). William Butler Yeats's "The Symbolic System" of William Blake. *Estudios Irlandeses, 3*: 10–28.

Ballard, J. G. (1981). *The Unlimited Dream Company*. London: Triad/Panther.

Bentley, Jr., G. E. (1977). *Blake Books*. Oxford: Clarendon Press.

Carter, A. (1977). *The Passion of New Eve*. London: Virago.

Carter, A. (Ed.) (1991). *The Virago Book of Fairy Tales*. London: Virago.

Carter, A. (1998). *Shaking a Leg: Collected Journalism and Writings*. London: Vintage.

Cary, J. (1944). *The Horse's Mouth*. New edition. Harmondsworth: Penguin.

Clark, S. (2007). "There is no competition": Eliot on Blake, Blake in Eliot. In: S. Clarke and J. Whittaker (Eds.), *Blake, Modernity and Popular Culture*. Houndmills: Palgrave.

Damon, S. F. (1924). *William Blake: His Philosophy and Symbols*. Boston: Houghton Miffin.

Damrosch, L. (1980). *Symbol and Truth in Blake's Myth*. Princeton: Princeton University Press.

Davies, K. (2006). The lost Moravian history of William Blake's family: snapshots from the archive. *Literature Compass*. http://www.blackwell-compass.com/subject/literature/article_view?article_id = lico_articles_bpl370, accessed 15 December, 2010.

Dorfman, D. (1969). *Blake in the Nineteenth Century: His Reputation as a Poet from Gilchrist to Yeats*. New Haven: Yale University Press.

Eaves, M. (1995). On Blakes we want and Blakes we don't. *Huntington Library Quarterly, 58*: 413–439.

Eliot. T. S. (1924). *The Sacred Wood: Essays on Poetry and Criticism*. New edition. London: Faber and Faber.

Ellis, E. & Yeats, W. B. (Eds.) (1893). *The Works of William Blake, Poetic, Symbolic, and Critical*. 3 vols. London: Bernard Quaritch.

Erdman, D. V. (1988). *The Complete Poetry & Prose of William Blake*. Revised edn. New York: Bantam Doubleday.

Frye, N. (1947). *Fearful Symmetry: A Study of William Blake*. Princeton: Princeton University Press.

George, D. H. (1980). *Blake and Freud*. Ithaca: Cornell University Press.

Grant, K. (1975). *Images and Oracles of Austin Osman Spare*. London: Frederick Muller.

Holliday, M. (2007). A home and a grave: Mike Holliday on *The Unlimited Dream Company*. *Ballardian*, 17 July 2007. http://www.ballardian.com/home-and-a-grave, accessed 23 December 2010.

Larrissy, E. (2006). *Blake and Modern Literature*. Houndmills: Palgrave.

Lincoln, A. (Ed.) (1991). *The Illuminated Books of William Blake, Volume 2: Songs of Innocence and of Experience*. London: Tate Publishing.

Masterson, D. & O'Shea, E. (1985). Code breaking and myth making: the Ellis-Yeats edition of Blake's works. *Yeats's Annual, 3*: 53–80.

Prothero, S. (2010). *God is Not One: The Eight Rival Religions That Run the World—And Why Their Differences Matter*. London: Harper Collins.

Quinney, L. (2009). *William Blake on Self and Soul*. Cambridge, MA: Harvard University Press.

Ranger, C. (2007). Friendly enemies: a dialogical encounter between William Blake and Angela Carter. In: S. Clarke and J. Whittaker (Eds.), *Blake, Modernity and Popular Culture*. Houndmills: Palgrave.

Rich, A. (1995). *On Lies, Secrets, and Silence: Selected Prose, 1966–1978*. New York: Norton.

Schuchard, M. K. (2006). *Why Mrs Blake Cried*. London: Century.

Singer, J. (1973). *The Unholy Bible: A Psychological Interpretation of William Blake*. New York: Harper & Row.

Spare, A. O. (1993). *From the Inferno to Zos: The Writings and Images of Austin Osman Spare*. A. R. Naylor (Ed.). Seattle: First Impressions.

Swinburne, A. C. (1868). *William Blake: A Critical Essay*. London: John Camden Hotten.

Tanner, T. (1971). *City of Words: American Fiction, 1950–1970*. London: Harper Collins.

Thompson, A. (2010). *The Existential Detective*. Isle of Lewis: Two Ravens Press.

Whitson, R. & Whittaker, J. (2012). *William Blake and the Digital Humanities: Collaboration, Participation, and Social Media*. New York: Routledge.

# PART II

## OEDIPUS RECONSIDERED

## CHAPTER THREE

# The Yayāti complex: a contra-oedipal take on myth and the unconscious

*Saugata Bhaduri*

It is likely that when one sets to examine the connections between myth and the unconscious, the figure of Oedipus would be the first to come to one's mind. How Freud interpreted the myth of Oedipus to stand as a metaphor for the unconscious of everyman is indeed spectacular. Let me quote here how Freud narrates the myth in question, connects it to the unconscious, and also claims it to be of universal import:

> And now you will be eager to hear what this terrible Oedipus complex contains. Its name tells you. You all know the Greek legend of King Oedipus, who was destined by fate to kill his father and take his mother to wife, who did everything possible to escape the oracle's decree and punished himself by blinding when he learned that he had none the less unwittingly committed both these crimes … To this extent it has a certain resemblance to the progress of a psychoanalysis … He reacts as though by self-analysis he had recognized the Oedipus complex in himself and had unveiled the will of the gods and the oracle as exalted disguises of his own unconscious. It is as though he was obliged to remember the two wishes—to do away with his father and in place of him to take his

> mother to wife—and to be horrified at them ... There can be no doubt that the Oedipus complex may be looked upon as one of the most important sources of the sense of guilt by which neurotics are so often tormented. But more than this: in a study of the beginnings of human religion and morality which I published in 1913 under the title of *Totem and Taboo* ... I put forward a suggestion that mankind as a whole may have acquired its sense of guilt, the ultimate source of religion and morality, at the beginning of its history, in connection with the Oedipus complex. (Freud, 1916–1917, pp. 330–332)

But can what Freud named the Oedipus complex be really considered a universal model, for "mankind as a whole" as he puts it, or is it another instance of blatant Eurocentrism in our hermeneutic practices? Can one find, in non-European sources, linkages between myth and the unconscious that are not oedipal, or that are even contra-oedipal? It is this query that leads me to look into classical Indian mythology at what is acknowledged in some circles as the Yayāti complex, a potent instance of reverse-oedipality that connects myth and the unconscious.

The "Yayāti complex" is, as indicated above, not a neologism coined by myself, but a concept that has been around for some time now. For instance, Anand C. Paranjape claims, in an influential study that, "it is tempting to suggest that a 'Yayāti Complex' is as central a feature of the Indian civilization as Freud thought the Oedipus Complex was for the whole of humanity" (Paranjape, 1998, p. 254). Extending the scope of the function of the Yayāti complex further into what I call its "reverse-oedipality", Devdutt Pattanaik notes that "[t]ales in Hindu scriptures suggest a reverse-oedipal, or Yayati complex" (Pattanaik, 2003, p. 190). But, what is the "Yayāti complex"? This essay seeks to address four central issues that arise from the above quotes, namely, first, that Yayāti is a figure in classical Indian philosophy; second, that he (or at least the "complex" that is derivable from his story) is "central" to "Indian civilization"; third, that this "complex" is "reverse-oedipal"; and fourth, that this "complex" holds the key to understanding the functioning of the unconscious and the connection between myth and the unconscious in ways that are different from Freudian.

First, then, let me introduce the story of Yayāti. The well-known classical Indian myth of Yayāti provides an interesting counterpoint to the Oedipus myth. It was originally narrated in the *Mahābhārata*,

Book I, i.e *Ādi-parva*, Sections 75–93 (*Mahābhārata*, the great Sanskrit epic usually attributed to Vyāsa, was begun sometime in the ninth century BCE and completed in its current form by the fourth century CE) and followed up in other sources such as the *Harivaṁśa* (an appendix to the *Mahābhārata* narrating the genealogy of Kṛṣṇa, composed around the first century CE), *Viṣṇu-purāṇa* (a compilation of legends of ancient kings and stories pertaining to the different incarnations of the Hindu god Viṣṇu, believed to have been composed around the fourth century CE), *Padma-purāṇa* (a later text composed between the eighth and eleventh century CE, which depicts myths concerning the creation of the cosmos and Bhārata or India), and *Bhāgavata-purāṇa* (or *śrīmad-bhāgavatam*, an even later text, composed around tenth to eleventh century CE, depicting the different incarnations of the Hindu god Viṣṇu, especially Kṛṣṇa). Unlike the Oedipus myth, where the son has to kill the father in a foreboded game of contested sexuality, Yayāti's is the reverse story of a son giving up his own youth and sexual prowess to provide the same to his father.

The complex and rather long story involves King Yayāti's bigamous dalliance with the Asura princess Śarmiṣṭhā (who, due to certain circumstances, not necessary to be narrated here, had been reduced to the status of a maid to his first wife), and the first wife Devayānī's father, the sage Śukrācārya, cursing Yayāti for this marital breach with infirmity and decrepitude, but with a very interesting redemptive rider. To quote from a concise account of the originally nineteen-chapter-long story in the *Mahābhārata*:

> Sharmishtha continued to stay as Devayani's handmaid. Yayati made a palace for Sharmishtha at the request of Devayani. One day Sharmishtha secretly met Yayati and told him what happened between her and Devayani. Yayati was sympathetic. Sharmishtha begged Yayati to take her as the second wife. Yayati agreed and married her but without the knowledge of Devayani. Sharmishtha had three sons. One day, Devayani met the three sons of Sharmishtha. She asked the boys the name of their father. They pointed to Yayati. Devayani was shocked. She felt deceived and ran to her father's hermitage. Sukracharya was enraged and cursed Yayati with premature old age. Yayati begged for forgiveness. Sukracharya and Devayani felt sorry for him. Sukracharya then said, "I cannot take back my curse, but if any of your sons is ready to exchange his

youth for your old age, you will be young again as long as you wish".

Yayati, now an old man, quickly returned to his kingdom and called for his eldest son. "My dutiful son, take my old age and give me your youth, at least for a while, until I am ready to embrace my old age". The eldest son turned down his father's request and so also the next three older brothers. Then came the youngest, Puru. He agreed and immediately turned old. Yayati rushed out as a young man to enjoy his life. After years spent in vain effort to quench his desires by indulgence, Yayati finally came to his senses. He returned to Puru and said, "Dear son, sensual desire is never quenched by indulgence any more than fire is extinguished by pouring oil on it. Take back your youth and rule the kingdom wisely and well".

Yayati then returned to the forest and spent the rest of his days in austerities, meditating upon Brahman, the ultimate reality. In due course, he attained heaven. ("Story of King Yayati")

The above is the "original" version of the Yayāti myth as narrated in *Mahābhārata* and extended with slight variations in *Viṣṇu-purāṇa* and *Bhāgavata-purāṇa*. However, *Harivaṁśa* gives an additional piece of information about Yayāti—that he received a celestial chariot from Indra, the king of the gods, with which he conquered the whole world and even defeated the gods. The Indra-chariot connection leads to a somewhat different version of the Yayāti myth in *Padma-purāṇa*:

Yayāti was invited to heaven by Indra, who sent Mātali, his charioteer, to fetch his guest. On their way they held a philosophical discussion, which made such an impression on Yayāti that, when he returned to earth, he, by his virtuous administration, rendered all his subjects exempt from passion and decay. Yama complained that men no longer died, and so Indra sent Kāma-deva, god of love, and his daughter, Aśruvindumatī, to excite a passion in the breast of Yayāti. He became enamoured, and in order to become a fit husband for his youthful charmer he made application to his sons for an exchange of their youth and his decrepitude. All refused but Puru, whose manly vigour his father assumed. After a while the youthful bride, at the instigation of Indra, persuaded her husband to return to heaven, and he then restored to Puru his youth. (Dowson, 2004, p. 377)

To be noted in these two rather different versions of the Yayāti myth is that whether he was just another king or an immensely powerful one who defeated even the gods, whether his amorous exploits involved Devayānī and Śarmiṣṭhā or Aśruvindumatī, what is common is that he bartered his son Puru's youth for his decrepitude to fulfil his own desires. Thus, whether the maritally unfaithful Yayāti was cursed by his father-in-law to suffer loss of youth and virility, with the condition that he could regain the same if one of his sons were to barter his own youth for his decrepitude, or whether he did so to enjoy a relationship with the daughter of Yama, the god of death, what is certain is that Yayāti's youngest son Puru gives up his youth for the sake of his father, and the father, after years of enjoying the fruits of young age loaned by his son, finally restores the same to his son and retires to the forest to die. This, therefore, is the crux of the Yayāti myth: that the son, rather than endeavouring to supplant the father to fulfil his sexual desire, instead gives up his own youth and virility to help fulfil the father's sexual quest.

Let me now move from the story of Yayāti to my second point: the significance of this myth in Indian culture down the ages. Not only has the myth been told and retold in several canonical texts of classical Indian literature and religion, but the story of Yayāti has also occupied a central place in contemporary Indian culture. It is not possible to list all the instances where modern Indian literature has recreated the Yayāti myth, but a contextualising passage from Sisir Kumar Das's authoritative *History of Indian Literature 1911–1956* may suffice to demonstrate how much the myth has been an obsession for Indian modernity:

> The earliest work on the subject in this century is *Yayāti* (1908) by the prolific Tamil playwright P. Sambandha Mudaliyar. He was followed by Srikanta Satpathy, the author of the Oriya narrative *Yayāti* (1927), and Govinda Ballabh Pant (Hindi play *Yayāti*, 1951) and V. S. Khandekar whose novel *Yayāti* (1959) has been hailed as one of the greatest works in Marathi literature. Sudhindranath Datta's 'Yayāti' included in *Sambarta* (1953) is one of the memorable poems in modern Bengali literature. Similarly, Umashankar Joshi's *Prācīna* (1944), a collection of seven dialogues [including Yayāti], created a new form of verse plays on themes borrowed from mythology. (Das, 1995, pp. 140–141)

While the above list shows how the story of Yayāti captured the imagination of a fledgling colonial modern Indian literary culture from all corners of the subcontinent—north (Hindi), south (Tamil), east (Oriya and Bengali) and west (Marathi)—the most influential among these has surely been Khandekar's novel *Yayāti*. Not only has the novel won the author the highest national literary awards of India—the Sahitya Akademi Award (1960) and the Jnanapith Award (1974)—but it also reinterprets the classical myth in an original way by defending Śarmiṣṭhā and Yayāti and putting the blame on Devayānī, thus showing signs of how appropriations of the text have kept in tune with changing times.

An equally influential adaptation, and an important representative of the contemporary canon of Indian literature (published after the period Das discusses, though) is Girish Karnad's first play *Yayāti*, originally composed in Kannada in 1961 and translated into English by the author in 2008. Incidentally, the play was composed by a twenty-two year old Karnad during his three-week voyage from India to England and his initial days in Oxford. He had come to pursue a Masters degree there, thus marking a curious correspondence of the myth with the angst a postcolonial intellectual typically bears—the tussle between belonging to one's native roots and experiencing affinity with the coloniser's culture. Explaining how relevant the story of Yayāti is to the postcolonial Indian sensibility, at least as exemplified in his own experiential version of the same, Karnad says in an interview:

> While I was writing the play, I saw it only as an escape from my stressful situation. But looking back, I am amazed at how precisely the myth of Yayati reflected my anxieties at that moment, my resentment with all those who seemed to demand that I sacrifice my future. By the time I had finished working on Yayati—during the three weeks it took the ship to reach England and in the lonely cloisters of the University—the myth had enabled me to articulate to myself a set of values that I had been unable to arrive at rationally. Whether to return home finally seemed the most minor of issues; the myth had nailed me to my past. (Ganesh, 2007)

This engagement with the myth thus presented young Karnad with an occasion to experience and assess the postcolonial angst of being caught between his being shipped to a British university and his being "nailed" to his past. Beyond this constellation, there is the circumstance of the English translation of *Yayati* almost four decades later, which highlights some other lines of mooring of the myth to quotidian facets of the Indian way of life. Karnad says in the same interview:

> There was more than one temptation to go back to it … [T]here was my own lived experience. From 22 to 70, I have grown and my perceptions have changed. For instance, when Yayati tells Sharmishta, "I'll make you my queen", she is so overwhelmed by the offer that she bursts into tears. This is something that didn't occur to me when I was 22. Also, when the newly-married Pooru says he wants to be left alone in his room … they were exactly my feelings when I went to my home in Dharwar with my wife. I wanted to be left alone in my room, it was my private space. (Ganesh, 2007)

What is interesting here is that, in recounting this dual relationship that he had with his own composition and re-composition of the myth at two different points of time in his life, and in theorising through the same the centrality of this myth to the Indian way of being, Karnad himself actually uses the term "Yayāti complex" and characterises it as reverse-oedipal. As the interviewer Deepa Ganesh puts it, paraphrasing Karnad's words, "If the West has its obsessions with the Oedipus complex, in India the engagement works in the reverse, which could perhaps be described as the Yayati complex. Karnad cites the Shantanu-Bheeshma story, Ganesha story, and the story of Rama from mythology as [further] examples" (Ganesh, 2007).

Yayāti finds prominence not only in Indian literature, but in contemporary Indian visual culture, too. The latter has its own re-interpretations of the myth to offer, as the 1987 painting *Yayati* by the celebrated Indian painter Bhupen Khakhar shows (see http://www.queer-arts.org/khakhar/yayati_lg.htm). This painting is very significant not only because it shows the prominence of the myth of Yayāti in the domain of modern Indian visual arts, but also because of the re-interpretation of the myth that it demonstrates. The first thing that strikes one is the frieze on the top comprising mundane activities of day-to-day Indian life, against whose backdrop one sees the act of Yayāti and Puru exchanging their youth. This backdrop frieze suggests a connection to the quote from Karnad above as to how there is an often imperceptible continuity between the Yayāti myth and the quotidian facets of Indian life. More important, however, are the two figures in the foreground. Whether the old decrepit figure at bottom is Yayāti receiving youth from his angelic son on top of him, or the sylphic figure on top is Yayāti taking off on his wishful wings borrowed from a freshly oldened Puru at bottom, is not the question. What is crucial is that this transference of youth and identity takes place through the two male figures—a father and a son—bringing their erect penises in contact with each other, in an unmistakably homosexual act. Without going into Khakhar's status and reception as a gay artist, what can be noted is how this adaptation of the Yayāti myth inverts a basic premise of the Oedipus complex: rather than the well-known narrative of incest between a parent and child of the opposite sex, what is foregrounded in the painting is the incestuous act itself between the father and the son, parent and child of the same sex. Thus, the Yayāti myth poses the possibility of a reverse-oedipality not only in terms of the son's giving up his youth for his father's sexual gratification—as generally presumed above—but also in terms of queering and reversing the very heteronormative basis of socialisation that Oedipus presumes. I will later connect the two theoretical insights that we have gained so far—Khakhar's appropriation of the Yayāti myth into queer discourse and Karnad's extrapolation of the same to postcolonialism.

Here, however, I would like to move on to the third point of this essay—that which concerns the possibilities, and actual existence, of a "reverse-oedipal" complex in the Indian context. The question whether one could find a general insistence on a reverse-oedipal complex in Indian mythology (of which Yayāti is but a symptom) has been the object of significant academic deliberation. A. K. Ramanujan, probably the best known modern Indian folklorist, writes in a 1972 article called "The Indian 'Oedipus'" the following: "Searching for stories of the Oedipus type some years ago in Indian myth and folklore, I found very little that looked like the Sophocles play" and adds: "Others had searched before me (e.g. Spratt, 1966) and concluded that Indian narrative has no Oedipal tales and therefore, of course, Indians have no Oedipus complex" (Ramanujan, 1972, p. 127). This leads us to the cited Spratt himself who, in his influential *Hindu Culture and Personality: A Psychoanalytic Study*, suggests that rather than "positive oedipal" stories of sons going against fathers, Indian mythology primarily presents "negative oedipal" tales of "narcissistic" fathers attacking, killing, or castrating sons. He argues:

> In judging between the hitherto accepted view that the typical Hindu psyche is punitive and the contention that it is narcissistic, the simplest criterion is the manifestation of the positive Oedipus complex. If sons frequently hate, attack, castrate or kill their fathers, then the accepted view is sound; if they seldom do but normally submit to their fathers, adopt the passive homo-sexual attitude, or castrate themselves in order to win his goodwill, then the view of this book is substantiated. (Spratt, 1966, p. 105)

Spratt and Ramanujan recognise that some Indian myths do contain "positive oedipal" content, and Ramanujan in his article collects quite a few narratives, both folk and classical, that are somewhat oedipal. Possible examples include the myths of Arjuna/Babhruvāhana, Prajāpati/Rudra, Rāvaṇa/Sītā, and Rāma/Lava-Kuśa, for instance. In *Mahābhārata*, Arjuna is killed by his son Babhruvāhana and later resurrected. The *Veda*s mention how Prajāpati Brahmā had intercourse with his daughter and was pierced during the act by his enraged son Rudra. In certain Jaina versions of the *Rāmāyaṇa*, Sītā was Rāvaṇa's daughter, whom he abandoned since it was ordained that she would be the cause of his death, but his later desire for, and abduction of, her makes the prophecy come true with Sītā's husband Rāma being the instrumental cause of Rāvaṇa's death. In the Bengali *Rāmāyaṇa*, Rāma is killed by his twin sons Lava and Kuśa and later revived. However, both Spratt and Ramanujan are of the opinion that such stories are few and far between, or belong to obscure sources, and that, generally, the better-known Indian myths always reverse the oedipal pattern.

Some other scholars, however, differ. George Devereux, for instance, in his influential article "The Oedipal situation and its consequences in epics of ancient India", writes that "[t]he Great Epics of Indian literature seem to reflect in an almost undisguised form a cluster of attitudes and fantasies which center about the Oedipus complex, the primal scene, the latency period, and the revival of the Oedipus conflict during puberty" (Devereux, 1951, p. 5). Similarly, Robert P. Goldman in his much-cited essay "Fathers, sons and gurus: Oedipal conflict in the Sanskrit epics" suggests that canonical Indian myths too have their share of oedipal tales:

> Although it has been occasionally argued that the Indian literature, written and oral, literary and folk, contains no truly Oedipal myth or legend, and that Indian children are somehow thereby exempted

> from what is otherwise a universal element of the human psyche, the existence of even the scanty literature ... at least absolves me from the need to once more refute this preposterous notion. Let us accept as a starting point that Indian literature, from its most ancient surviving period, *does* contain at least some Oedipal material. (Goldman, 1978, p. 325)

For Goldman, the failure on the part of some scholars to recognise the prominence of oedipal narratives in such seminal pieces of literature as *Rāmāyaṇa* and *Mahābhārata* is due to the fact that they look for the oedipal conflict too literally—in other words, they look for the precise father–mother–son triangle—rather than expanding its metaphorical scope across other forms of cross-generational incestuous or conflictual relationships. He argues that "[i]t is possible, if we are willing to abandon a fixation on the actual father, mother, son triangle of the famous Greek story, to demonstrate that the Oedipal struggle is to be found represented in and is in fact the central issue in a fairly large number of the most widely known, often retold, and most popular of India's traditional legends" (Goldman, 1978, p. 327). Accordingly, Goldman analyses in his article numerous classical Indian stories, and shows how they have material that is oedipal. In fact, on his reading, the story of Yayāti is also "positive oedipal", rather than "negative oedipal", "reverse oedipal", or "contra-oedipal", as we have otherwise interpreted it. For Goldman, Puru's surrender to Yayāti is only "temporary" and ultimately it is he who emerges victorious, and his initial suspension of virility is in fact quite akin to the oedipal suppression of one's desire out of fear of castration at the hands of the father (Goldman, 1978, pp. 344–347). Goldman highlights this "temporary" nature of the Puru-Yayāti transaction in his article, "Transsexualism, gender, and anxiety in traditional India", where he places it within a wider context: "[M]ost important Bhārata dynasts and heroes including Ila, Yayati, Puru, Pandu, and Arjuna are forced, either through a curse or as an act of filial devotion, to lose or suppress their virility temporarily" (Goldman, 1993, p. 380).

While the debate as to whether there are or are not oedipal tales in classical Indian mythology may continue, my concern here is just the reverse—whether there are, the number of oedipal stories notwithstanding, several important instances of what is ostensibly a reversal of the oedipal situation, and whether these instances could shed some light on the (particularly Indian) unconscious. In fact, Ramanujan, in a later essay of his—"The Indian Oedipus" (1983)—acknowledges Goldman's supplementations: "Goldman (1978) ... takes issue with my point regarding the 'reverse-Oedipus' in India. He enlarges on some of my examples (and adds several more) with great erudition, makes several acceptable corrections (which I have incorporated here), and points to an important displacement of the 'positive' Oedipal" (Ramanujan, 1983, p. 245). He, however, still generally holds his earlier position concerning "reverse oedipality" and gives several major illustrations of the same—stories of Bhīṣma, Gaṇeśa, and, of course, Yayāti:

> There are very, very few stories of actual patricide in Hindu myth, literature, and folklore ... But such stories are rare or little known .... But another pattern is very common: the aggression of the father towards the son. In all these stories the son willingly gives up (often transfers) his political and sexual potency. In the epic *Mahābhārata*, Bhīṣma, the first son of Śāntanu, renounces both kingdom and his reproductive sexual life so that his father may marry a fishergirl and continue his (father's) sexual/reproductive life ... Yayāti, a king cursed by a sage to suffer senility, wishes to prolong his life of pleasure and asks his five sons to transfer their youth to him ... Many more instances may be cited of the father-son conflict with the father as victorious aggressor. I shall add only one more: the story of Gaṇeśa, the elephant-headed god. Pārvatī went to bathe, and stationed Gaṇeśa, her son, at the door, telling him to let nobody in. (In the *Śiva Purāṇa*, the scene is set in the bedchamber.) Her husband Śiva wanted to enter; and when Gaṇeśa tried to stop him, Śiva cut off his head, which was later replaced by an elephant head. (Ramanujan, 1983, pp. 244–245)

One could go on documenting the contra-oedipal possibilities that so many classical Indian narratives have to offer, but it is time to move on to my fourth and final point—the implications of this "complex" for the "Indian unconscious". Can one generalise this abundance of stories of the son giving in to the father's wishes as a "Yayāti complex" that marks the "Indian" psyche, as distinct from the "Western" one? Devdutt Pattanaik definitely thinks so, and writes in a 2010 article:

> In Greek mythology, a recurrent theme is one where fathers are killed by their sons. Uranus is killed by his son, Cronus, the Titan.

> Cronus, in turn, is killed by his son, Zeus, the Olympian. The first to lead the gods is Uranus. When he is killed, Cronus takes his place. When Cronus is killed Zeus takes his place. Thus, succession takes place by the death of the father … Sons have to revolt against their father and claim the universe … In Hindu mythology, however, a different recurring theme is seen. Here, it is the father who triumphs and the son loses. And the defeat of the son, often voluntary, is glorified. What scholars have observed in India is the Yayati complex, which is rather the opposite of the Oedipus complex … Son sacrifices himself for the pleasure of the father and for this he is glorified as a hero. Yayati complex is then about the younger generation submitting to the older generation. (Pattanaik, 2010)

Ramanujan also seems to hold the view that the contrariness in the tropes of the two sets of myths suggests a fundamental difference between the two cultural modes of being, two types of psyches, and, most specifically, two different models for the unconscious. Arguing how the "reverse" or "negative" oedipality in Indian tales like Yayāti shows that the Freudian model cannot be taken as "universal", and a people's unconscious "quest" has to be understood in culturally specific terms, he asks:

> Why do the Indian tales cited here present the reverse, defensive, "negative" Oedipus-type? And the Greek Oedipus the "positive" (son-marries-mother, etc.) type? … The problem of psychoanalytic universals is a difficult and important one. Is the Oedipus complex universal? Does it take the same form regardless of culture? People in all cultures have fathers, mothers, sons and daughters. But the relations between them are not culture-free. Kinship patterns, property laws, the dominance of male or female in power, lineage or residence, attitudes to old age or childhood, and more, are all influential in deciding psychological patterns. While intergenerational competition … seems universal, the direction of aggression and desire, and the outcome seem different in different cultures … Indian conceptions of heroes and heroism are also quite different from the Greek or other European notions. Freud says, "A hero is someone who has had the courage to rebel against his father and has in the end victoriously overcome him"… The modern Western

> quest is individuation, achieved through an overthrow of the father, whereas the Indian hero's quest is to fulfil his father, his family. (Ramanujan, 1983, pp. 253–254)

Ramanujan's interpretation holds that the recurrence of reverse-oedipal motifs in Indian mythology can provide vital insights into the nature and constitution of the Indian psyche and the workings of the Yayāti complex in contradistinction to the Oedipus complex. Goldman is likewise of the opinion that these narratives, though oedipal and not contra-oedipal for him as explained above, can provide significant insight into the cultural, social, and psychological makeup of the Hindus:

> By studying the Oedipal episodes of the *Rāmāyaṇa* and the *Mahābhārata* we can at the same time gain important insights into many phenomena of Indian familial, social, and spiritual life. Serious research can and should trace the connections between recurrent and characteristic mythic and legendary material in the sagas of the epic heroes and well attested characteristic, though poorly understood, phenomena of Hindu culture such as the subservience to authority … nonviolence … and the high value placed on renunciation. It is through a careful pursuit of such connections that we may hope to further advance our knowledge and understanding of Indian life as well as Indian literature. … The reverse is also true. Only through insights into the psychological dynamics of Hindu family and social life can such curious and recurrent epic motifs as … the degradation of one's sons, the disqualification of the heir-apparent … be understood. (Goldman, 1978, p. 365)

But what constitutes the features of this differential, perhaps reverse-oedipal, collective unconscious, and what would have been its historical fallout? Probably the most convincing, if also the most controversial attempt to connect such narratives of self-mortification—by a young male to a senior family member—to the collective unconscious of Indians, or Hindus to be precise, is found in G. Morris Carstairs's classic *The Twice Born* (1951), where he argues that in India,

> [i]n effect all those who occupy the status of sons or younger brothers are required to enact a symbolic self-castration, denying themselves the right to lead an emotional or sexual life of their own

> so long as the father-figures still live and dominate them. On the other hand he expects a similar unquestioning subservience from all those who are below him in rank and authority. (Carstairs, 1951, p. 160)

Carstairs's general thesis of the "unquestioning subservience" of the Indian male psyche, based on such narratives, leads him to theorise Indian male psychosexual development as one where the growing self is always desirous of its subordination to powerful male others, as opposed to the oedipal development of the Western self which primarily resists subordination and engages with authority. Carstairs extends this to a study of the "genesis of national character" in India through "events which occur in the earliest stages of psychological maturation" (Carstairs, 1951, pp. 138, 153). In fact, for Carstairs, it is this subordination to the father—or Yayāti complex, as we have had it—that can explain the Indian's general psychological propensity for submission before authority:

> From this time on his father's voice will be associated with commands which must be obeyed … he has no choice other than that of unconditional surrender before this strong intruding stranger, his father. He must not only submit before this rival, but must deny any wish to compete with him. This is clearly reflected in the Hindu's later attitude towards his fellow men. To his father, and to figures of authority in general he owes unquestioning obedience … In effect all those who occupy the status of sons or younger brothers are required to enact a symbolic self-castration, denying themselves the right to lead an emotional or sexual life of their own so long as the father-figures still live and dominate them. This is implicit in the Hindus' willing subservience to autocratic Rajahs, to the rich, and to important officials. (Carstairs, 1951, pp. 158–160)

The argument that passive acceptance of older male authority, or the Yayāti complex, is fundamental to the Indian male psyche is further developed by Sudhir Kakar in *The Inner World* (1981). The image of the submissive Indian male, desiring and giving himself up to the figure of a stronger male authority—the Yayāti complex itself—has also been interpreted in homosexual terms, not only by Kakar, but also as shown in my earlier reference to Khakhar's painting, or to an earlier quote in this article from Spratt. The political problem of such a construction of the Indian unconscious as passive lies in its easy extrapolation into a rationalisation of colonialism—that is, into the construction of the figure of the submissive Indian, psychologically oriented towards desiring the rule of the colonising father figure. The critique of such an interpretation has been proposed by Ashis Nandy in *The Intimate Enemy*. Here Nandy talks about "the homology between sexual and political dominance which Western colonialism invariably used—in Asia, Africa, Latin America", which makes one internalise "the idea of colonial rule as a manly or husbandly or lordly prerogative" (Nandy, 1983, pp. 4–5).

However, the interpretation of the "homosexual" incest and the resultant surrender of the son to the father as necessarily passive and effete itself possibly emerges from a homophobic position that fails to understand the subversive power of the queer. Cannot the "queering" that the reverse-oedipal Yayāti complex undertakes be seen as a potential undercutting of models of heteronormative Eurocentric universalisation, a reading which may furthermore allow for a radical "postcolonial" subversion of the same? It can certainly be argued that the pacifist and passivist, non-violent, self-castigating, and renunciatory attitude that Gandhi coaxed Indians to have towards their colonial masters effectively led India to her decolonisation, however "queer" such methods may seem to Manichean oedipal models of a violent, contestatory, and acquisitory model of interpersonal and international strife. The Yayāti complex, though, is indeed queer, and its reversal of the oedipal universal, of heteronormative commonsense, of the commonly and unquestioningly accepted principles of strife, competition, acquisition, violence, is potentially radical. Furthermore, far from the usual belief that the one who sacrifices loses, does not the Yayāti myth demonstrate succinctly that it is the one who submits, surrenders, renounces, that eventually, but assuredly, emerges as the "hero"? But, rather than going gaga (or "Yaya", if you will) over these somewhat hyperbolic statements of mine about the radical potential of reverse-oedipality, let me end this article with three cautionary notes.

First, any generalisation is problematic. As Goldman's and Devereux's studies referred to above show, it is not that every classical Indian narrative showing intergenerational incest or conflict is necessarily "contra-oedipal" and demonstrative of the Yayāti complex; quite a few are straightforwardly, or by extension, oedipal—including, as in Goldman's interpretation, the Yayāti myth itself. Moreover, even in narratives that do exhibit the Yayāti complex, like the story of Yayāti himself, not all sons are necessarily submissive to the father—for each Puru there are four other older sons who turn down their father's request. Furthermore, the father does not rule forever, as Yayāti's eventual surrender of his loaned youth to its rightful owner, the son, suggests. Lawrence Cohen succinctly sums up this situation:

> Old fathers cannot claim their sons' hot bodies for long. Their cooling and weak physiologies prevent them from exercising adequate control, and their demands for continued authority become empty and inappropriate, *bakbak*—so much nonsense or hot air. Sixty-ishness points to the contested authority between generations, embodied as a disjunction between a cooling body and a will or brain that cannot recognize the process. From this perspective, the heat of old brains is a reaction to the reality of old and cold; it is the proverbial rope of Indian philosophy, mistaken for a snake along the road at dusk, the symptom of false consciousness. (Cohen, 1998, p. 170)

Second, the potential polemic as to whether the Yayāti complex (based apparently on surrender and renunciation, by one son at least) is in any way "better" than the Oedipus complex (based on the desire to overpower), and, as a corollary, whether Eastern civilisations, steeped as they apparently are in the former, are "holier" than the acquisitive Westerners, is a specious, tortuous, and potentially meaningless debate. I have already shown how the complex can be and has been interpreted both positively and negatively. Moreover, one should always remember that the "complex" in question is named after the impossibly selfish Yayāti and not the self-effacing Puru, and thus it is ambiguous, at the very least, as to whether the term semantically invokes images of the renunciatory tendencies of Puru or the hyper-acquisitory tendencies of Yayāti. Interestingly, while the "complex" as discussed above does connote submission and sacrifice, there is also an equally established problematic concept called the "Yayāti syndrome", which some recent studies in management and politics have identified with self-aggrandising behaviour that does away with conscience for personal gain. Wikipedia, a good indicator of popular perception of terms, describes the syndrome as follows: "In modern language and usage, trading conscientious behaviour for external gain is sometimes called Yayati Syndrome". This "syndrome" cannot be taken as a sign of Indian moral superiority either, given that for every Puru to function, the East necessarily has a Yayāti at work.

Finally, one should refrain from the temptation of over-theorisation. It should be noted that, while describing the Yayāti complex, I have used epithets like "contra-oedipal", "reverse-oedipal", "negative-oedipal", even "otherwise-than-oedipal", but have deliberately refrained from using the established term "anti-oedipal", because—even if there may exist possibilities for such a comparative study—I believe it would be a bit of a theoretical overkill to connect the pre-capitalist contra-oedipal modes of subjectivisation presented in the Yayāti complex with the post-capitalist "anti-Oedipus" that Deleuze and Guattari propose in their monumental eponymous trans-Freudian study (1972).

In the context of the connection established in Freudian psychoanalysis between the Oedipus myth and the unconscious and its presumption of a universalism for the same, this essay proposed to scrutinise the reverse myth of Yayāti, and similar narratives in Indian sources, to establish whether the relationship between mythology and the unconscious can be otherwise than oedipal—whether there can be the case for a contra-oedipal Yayāti complex. To do so, I traversed four stages: I narrated the Yayāti myth, looked at the centrality it, and the trope itself, enjoys in the Indian context, showed how the narrative proposes "reverse-oedipal", "negative-oedipal", or even "contra-oedipal" possibilities, and then analysed how this "complex" can be seen as the founding block of the very development—often problematically so and often demonstrating possibilities of radical subversion of the global normative—of the Indian psyche and collective unconscious. Having further provided cautionary notes as to how one should not take the Yayāti complex as a theoretically indulgent point of departure for an alternate generalisation, let me end by reiterating the objective of this essay. My simple aim has been to show that, rather than Oedipus being presumed as a universal model for connecting myth and the unconscious, there are other models, available from other cultural universes, which connect myth and the unconscious in ways that are quite different, if not altogether the obverse of, the oedipal—and Yayāti is a fitting example of the same.

## *References*


Carstairs, G. M. (1957). *The Twice-Born: A Study of a Community of High-Caste Hindus*. London: Hogarth.

Cohen, L. (1998). The anger of the rishis. In: *No Aging in India: Alzheimer's, The Bad Family, and Other Modern Things* (pp. 153–187). Berkeley, CA: University of California Press.

Das, S. K. (1995). *A History of Indian Literature 1911–1956—Struggle for Freedom: Triumph and Tragedy*. New Delhi: Sahitya Akademi, 2006.

Deleuze, G. & Guattari, F. (1972). *L'anti-Oedipe*. Paris: Éditions de Minuit.

Devereux, G. (1951). The oedipal situation and its consequences in epics of ancient India. *Samīkṣā, 5*: 5–13.

Dowson, J. (2004 [1879]). Yayāti. In: *A Classical Dictionary of Hindu Mythology and Religion, Geography, History and Literature*. New Delhi: Asian Educational.

Freud, S. (1916–1917). *Introductory Lectures on Psycho-Analysis (Part III). S. E., 16*. London: Hogarth.

Ganesh, D. (2007). The time loop: interview with Girish Karnad. In: *The Hindu*, 19 November 2007. http://www.hinduonnet.com/thehindu/mp/2007/11/19/stories/2007111950880100.htm, accessed 25 August 2010.

Goldman, R. P. (1978). Fathers, sons and gurus: oedipal conflict in the Sanskrit epics. *Journal of Indian Philosophy, 6*: 325–392.

Goldman, R. P. (1993). Transsexualism, gender, and anxiety in traditional India. *Journal of the American Oriental Society, 113*: 374–401. http://en.wikipedia.org/wiki/Yayati, accessed on 25 August 2010.

Kakar, S. (1981). *The Inner World: A Psycho-Analytic Study of Childhood and Society in India*. Delhi: Oxford University Press.

Karnad, G. (1961). *Yayati*. G. Karnad (Trans.). Delhi: Oxford University Press, 2008.

Khakhar, B. (1987). *Yayati* (Painting, Oil on Canvas 91 X 122 cm). Collection of Mr. & Mrs. James Kirkham, London. http://www.queer-arts.org/khakhar/yayati_lg.htm, accessed on 25 August 2010.

Khandekar, V. S. (1959). *Yayati: A Classic Tale of Lust*. Y. P. Kulkarni (Trans.). Delhi: Orient Paperbacks, 2008.

Nandy, A. (1983). *The Intimate Enemy: Loss and Recovery of Self under Colonialism*. Delhi: Oxford University Press.

Paranjape, A. C. (1998). *Self and Identity in Modern Psychology and Indian Thought*. New York: Plenum.

Pattanaik, D. (2003). *Indian Mythology: Tales, Symbols and Rituals from the Heart of the Subcontinent*. Rochester, VT: Inner Traditions International.

Pattanaik, D. (2010). Fathers and sons. In: *Corporate Dossier*, 27 February 2010. http://devdutt.com/fathers-and-sons/, accessed on 25 August 2010.

Ramanujan, A. K. (1972). The Indian "Oedipus". *Transactions of the Indian Institute of Advanced Studies, 16*: 127–137.

Ramanujan, A. K. (1983). The Indian Oedipus. In: L. Edmunds and A. Dundes (Eds.), *Oedipus: A Folklore Casebook* (pp. 234–261). Madison, WI: University of Wisconsin Press, 1995.

Spratt, P. (1966). *Hindu Culture and Personality: A Psycho-Analytic Study*. Bombay: Manaktala.

"Story of King Yayati" (2010). http://www.mahabharataonline.com/stories/mahabharata_story.php?id=13, accessed on 25 August 2010.

CHAPTER FOUR

# The slaughter of Isaac: oedipal themes in the Akedah narrative revisited

*Paul Cantz*

Biblical narratives have historically been maligned or entirely ignored within the development of western thought in general and psychoanalytic metatheory in particular (Cantz, 2012; Cantz & Kaplan, 2013; Hazony, 2012; Kaplan, 1990, 2002; Wellisch, 1954). Sigmund Freud, despite his familiarity with biblical material as well as Jewish customs and rabbinic literature (Bakan, 1958; Küng, 1979; Yerushalmi, 1991; Gresser, 1994), chose to orient his theoretical writings and clinical jargon with myths and loan-words from Classical Greece (e.g. Oedipus, Narcissus, Eros, Kronos, catharsis), which he purported best captured the universal human condition (Downing, 1975). Freud's reliance on Greek-based metaphors, in all likelihood, derived from the ideological idealisation of Hellenic values imparted to him during his formative years attending the patently secular Viennese Gymnasium (Gay, 1987; Winter, 1997–1998; Winter, 1999). Sarah Winter (1999) and Arnold Richards (2006, 2008) have both highlighted Freud's implicit commitment to the German pedagogical spirit of *Bildung*, which, while not lending itself to a clean translation, broadly means "formation" or "self-cultivation", but more specifically refers to the post-enlightenment, neo-humanist tradition that became the intellectual home of German scholars and the surest route for aspiring Jewish academics to achieve social respectability and professional advancement. The cosmopolitan, ardently secular ethos of *Bildung* would have made it unconscionable for Freud to interpret the Bible favourably. In a sense, the cultural pressures of *Bildung* blinded Freud, constricting him to draw narrowly upon the classical Latin, Greek, and European literature that conformed to the intellectual sensibilities of the Viennese bourgeois.

Freud's determination for psychoanalysis to be accepted as a bona fide scientific discipline, rather than merely a "national Jewish affair" (eine jüdische nationale Angelegenheit)—a concern that he privately shared with Karl Abraham—led him to ensure the installation of Carl Gustav Jung (a gentile) as the first president of the International Psychoanalytic Association. In 1913, after Jung abdicated his presidency from the International, Freud quickly found a replacement in another non-Jewish analyst, the Englishman and his future biographer Ernest Jones.

As a consequence of Freud's reductive and materialistic treatment of religion, there unfortunately has been a limited effort to thoughtfully synthesise conventional psychoanalytic theory with the biblical tradition (Cantz & Kaplan, 2012; Fromm, 1966; Kaplan, 2002; Skolnick, 2009; Spero, 1992; Wellisch, 1954). Several recently published letters from Freud reproduced by Rolnik (2012) confirm Freud's limited understanding of biblical and Hebrew thinking. A short time after the publication of *The Interpretation of Dreams*, the Jewish historian and folklorist Alter Druyanov (then of Odessa) wrote to Freud suggesting that many of Freud's ideas align with those of the early Hebrews found in the Talmudic and Kabbalistic writings. Freud coolly replied that "[t]he remarks in the Talmud on the dream-problem have frequently been brought to my attention. It seems to me, however, that the similarities with the ancient Greek understanding of dreams are far more striking" (Rolnik, 2012, p. 13). In a second, equally illuminating exchange, the neo-Kantian Jewish philosopher Jakob Klatzkin requested a meeting with Freud to discuss his bio-philosophical essay, "The Urge to Know and the Principle of Life and Death", a copy of which he sent to Freud. Freud denied Klatzkin the opportunity to discuss his Hebraically-tinged hypothesis that consciousness could be traced to a vital power—a premise that was utterly incongruent with Freud's neo-Romantic proclivities—, flippantly responding that "the exchange between us would be equivalent to that between a polar bear and a whale" (Freud to Klatzkin, 14 February 1935, cited in Rolnik, 2012, p. 26).

Although implicitly influenced to a certain degree by his Jewish roots (Bakan, 1958), Freud adopted the Hellenic-Latin world of *Bildung* as his primary cultural frame of reference. Lowenberg has identified four domains that qualify Freud as what he describes as an "Hellenic pagan" (Lowenberg, 1994, p. 139): the oedipal triumph over his poor Jewish merchant father, his admiration of Greek aesthetics and Mediterranean antiquity, his plea for non-judgmental sexual morality and his personal philosophy of stoicism, particularly in the manner in which he faced his own physical decline and death. In these ways and others, Freud can be considered a Western thinker *par excellence*, and thus we should be reminded of Slater's blunt assessment that "buried beneath every western man is a Greek" (Slater, 1968, p. 451).

The privileged, intellectually entrenched position that the Greek worldview maintains within the ethos of psychoanalysis has encouraged a trend of approaching the Bible as a book to psychoanalyse rather than accommodating it as a valued, valid source for alternative cultural narratives. Although there can be little disagreement that Greek mythology reflects truths regarding core conflicts of the human condition, there must be room to question whether the resolutions promoted by these narratives represent the highest ideals of psychomoral progression, or if they merely represent the best solutions that could be expected from the Greek worldview. The rich dynamism of Hebraic thought remains pregnant with potential contributions to the theoretical edifice and clinical practice of psychoanalysis. I argue that as a genre, biblical stories should generally be appreciated as psychologically advanced narratives meant to both reflect and impart progressive Western cultural values, such as the ability to psychologically individuate from one's family of origin and form healthy social boundaries and mature interpersonal attachments. In this vein, I argue that prototypical myths from the Greek and biblical cultures can be aptly situated on a psycho-mythological continuum, with Hellenic myths representing a less psychologically integrated, good-enough level of psychic development, while Hebraic myths denote an unambivalent, higher level of psychological achievement. Furthermore, a continuum of myths that exemplify varying measures of psychological integration can likewise be identified in the Greek and biblical literature, allowing for the cultural phenomenon of a minority of "Hebraicised" Greek mythologies as well as "Hellenised" Hebraic mythologies.

The foundational status that the myth of Oedipus Rex enjoys within psychoanalytic metatheory makes this the obvious starting point for the exploration of the cultural assumptions upon which Freud developed his science. Similarly, the centrality of the biblical story of the binding of Isaac (Genesis 22),[1] commonly referred to in Hebrew as the "Akedah", in each of the major Western religions (Judaism, Christianity, and Islam) invites us to explore the unique cultural attraction of this myth and its own potential contributions to the continuing development of psychoanalytic theory and practice. Indeed, the psychoanalytic comparison between the Oedipus and Isaac mythologies has become a pastime in and of itself (see Arieti, 1981; Kaplan, 1990, 2002, 2007; Kaplan & Algom, 1997; Rank, 1912; Reik, 1961; Stucken, 1896–1907; Wellisch, 1954), and much of this present inquiry has been inspired by the provocative suggestions of those individuals who have boldly advocated a "biblical psychology".

### *Hebraism and Hellenism redux*

The acclaimed German poet and satirist Heinrich Heine can be credited for sparking the modern discussion concerning Hebraism and Hellenism. One of Heine's biographers, Israel Tabak (1948), identified his ambivalent feelings towards his Jewish roots as contributing to a certain *Zerrissenheit*—a fundamental rift in his soul—commenting that "in his appraisal of Jews and Judaism, and in his analysis of the Jewish problem, we find conflict and contradiction, praise and blame, glorification and ruthless denunciation side by side" (Tabak, 1948, p. 189). Nevertheless, in one of Heine's more famous appraisals we can find little doubt about his general cultural allegiances: "All men are either Jews or Hellenes, men ascetic in their instincts, hostile to culture, spiritual fanatics, or men of vigorous good cheer, full of the pride of life, naturalists" (Heine, 1840, p. 10). Like Heine, Freud traversed his professional career by walking an intellectual tightrope, as it were, between his assimilative strivings and his own Hebraic birthright and therefore it should come as little surprise that Freud was absolutely smitten with Heine's work, entertaining an intellectual kinship with the man whom he once listed among his all-time favourite authors (Freud, 1906f).

A generation later, the English poet and cultural critic, Matthew Arnold, in his own celebrated essay on Hebraism and Hellenism (1869), advocated a more inclusive approach to this subject, hoping that the critical integration of these two currents of Western thought would lead to the ideal society.

In consideration of the mutual influence that biblical and Hellenistic attitudes have had on a cultural level, it may be warranted to extend this dialectal interplay into the realm of individual psychology, in the process delimiting a space in which psychoanalysis and the biblical attitude can constructively coexist. In order to demonstrate the synergetic potential of theoretically marrying biblical and Hellenistic psychological paradigms, the biblical story of the binding of Isaac will be interpreted in concert with the mythology of Oedipus as well as with the rich post-biblical rabbinic traditions (midrashim) that reflect Hellenistic themes concerning the sacrifice of Isaac. The hopeful and optimistic biblical (Hebraic) narrative interpreted in tandem with the tragic and pessimistic (Hellenistic) post-biblical traditions represents an intercultural movement towards a more psychically integrated brand of folklore.

## *Biblical psychology*

It was Erich Wellisch's book *Oedipus and Isaac* (1954) that first produced a comprehensive comparison between these two cultural stories and truly welcomed a positive interest in the psychoanalytical study of the Bible. Wellisch, a British psychiatrist and psychotherapist, maintained that Freud's "Oedipus complex" portrayed an incomplete, underdeveloped and hopelessly Greek picture of mental health. To compensate for this perceived deficit in psychological theory, Wellisch focused on the story of the Akedah as the quintessential example of oedipal mastery.

According to Freud (1914c, 1923b, 1923e, 1924d), the critical event signalling the successful resolution of the Oedipus complex occurs when the child introjects parental values to form what becomes their ego ideal—a vital component of the superego. More specifically, Freud maintained that the ego ideal develops through the channelling of the libidinal object-love previously reserved for the opposite-sex parent into a narcissistic libido, resulting in a more realistic, balanced, and independent mental organisation of the self.

Although Wellisch subscribed to Freud's theory of superego development, the "Akedah motif", as he termed it, chiefly focused on the father's experience (the "Laius complex") and radically extended the introjection process by including the impact of an "assum[ed] external moral force" (Wellisch, 1954, p. 78), which "we are accustomed to call God" (ibid., p. 91) into the constellation of superego development. Abraham, by yielding to God's ninth-hour plea to "[l]ay not thy hand upon the lad, neither do thou any thing unto him" (Gen. 22:12), rejected the path of psychological determinism and internalised the life-affirming message of his Deity. This provision effectively makes Wellisch's theory one of "instinctual modification" rather than compromise formation, corresponding to a fundamental transformation of the instinctual architecture of the psyche and negating the need for further superego refinement since the Akedah motif offers a complete solution to conflict-laden, filio-parental dynamics.

Wellisch argued that parent-child dynamics were biblically codified in the covenantal resolution of the Akedah narrative, that they are characterised by the wholesale abandonment of paternal aggression and possessiveness, which are replaced by a peaceful, unambivalent bond of love and trust. Wellisch understood this moral development as being facilitated by Abraham's introjection of a divine imago—a paradigm-shifting event that effectively catalysed the life instinct against the death instinct, thereby deflating father–son rivalries and ensuring that intergenerational continuity is maintained (Wellisch, 1954, p. 114). Here we can also discern a parallel process between God/Abraham and Abraham/Isaac; similar to how Abraham's willingness to sacrifice his most beloved son concretised God's love and trust in Abraham and ended the series of trials of faith that Abraham had endured, Isaac's willingness to be bound on the altar demonstrated his own faith and trust in his father, Abraham. It therefore seems plausible that Isaac's submission encouraged Abraham's psychological progression. Alternatively stated, the covenantal relationship between Abraham and God extended into Abraham's relationship with Isaac. In essence, Abraham's relationship with God became prototypical for the intergenerational investment between fathers and their sons in the Hebrew tradition.

Offering a "new approach to psychiatry" (1954, p. 79), Wellisch believed that the conventional, Greek-influenced, psychoanalytic theory was passé at best and counter-therapeutic at worst, presenting his "biblical psychology", with its focus on the Akedah motif, as the natural extension of the Hellenistic paradigm of the psyche.

Unfortunately, during the printing of *Oedipus and Isaac*, Wellisch unexpectedly died. His work was mainly ignored by his contemporaries, with the notable exception of Theodore Reik (1961), who dismissed Wellisch's conclusions on the grounds that such a "venturesome assumption" of instinctual modification betrays all known historical and psychological data, although eventually conceding that the episode of the Akedah offers a "partial and provisional adaptation" of the aggressive tendencies between fathers and sons (Reik, 1961, p. 226).

Kalman Kaplan and his associates have generated a renewed interest in a non-theological Bible-based metapsychology and placed the Akedah motif as the cornerstone of their conceptual efforts (Cantz, 2012; Cantz & Kaplan, 2013; Kaplan, Schwartz, & Markus-Kaplan, 1984; Kaplan & Schwartz, 1993; Schwartz & Kaplan, 2004; Kaplan & Schwartz, 2006; Schwartz & Kaplan, 2007). Kaplan's critique (2002) undercuts Freudian theory by suggesting that the Akedah represents a binary alternative to, rather than a developmental extension of, the Oedipus complex. Following Slater's (1968) seminal work in ancient Greek family systems, Kaplan (2002) suggested that social psychological forces offer an alternative explanation for the morally superior and psychologically more mature father–son relationship described in the Akedah narrative. For Kaplan, the myth of Oedipus reflected merely the depraved social mores and misguided values of Classic Greek society and did not, as Freud maintained, represent a universal psychological condition. Asked Kaplan:

> What kind of society is it where: (1) the son is seen as a threat to the father's position and the father is seen as a block to the son's development; (2) the son's only means of redressing this grievance is through displacing the father through the aid of the mother; [and] (3) the father keeps his power through implicitly or explicitly threatening castration? (Kaplan, 2002, p. 711)

Although Kaplan rejects the strict Wellischian interpretation of "instinctual modification", he affirms the possibility of culturally-mediated psychosocial transformations. Biblical society and its covenantal structure, asserts Kaplan, stymied the historical pattern of paternal competition, replacing this longstanding familial tension with a social system that promoted mutual benefit for both father and son, since "[t]he two generations have a vested interest in each other's well-being. The son wants a teacher, the father wants an heir" (Kaplan, 2002, p. 715). As a result of the unbalancing of these fatalistic familial power dynamics, Abraham achieved a level of psychological maturity that enabled him to replace his aggressive paternal tendencies with an unapologetic covenantal parent-son relationship forged in love and trust instead of a conflict-laden psychological paradigm based on fear and aggression.

This covenant, according to Kaplan, becomes symbolised through ritual circumcision, which he interprets as a non-injurious, sanctified cross-generational reminder of the modulated aggressive instinct—a "concrete physical act ... which internalizes this spiritual transformation" (Kaplan, 2002, p. 17). There is no need to fear a father who has demonstrated filicidal restraint and who expressly desires for his son to surpass him.

## *The psycho-mythological continuum*

The French philosopher and Nobel Laureate Henri Bergson (1932) suggested that the historical record of religions, which he felt were a natural extension of myths, could be effectively reduced into two camps: the "static" and the "dynamic". The former and relatively primitive "static" religions relied upon social pressure to enforce moral codes, while the latter, more sophisticated "dynamic" religions broke free of external demands and attracted fully cognisant followers. In effect, Bergson suggested that there exists a spectrum of mytho-religious expressions that displays static, deterministic tendencies on the low end, and dynamic, progressive impulses, on the high end.

Commenting on Bergson, another philosopher, Ernst Cassirer (1944), applied these discrete categories to Greek mythologies and Semitic religions, respectively, noting a progression from functional, concrete deities to more personal gods, such as Zeus, Hera, and Apollo, to finally a generalised, universal God, specifically the God of Israel. Cassirer's explanation highlighted the psychological progression from an external to an internal locus of control, writing that a "change of meaning" began with the prophetic books of the Hebrew Bible, whereby the potential purity or impurity of physical actions that constrained the behaviour of those primitive religionists became minimised and secondary to an individual's personal motivation, explaining that within the higher religion "[t]he only purity that has a religious significance and dignity is purity of the heart" (Cassirer, 1944, p. 107). The concrete taboo system that reigned in periods of more primitive religions had effectively become sublimated by the higher religions, creating a "more profound sense of religious obligation that instead of being a restriction or compulsion [became] the expression of a new positive ideal of human freedom" (ibid., p. 108).

Cassirer's philosophical elucidation of the complementary ethico-moral evolution of myth and religion provides a conceptual matrix for exploring the psychoanalytic vicissitudes of this mytho-religious progression, especially as it relates to the movement from Greek to biblical psychological attitudes.

Although the earliest psychoanalysts viewed myths and fairytales as intrapsychically synonymous with dreams inasmuch as both derived from the same intrapsychic pressures aimed to satisfy infantile wishes (Riklin & White, 1915; Rank, 1912), perhaps one of the most innovative contributions to the psychoanalytic understanding of myths came from the ego-psychologist Jacob Arlow (1961, 1964). Arlow stressed that myths can be better interpreted outside the topographic model of psychic functioning, contending that along with serving the fulfilment of id-based instinctual pressures, myths can function as shared cultural fantasies that both encourage and support defensive and adaptive ego functions in the service of personality organisation and superego development. Accordingly, cultures invariably craft and mobilise these shared cultural fantasies in the service of socialisation, buffering and cathecting the instinctual pressures enacted by the id into reality-promoting mythological expressions that adaptively integrate with societal mores.

In consideration of the common instinctual wishes that enact themselves in the fantasy life of the unconscious, Arlow (1961) maintained that each individual possesses a hierarchy of adaptive and defensive personal fantasies that become more or less prominently expressed at different developmental stages of ego-integration. Each culture offers its members a vicarious outlet to engage common unconscious fantasies, usually in temporal psycho-moral succession relative to the individual's stage of ego development. Arlow illustrates this point by contrasting three genetically identical expressions of mythology representing the common childhood wish to castrate, steal, and subsequently devour the phallus of the father. These are: the English fairy tale of Jack and the Beanstalk, the Greek myth of Prometheus stealing fire from Zeus, and the biblical story of Moses receiving the Law from God. In broad strokes, each of these three myths concerns a relationship to an authoritarian paternal figure that possesses something desirable to the protagonist. The figures of Jack and Prometheus, who each represent cultural heroes that resonate with either pathologically regressed or developmentally appropriate levels of primitive psychic integration (for example, pre-oedipal children), encountered malevolent and dictatorial patriarchal figures, and therefore were forced to resort to theft and deception to satisfy their wishes and to triumph over obvious personal trespasses. For Jack, as is typical for most fairy tale heroes, his mission was unambiguously righteous since in the concrete, part-object world of primitive ego development fairy tales reinforce what the folklorist André Jollés (1958) has called *"naïve moralité"*, in which the climactic endings almost always uphold conventional, if not immature, moral ideals. In both instances, Jack and Prometheus were burdened by an overwhelming fear of authoritarian (paternal) retaliation, and while Jack, in the manner of all fairytale endings, lived "happily ever after" in libidinal bliss, Prometheus was not as fortunate, and subsequently suffered severe punishment for his transgressions, being chained in the Caucasus mountains and having his daily-regenerating liver eaten-out by an eagle. Nevertheless, Prometheus' suffering corresponds to an incrementally more advanced form of ego development.

Of particular relevance to the Oedipus-Isaac/Hellenism-Hebraism exchange, however, is Arlow's evaluation of the tragic myth of Prometheus in contradistinction to the story of Moses receiving the Law. In Wellischian fashion, Arlow presented this biblical variant of the Jack and Prometheus myth as emphasising the integral role of positive identification with the (paternal) God in the formation of a higher order of psychic integration. Rather than encountering divine resistance after ascending Mount Sinai, Moses was freely given God's greatest gift—the Law:

> What was originally a crime of defiance and aggression against the gods is, in this later version, presented as carrying out the wishes of God himself. What has intervened is the process of identification, the identification between a mortal and a God (between father and son). *The identification is on a moral, rather than on an instinctual,* level. (Arlow, 1961, pp. 383–384; emphasis added)

Displaying an uncanny similarity with Wellisch's characterisation of Abraham's post-Akedah relationship with Isaac, Arlow portrayed Moses' identification with God as being based on a "moral, rather than instinctual level" (ibid., p. 383)—a thematically unique distinction. Whereas the Greek gods maintained power through sadistic manoeuvres, punishing the hubris of mortals, biblical society promoted—indeed commanded—complete *imitatio Dei.*

Although drawing conclusions different from those made by Wellisch, Arlow clearly displayed sensitivity to the type of instinctual shift communicated in biblical stories. Unlike Greek myths, biblical folklore presents narratives in which the superego ultimately attains psychic dominance, achieving a culturally adaptive level of instinctual sublimation and renunciation while concurrently allowing a modicum of expression for id-based wishes (Arlow, 1964). Of particular distinction, however, is that while Freud described the superego as the "heir of the Oedipus complex" (Freud, 1940a, p. 205), the moral element and the accompanying emphasis on righteous conduct within Hebraism do not simply represent the psychic by-products of an overdeveloped and punitive superego, but rather correspond to an instinctually disarmed psychic agent that behaves, as Arlow later suggested, more like the ego: "Such a superego", he writes, "would function judgmentally in a controlled, objective way ... that is, with no driving, compelling quality" (Arlow, 1982, p. 236). In an adaptation of one of Freud's better-known quotes, it may be warranted to say that in a biblical psychoanalysis: "where the superego was, ego shall be", or alternatively stated, that there exists a higher form of ego integration that extends the Hellenic-analytic ideal of the perfect id-ego-superego dialectic, perchance sequencing into a "supra-ego". This supra-ego functions as a qualitatively distinct psychic agent that supports the transcendence of instinctual proclivities in the service of attaining an enhanced ability to individuate, as well as a greater capacity to form mature attachment relationships. In the biblical psychic economy moral behaviour need not necessarily stem from a complex series of compromise formations fuelled by a sense of incestuous guilt, but instead is shaped by unambiguous, covenantal post-oedipal object relations that promote an individuated and morally robust ego.

It should not be ignored, however, that even in the Greek mythological tradition there can be found counter-normative mythological examples that display an incrementally higher order of familial object relations. Kohut (1982), for instance, suggested that the paternally responsible actions of Odysseus (who chose to save his infant son Telemachus from being crushed by his advancing plough) demonstrated the value of intergenerational harmony, which he considered to be reflective of normal human tendencies rather than an exceptionally moral psychology (that is, the "Telemachus complex"). Later in this Homeric epic we find Telemachus reciprocating Odysseus' sentiments when, while lamenting the absence of his father, he confided to his friend Eumaeus that, "if men could have anything for the asking, my father's return would be my first choice" (Homer, 1909–1914, Bk. XVI.148–149). We can also observe a psychologically progressed father–son relationship in Ovid's version of the myth of Medea and Aeson: Jason, upon returning from his adventures of retrieving the Golden Fleece, finds his father, King Aeson, close to death and beseeches his newly claimed wife, Medea (a sorceress), to intercede by supernaturally transferring a portion of his own vitality to his father, thereby extending his life (Ovid, 1993, Bk. VII).

It is worth noting, however, that while the relationship between Jason and Aeson surely demonstrated an increased measure of filial piety, Medea, impressed with Jason's overtures, rejected his plan and offered her own: she instead killed Aeson and drained his blood, subsequently reviving him with the use of a secret potion. This magical intervention not only staved off Aeson's demise, but erased forty years of aging, returning to him his former youthful energy and beautiful countenance. Unlike the covenantal bond that existed between Abraham and Isaac, Aeson's supernatural renewal ensured that his Corinthian monarchy was secure, thus implicitly reinforcing the intergenerational mistrust that fathers harboured against their sons.

Further advanced on the psycho-mythological continuum, however, lies the Akedah, which represents a progression on the oedipal motif that fully resonates with the Hebraic attitude towards healthy family relations. Within the context of a trusting relationship with a paternal imago (God), Abraham achieved a higher order of psychic integration that facilitated the modulation of unconscious, aggressive, filicidal impulses, allowing him to exercise instinctual restraint against the seemingly insurmountable opposition of fate. In so doing, he presented a psychically advanced resolution that released Isaac from the punishment (castration) that he would otherwise have been expected to receive as a consequence of, as Sugar (2002) has speculatively argued, implied incestuous phantasies directed towards his mother, Sarah.

As far as the dynamics underlying myth-identification are concerned, the reasons why the episode in Genesis 22 has not been semantically codified as "the test of Abraham", or a similarly descriptive variant, but rather as "the binding of Isaac", become clear. By identifying with Isaac, those communities that emphasise the story of the Akedah, whether they be Jewish, Christian, or Muslim, viscerally trust their intergenerational covenantal relationship with their actual parents as much as their metaphorical parent, that is, God. The id-based dynamics that drive oedipal triangulations do not inform their morally sophisticated psychic architecture, but rather the intergenerational covenantal bond empowers the conscious agency of the superego into mobilising the self towards a higher-order of conflict-free constellation of introjected familial object relations.

However, since the universal instinctual transformation of incestuous and murderous impulses eludes mankind, the biblical narrative presents a reverse-negative of the tragic Oedipus myth, although instead of exclusively marketing this story to children, like most fairy tales, it facilitates several levels of psychological maturity. For children, by identifying with the "lad" Isaac who narrowly escapes being murdered by his father, the Akedah functions as a simple fairy tale that communicates a fantastical escape from filicidal rage. For the adult who has attained the covenantal level of psychic integration, the Akedah represents a textured legend that exemplifies the attainment of instinctual transcendence and the promise of intergenerational familial harmony. In this vein, fairy tales and biblical stories, although conversely situated on opposite ends of the psycho-mythological continuum, both present unambiguous psychic resolutions to fundamental human conflicts.

## *Psycho-moral regressive identification*

In varying degrees, the psychoanalytic community generally acknowledges that oedipal triangulations represent a universal psychological construct, albeit with variations, cross-culturally and without major exceptions (Edmunds & Dundes, 1984; Johnson & Williams, 1996; Rank, 1907; Sugar, 2002; Tang & Smith, 1966). Indeed, even while appreciating psychologically progressive elements in the Akedah narrative, within the biblical economy of the psyche we can nevertheless discern deep-seated psychological paradigms that drive aggressive and incestuous wishes.

Lending further credence to the mythological-progressive nature of the biblical Akedah is the host of post-biblical rabbinic legends (midrashim) that portray the actual slaughter and subsequent resurrection of

Isaac at the hands of his father, Abraham (Spiegel, 1968). If we consider the biblical Akedah as existing at the apex of the psycho-mythological continuum of familial object relations, we should expect the regressive manifestation of a developmentally analogous biblical version of the Greek-based Oedipal tragedy, as Arlow indicated: "Regressive reactivation of repressed wishes of an earlier phase may be permitted expression by the ego if certain conditions are satisfied" (Arlow, 1961, p. 384). According to Spiegel (1968), these legends enjoyed their widest popularity during the Middle Ages as the devastation of many Jewish communities demanded a model of martyrdom that inspired faith and encouraged resilience. These Jewish communities were searching for meaning in their suffering—suffering that, consistent with their religious ideation, was delivered by a presumably loving God.

The myriad of artistic expressions of Isaac portrayed as a young boy—a chronological assumption that is not supported by a careful biblical accounting or mainstream rabbinic sentiment—further buttresses the developmentally adaptive nature facilitated by the post-biblical Akedah material, suggesting that the constellation of phantasies that inspired these artistic renderings relates to a developmentally regressive matrix of object relations. Parallel with the historical emergence of the counter-scriptural rabbinic legends of the slaughter of Isaac, renderings of Isaac as a young child are especially abundant within ancient, medieval, Renaissance, and Baroque Jewish and Christian artistic expressions of the Akedah (see Caspi & Greene, 2006; Gutmann, 1987; Smith, 1922). Although the Bible neglects to explicitly mention the age of Isaac at the time of the Akedah, various post-biblical exegetic sources conclude that Isaac was at least thirty-seven years of age during this ordeal—a mature man who had the moral agency and physical fortitude to resist his father had he sensed any hints at nefarious motives (Spiegel, 1968).

With the understanding of how the post-biblical Akedah material arose to release the oedipal hostility suppressed in Genesis 22, it is only natural that those artists choosing to iconize this scene depicted Isaac as a child at the pinnacle of his oedipal conflict—a puerile figure submissively docile to his own fateful sacrifice and immolation.

Extending Arlow's (1961) dual emphasis on the role of myth-identification in the process of individual and social psychological integration, Rollo May (1991), in his last published book, eloquently captured the functional essence of myths—particularly those that appeal to the base instincts of mankind:

> [i]n myths ... we experience catharsis by identifying with the performers on stage ... This is the openness of the myth: it spreads its arms, and all whom it takes in gain some of the power of the catharsis. There is also in the catharsis the social effect, the cleansing of the community ... [a] shared 'id' experience. (May, 1991, pp. 232–233)

We see from here that developmentally regressive mythologies—myths that remain situated relatively lower on the psycho-mythological continuum compared to the highest point achieved by a culture—also display defensive and adaptive qualities, much as individuals regress into developmentally earlier defensive operations when the ego becomes overwhelmed. The cultural emergence of these various aggadic legends that straightforwardly related the actual death of Isaac at the hands of Abraham was inevitable, similar to repressed traumatic psychic material manifesting itself in neurotic behaviours. This phenomenon of cultural repression, and the compensatory action of the unconscious, was discussed from a Jungian perspective by Rollins (1999), who commented that:

> A keystone of Jung's psychology is that the unconscious spontaneously produces images of direction or integration for individuals and cultures. Classical religions characteristically traffic in such images, which in the end have to do, not just with history "back then" or "out there" but with the "now" and the "within." ... [T]he purpose of these images within the economy of the psyche is to correct the "course" of the psyche when it has become "one-sided or adopts false attitudes". This serves as a corrective not only to the individual psyche, but to the psychic attitude of an entire culture or age when it has become sidetracked or when it forgets its *raison d'être*. (Rollins, 1999, p. 54)

If we consider the Jungian notion of the compensatory function of archetypical myths in union with Arlow's and May's complementary idea of cathartic identification and ego adaption, these post-biblical Akedah legends may have served a corrective function for the Jewish people, keeping in check the psychologically progressive oedipal resolutions promoted by the plain scriptural narrative. Using May's language, the accommodation of these legends within Jewish tradition acted to "cleanse" individuals from the shame and guilt associated with aggressive and filicidal urges—urges that were supposed to have been spiritually and psychologically neutralised by Abraham's instinctual restraint. The counter-scriptural mythology that arose from the story of the Akedah should not be surprising since, much like the unconscious material of the individual psyche, a "return of the repressed" occurs, which in this case allows for a religiously sanctioned liberation of viscerally experienced emotions of aggressiveness, seductiveness, and jealousy relating to an earlier, less integrated version of oedipal fantasy formations. In agreement, Bergmann (1992) suggested that in developmentally normative stages of psychological maturity, particularly in young boys, this consummated slaughter phantasy provides an outlet for sadomasochistic impulses. In effect, the counter-scriptural Akedah tradition represents the Jewish version of the Greek Oedipus myth and not the actual biblical narrative, as many have commonly suggested.

Nevertheless, we see the therapeutic limits of these paradoxical midrashic myths since even they could not offer an unpolluted emotional liberation, needing to yield to the biblical reality of Isaac's enduring vitality; Isaac would not have been resurrected in a completely cathartic mythological legend. This mytho-theological failsafe, as it were, perhaps ensured that the Hebraic attitude would give prominence to the biblical Akedah, with its accompanying message of hope, trust, and instinctual mastery.

With this updated consideration, the Greek myth of Oedipus and the counter-scriptural rabbinic traditions that portray the filicidal slaughter of Isaac appeal to a decidedly unconscious brand of pre-oedipal wish-fulfilment and phantasy formation that is aligned with primitive aggressive drives, that is, with thanatos. In direct contradistinction, the biblical Akedah can be understood as promoting the transcendence of these pre-oedipal wishes, reinforced *pari passu* with the life-instinct, eros.

## *A call for a biblical psychoanalysis*

Had Freud drawn upon biblical narratives to construct the theoretical wireframe of psychoanalysis the trajectory of psychotherapeutic developments over the past century might well have unfolded in a dramatically different fashion. Of course, had Freud withstood the cultural pressures of *Bildung* and chosen this path he would certainly have encountered insurmountable resistances from within and without the Viennese medical establishment, and his new science would have in all likelihood remained in historical obscurity.

I have argued that the Greek tradition, similar to pre-oedipal psychic integration, generally endorsed a decidedly fatalistic, punitive, and psychologically limiting worldview. At this stage of psychological integration, a psychic compromise formation or sublimation may represent the best available solution for traversing familial conflicts. The Greek worldview, which orients the general psychoanalytic attitude, limits the goals of psychotherapy to good-enough solutions. In contradistinction, healthy, psychologically individuated ego development affords maximum freedom from instinctual forces, much as the biblical worldview remains "intrinsically open to the possibility of change and transformation" (Kaplan, 2002, pp. 214–215).

Few stories throughout history have left such indelible impressions upon western man as have the biblical legend of the Akedah and the Greek myth of Oedipus Rex. In his dramatisation of a prevalent Indo-European cultural myth, Sophocles memorialised the intolerably taboo seductive and aggressive undercurrents of familial triangulations. Jarring cultural mores, the explicit messages communicated in Genesis 22 created space for a teleological understanding of history by questioning whether humankind is governed by deterministic instinctual forces, such as those promoted by the Greeks, or whether it indeed harbours the potential to exercise personal agency and free-will, that is the will not only to neutralise but also to transcend deeply structured instinctual proclivities towards incest, aggression, and familial conflict all in the service of intergenerational continuity. The respective Akedah motifs advanced by Wellisch and Kaplan promoted a psychologically integrated, optimistic conceptualisation concerning oedipal dynamics, with each, in its own unique manner, suggesting that individual and societal transformation occurred as a result of the moral advances of biblical civilisation, with both advocating a renewed interest in a biblically informed metapsychology and psychotherapy.

The Bible, I would argue, has not inspired countless numbers throughout history because it communicates the turning point whereby human nature pivoted from base instinctual determinism to holy, all-encompassing spiritual freedom, but rather because it promises that there is the potential for such changes occurring on an individual and, during the so-called "messianic times", societal level.

Accordingly, the message of the Akedah—the "Akedah motif"—aligns with the expressed goals of clinical psychoanalysis, since it demonstrates the inherent capacity for the taming of instinctual forces through the reorganisation and restructuring of the psyche. There can be little doubt, though, that the Akedah motif, as with many biblical foundation stories, both indicates and promotes structural psychic change that progresses beyond the mere emboldening of the superego. In effect, these psychologically sophisticated stories reflect and support the transformation of the superego from a largely unconscious agent of compromise formation into an instinctually disarmed, psychologically-autonomous representative of the self, establishing what can at least provisionally be called a "supra-ego".

The paradoxical, counter-scriptural, post-biblical legends that relate the consummated sacrifice of Isaac at the hands of Abraham represent an inevitable rabbinic contribution functioning to regressively balance the mythological landscape by which humans experience a constellation of lesser-integrated fantasy formations. We find, for example, in Jewish history during times of heightened persecution that these same legends serve as rabbinically sanctioned avenues of emotional catharsis, offering partial sanitisation for culturally suppressed instinctual dispositions of incest and aggression. In this way, the Greek-based myth of Oedipus and the post-biblical, counter-scriptural, aggadic tradition, communicate equivalent developmental levels of psychic integration.

Oedipally progressive biblical myths such as Moses' receiving of the Law and the binding of Isaac signify more than lateral variants of Greek mythologies: they represent vertical movements towards an advanced level of ego integration. Nevertheless, Greek-based mythologies and biblical stories have both remained relevant in contemporary society because the psycho-cultural tendencies that these types of folklore represent metaphorically illustrate two distinct positions on the spectrum of the adaptive integration of the ego, with the former group highlighting the uncomfortably stubborn schematics of our instinctual heritage and the latter revealing the potential for instinctual transcendence.

## *Note*

1. As a test of faith, God commanded Abraham to sacrifice his most beloved son, Isaac. Abraham was willing to carry out God's wishes, but at the moment when he was to ritually slaughter and subsequently immolate his son, God interceded by sending an angel who commanded him to halt his actions. A ram was sacrificed in Isaac's stead.

## *References*

Arieti, S. (1981). *Abraham and the Contemporary Mind*. New York: Basic Books.

Arlow, J. (1961). Ego psychology and the study of mythology. *Journal of the American Psychoanalytic Association, 9*: 371–393.

Arlow, J. (1964). The Madonna conception through the eyes. *Psychoanalytic Study of Society, 3*: 13–25.

Arlow, J. (1982). Problems of the superego concept. *Psychoanalytic Study of the Child, 37*: 229–244.

Arnold, M. (1869). *Culture and Anarchy: An Essay in Political and Social Criticism*. New York: Macmillan, 1920.

Bakan, D. (1958). *Sigmund Freud and the Jewish Mystical Tradition*. Princeton, NJ: Van Nostrand.

Bergmann, M. S. (1992). *In the Shadow of Moloch: The Effect of the Sacrifice of Children in Western Religions*. New York: Columbia University Press.

Bergson, H. (1932). *The Two Sources of Morality and Religion*. R. A. Audra, C. Brereton, & W. H. Carter (Trans.). Notre Dame, IN: University of Notre Dame Press, 1977.

Cantz, P. (2012). Towards a biblical psychoanalysis: a second look at the first book. *Mental Health, Religion and Culture, 15*: 779–797.

Cantz, P. & Kaplan, K. J. (2013). Cross cultural reflections on the feminine "other": Hebraism and Hellenism redux. *Pastoral Psychology, 62*: 485–496.

Caspi, M. M. & Greene, J. T. (2006). *Unbinding the Binding of Isaac*. Lanham, MD: University Press of America.

Cassirer, E. (1944). *An Essay on Man*. New Haven, CT: Yale University Press.

Downing, C. (1975). Freud and the Greek mythological tradition. *Journal of the American Academy of Religion, 43*: 3–14.

Edmunds, L. & Dundes, A. (1984). *Oedipus: A Folklore Casebook*. New York: Garland.

Eigen, M. (1981). The area of faith in Winnicott, Lacan and Bion. *International Journal of Psycho-Analysis, 62*: 413–433.

Freud, S. (1906f). Contribution to a questionnaire on reading. *S. E., 9*: 245. London: Hogarth.

Freud, S. (1914c). On narcissism: an introduction. *S. E., 14*: 67–102. London: Hogarth.

Freud, S. (1923b). The ego and the id. *S. E., 19*: 12–59. London: Hogarth.

Freud, S. (1923e). The infantile genital organisations: an interpolation into the theory of sexuality. *S. E., 19*: 141–148. London: Hogarth.

Freud, S. (1924d). The dissolution of the Oedipus complex. *S. E., 19*: 173–179. London: Hogarth.

Freud, S. (1940a). An outline of psychoanalysis. *S. E., 23*. London: Hogarth.

Fromm, E. (1966). *You Shall be as Gods: A Radical Interpretation of the Old Testament and its Tradition*. New York: Harper and Row.

Fromm, E. (1980). *The Greatness and Limitations of Freud's Thought*. New York: Harper and Row.

Gay, P. (1987). *A Godless Jew: Freud, Atheism, and the Making of Psychoanalysis*. New Haven, CT: Yale University Press.

Gresser, M. (1994). *Dual Allegiance: Freud as a Modern Jew*. Albany, NY: State University of New York Press.

Gutmann, J. (1987). The sacrifice of Isaac in medieval Jewish art. *Artibus et Historiae, 8*: 67–89.

Hazony, Y. (2012). *The Philosophy of Hebrew Scripture*. Cambridge, MA: Cambridge University Press.

Heine, H. (1840). *Ludwig Börne: A Memorial*. J. L. Sammons (Trans.). Rochester, NY: Camden House, 2006.

Homer. (1909–1914). *The Odyssey*. The Harvard Classics, vol. XXII. S. H. Butcher & A. Lang (Trans.). New York: Collier & Son.

Johnson, A. & Williams, D. P. (1996). *Oedipus Ubiquitous: The Family Complex in World Folk Religion*. Stanford, CA: Stanford University Press.

Jollés, A. (1958). *Einfache formen*. Tübingen: Max Niemayer.

Kancyper, L. (2006). The role of pre-oedipal and oedipal factors in psychic life. *International Journal of Psycho-Analysis, 87*: 219–236.

Kaplan, K. J. (1990). Isaac and Oedipus: a re-examination of the father–son relationship. *Judaism, 39*: 73–81.

Kaplan, K. J. (2002). Isaac versus Oedipus: an alternative view. *Journal of the American Academy of Psychoanalysis, 30*: 707–717.

Kaplan, K. J. (2007). Isaac and Ruth: Biblical resolutions of the Oedipus and Electra complexes. *Annual of Psychoanalysis, 35*: 193–206.

Kaplan, K. J. & Algom, D. (1997). Freud, Oedipus and the Hebrew Bible. *Journal of Psychology and Judaism, 21*: 211–216.

Kaplan, K. J. & Schwartz, M. B. (1993). *A Psychology of Hope: An Antidote to the Suicidal Pathology of Western Civilization*. Westport, CN: Praeger.

Kaplan, K. J. & Schwartz, M. B. (2006). *The Seven Habits of the Good Life: How the Biblical Virtues Free us from the Seven Deadly Sins*. Lanham, MD: Rowman and Littlefield.

Kaplan, K. J., Schwartz, M. B., & Markus-Kaplan, M. (1984). *The Family: Biblical and Psychological Foundations*. New York: Human Sciences.

Kohut, H. (1982). Introspection, empathy, and the semi-circle of mental health. *International Journal of Psycho-Analysis, 63*: 395–407.

Küng, H. (1979). *Freud and the Problem of God*. New Haven, CN: Yale University Press.

Lowenberg, P. (1994). Freud's psycho-social identity. In: A. Haynal & E. Falzeder (Eds.), *100 years of Psychoanalysis: Contributions to the History of Psychoanalysis* (pp. 135–150). London: Karnac.

Markus-Kaplan, M. & Kaplan, K. J. (1979). The typology, diagnosis, pathologies and treatment-intervention of Hellenic versus Hebraic personality styles: a proposal on the psychology of interpersonal distancing. *Journal of Psychology and Judaism, 3*: 153–167.

May, R. (1991). *The Cry for Myth*. New York: Norton.

Miller, D. L. (2003). *Dreams of the Burning Child: Sacrificial Sons and the Father's Witness*. New York: Cornell University Press.

Ovid. (1993). *The Metamorphoses*. A. Mandelbaum (Trans.). New York: Harcourt.

Rank, O. (1907). *The Myth of the Birth of the Hero: A Psychological Interpretation of Mythology*. F. Robbins & S. E. Jelliffe (Trans.). New York: Journal of Nervous and Mental Disease Publishing Company, 1914.

Rank, O. (1912). *Das Inzest-Motiv in Dichtung und Sage: Grundzüge einer Psychologie des dichterischen Schaffens*. Leipzig: Franz Deuticke.

Reik, T. (1915). The puberty rites of savages. In: *Ritual: Four Psychoanalytic Studies*. New York: International Universities Press, 1946.

Reik, T. (1946). *Ritual: Four Psychoanalytic Studies*. New York: International Universities Press.

Reik, T. (1961). *The Temptation*. New York: George Braziller.

Richards, A. (2006). The creation and social transmission of psychoanalytic knowledge. *Journal of the American Psychoanalytic Association, 54*: 359–378.

Richards, A. (2008). Sigmund Freud's Jewish identity. Paper presented at "Judaism and psychoanalysis: A continuing dialogue" conference, October 2008, Chicago, IL.

Riklin, F. & White, W. (1915). Wish fulfilment and symbolism in fairy tales. *Psychoanalytic Review, 2*: 203–218.

Rollins, W. G. (1999). *Soul and Psyche*. Minneapolis, MN: Augsburg Fortress.

Rolnik, E. J. (2012). *Freud in Zion: History of Psychoanalysis in Jewish Palestine/Israel 1918–1948*. London: Karnac.

Schwartz, M. B. & Kaplan, K. J. (2004). *Biblical Stories for Psychotherapy and Counseling: A Sourcebook*. Binghamton, NY: Haworth.

Schwartz, M. B. & Kaplan, K. J. (2007). *The Fruits of her Hands: A Psychology of Biblical Women*. Grand Rapids, MI: William B. Eerdmans.

Skolnick, V. (2009). *The Biblical Path to Psychological Maturity*. Victoria, BC, Canada: Trafford.

Slater, P. E. (1968). *The Glory of Hera: Greek Mythology and the Greek Family*. Boston, MA: Beacon.

Smith, A. M. (1922). The iconography of the sacrifice of Isaac in early Christian art. *American Journal of Archaeology, 26*: 159–173.

Spero, M. H. (1992). *Religious Objects as Psychological Structures: A Critical Integration of Object Relations Theory, Psychotherapy, and Judaism*. Chicago: University of Chicago Press.

Spiegel, S. (1968). *The Last Trial: On the Legends and Lore of the Command to Abraham to Offer Isaac as a Sacrifice: The Akedah*. New York: Schocken.

Stucken, E. (1896–1907). *Astralmythen der Hebräer, Babylonier und Aegypter*. Leipzig: Eduard Pfeiffer.

Sugar, M. (2002). Commonalities between the Isaac and Oedipus myths: a speculation. *Journal of the American Academy of Psychoanalysis, 30*: 691–706.

Tabak, I. (1948). *Judaic Lore in Heine: The Heritage of a Poet*. Baltimore, MD: John Hopkins Press.

Tang, N. M. & Smith, B. L. (1966). The eternal triangle across cultures; Oedipus, Hsueh, and Ganesa. *Psychoanalytic Study of the Child, 51*: 562–579.

Wellisch, E. (1954). *Isaac and Oedipus: Studies in Biblical Psychology of the Sacrifice of Isaac*. London: Routledge and Kegan Paul.

Winter, S. (1997–1998). "Schoolboy psychology": Freud's classical education and the institutionalization of psychoanalytic knowledge. *Cultural Critique, 38*: 137–175.

Winter, S. (1999). *Freud and the Institution of Psychoanalytic Knowledge (Cultural Memory in the Present)*. Stanford, CA: Stanford University Press.

Yerushalmi, Y. (1991). *Freud's Moses: Terminable and Interminable*. New Haven, CN: Yale University Press.

CHAPTER FIVE

# From Oedipus to Ahab (and back): myth and psychoanalysis in science fiction

*Angie Voela*

Science fiction novels usually reflect contemporary concerns and anxieties in the form of things to come, and often contain didactic universal messages for the present and future of humanity. References to classical mythology and modern literary classics often reinforce these messages. But when Oedipus and Ahab are employed in the same contemporary novel, *Flashforward* (Sawyer, 1999), and appear to neither complement nor contradict one another, it is the reluctance or failure to settle for one or the other that becomes interesting.

The myth of Oedipus perhaps does not need an introduction. Let us, however, remind ourselves of the end of Sophocles' *Oedipus Rex*, in which the wise king, shocked by the revelation of his fate and his own blindness, stabs himself repeatedly in the eyes before taking the road to exile.

In Herman Melville's *Moby-Dick* (1851) Ahab is captain of the *Pequod*, the whaling vessel which the narrator, Ishmael, joins at Nantucket, Massachusetts. The novel defies simple classifications; it is a book about whaling, the sea, the community of men aboard the vessel, power relations and friendship, the pursuit of wealth and, in the case of Ahab, the obsessive pursuit of Moby Dick, the white whale. Ishmael first sets eyes on Ahab several days after the *Pequod* has sailed from Nantucket. He is impressed by the captain's physical appearance and intense silence.

As the *Pequod* continues her expedition, Ishmael describes the initial whaling successes in detail, along with encounters with other vessels. Ahab's obsession with Moby Dick is established gradually as he repeatedly asks other captains about the white whale's whereabouts. Tensions grow between Ahab and his officers, when they try to remind him of the commercial purpose of their journey and his obligation towards his crew and the owners of the vessel. Ahab's single-mindedness is dramatically described in chapter ninety-nine, entitled *The Doubloon*. The captain nails a large Ecuadorian golden coin to the mast and pledges it as reward to "whoever raises a certain whale" (Melville, 1851, p. 472). Soon afterwards, Ahab sets the *Pequod*'s course in pursuit of Moby Dick. Sightings of the whale, stories about his deadliness and even a request by the captain of the *Rachel* to help find his missing son, go unheeded by Ahab. The pursuit of Moby Dick ends with the destruction of the *Pequod* by the whale and the drowning of the crew. Entangled in the line of his own harpoon, Ahab is snatched from the last whaling boat and drawn to the bottom of the sea. Ishmael, the sole survivor, is rescued by the *Rachel*.

Despite their superficial similarity as single-minded individuals, Oedipus and Ahab express very different aspects of humanity and, more interestingly, belong to very different communities. The questions I would like to raise in this chapter are the following: how does contemporary culture employ them together in articulating emerging forms of individuality and collectivity? Does their simultaneous appearance mark a shift in the collective perception of the relevance of myth in representing the contemporary human condition?

These questions will be addressed with the following in mind: contemporary culture is imbued with Freudian psychoanalysis (Parker, 2010), in which the myth of Oedipus has an exceptional status. Popularised psychoanalysis contributes to mythologising and reinforcing stereotypical forms of thinking. This tendency must be made an object of inquiry alongside the deployment of the mythical figures through which it is usually expressed. Post-Freudians are, of course, aware of the pitfalls of popularisation and although they still draw on the oedipal myth for its symbolic value, they consider it to be an expression of the impossibility of desire (Grigg, 2006) rather than its illicit satisfaction or its fatal consequences. Deleuze and Guattari, on the other hand, criticise Freud for the use of the Oedipus myth and the concept of the Oedipus complex which, as they claim, reinforces familial-capitalist structures and reduces the complexity of human experience to a mere triangular relationship (Deleuze & Guattari, 1972). Thus, when they turn to literature for examples, they favour figures that venture into the unknown and go beyond the set coordinates of space and time. Ahab is one of them, for pursuing a "becoming" in unchartered territories, in proximity with an animal and away from the claustrophobic family. It is the trajectory of becoming rather than Ahab's obsessive nature that fascinates Deleuze and Guattari.

Below, I shall discuss Oedipus and Ahab, the space between them and their latent popular-psychoanalytic support, with reference to *Flashforward* (Sawyer, 1999). I shall start with a summary of the novel and a brief outline of the Lacanian and Deleuzian perspectives that form the theoretical backbone of my argument. Although critical of one another, these two perspectives also complement one another, illuminating different aspects of the novel and facilitating a better understanding of emerging cultural patterns.

* * *

The key event in *Flashforward* (Sawyer, 1999) is a scientific experiment with unpredictable consequences. At CERN's Large Hadron Collider physicists who try to locate the elusive Higgs boson perform a successful particle collision. Unexpectedly, however, this results in a three-minute blackout, during which the human population of the Earth experiences a "flashforward", a three-minute glimpse of their lives in thirty years' time. As the world tries to deal with the catastrophic consequences of the blackout (e.g., collisions, plane crashes, accidents), the main characters and leaders of the CERN team, Lloyd Simcoe and Theo Procopides, try to investigate the causes of the unexpected event. They seek permission to replicate the experiment in order to give humanity another glimpse of the future. Like everyone else, they also try to come to terms with the unexpected insight. Lloyd Simcoe will have to decide whether to go ahead with his planned marriage to colleague Mitsiko Komura, knowing that the marriage will eventually fail. Theo Procopides has no flashforward. Soon he learns why by phone calls coming from as far apart as South Africa and Canada: in 2030 he is dead. Theo's story is his effort to identify his killer and prevent his own death.

On one level, the novel can be read as a cautionary tale about the rapid advances of science and the possible side-effects of tampering with nature. On another level, the accident engenders an idiosyncratic universal equality: everybody is affected by it and in its aftermath everybody is implicated in coming to terms with the excessive sliver of knowledge it produces. Thus, millions of people respond to the *Mosaic*, a website created by Mitsiko Komura for sharing information about the future. Notably absent from the novel is any reference to ideological or socio-political circumstances before and after the accident. The *Mosaic*, however, chimes with the virtual internet communities we are already familiar with, and emerges as an anti-authoritarian, non-hierarchical space with no beginning and end, where no one's contribution is more valid than another's.

On the level of individuals, the pursuit of life after the event chimes with man's mythical desire to attain knowledge of the future. Ways of dealing with it vary. Lloyd Simcoe and Mitsiko Komura decide to get married come what may. Jake Horowitz, a junior researcher at CERN who, in his flashforward, sees that he has a passionate sexual relationship with a Canadian colleague, musters the courage to visit her. They start the passionate relationship in the present. Theo's younger brother, an aspiring writer, refuses to come to terms with the knowledge of his future failure and commits suicide. However this very event shows that the future remains fluid and changeable.

In that context, Theo's pursuit of his own fate is and is not an obsessive endeavour. Here are Theo's thoughts in 2030, after managing successfully to confront his killer, subverting the prediction of his death:

> Twenty-one years, obsessed by one thing. Did Ahab have sharp memories? Oh yes—losing his leg no doubt. But after that—after he'd begun his quest? Or was it all a blur, month after month, year after year, everything and everyone subsumed? But no—no. Theo was no Ahab; he wasn't hell-bent. He had found time for many things between 2009 and today, here in 2030. And yet—and yet he'd never allowed himself to make plans for the future. (Sawyer, 1999, p. 315)

And in relation to Oedipus:

> Twenty-one years overshadowed; even knowing that the future was mutable ... two decades had slipped by, mostly lost—if not actually skipped over, certainly dulled, reduced, lessened. No fatal flaw? It is to laugh ... That had been the most arrogant thought

> of all. Of course he had a fatal flaw; of course he had a *hamartia*. But it was the mirror image of Oedipus's; Oedipus had thought he could escape his fate. Theo, knowing the future was changeable, had still been dogged by the fear that he couldn't outwit destiny. (Ibid., p. 316)

We must believe Theo when he says that he is neither Oedipus nor Ahab. Indeed, there is no incestuous desire or other horrible transgression in his case. Theo is an innocent Oedipus, and in that sense tragic in his pursuit of knowledge. He is also a pioneer scientist who ventures into unchartered waters. Thus, it is the pursuit of scientific knowledge, which popular culture often perceives as obsessive, unregulated and unstoppable, that can be seen as arrogant.

* * *

Lacanian psychoanalysis, which generally upholds the validity of the Oedipus complex for individual development, also acknowledges the decline of the *Name of the Father* (Žižek, 1999), that is, of the symbolic paternal figure which normally translates the Oedipus complex into cultural values. In relation to the novel, therefore, the question I posed at the beginning amounts not to whether we can deploy myth to establish continuity with the past, finding Oedipus in his place, so to speak, but to observing the effects of the erosion of the *Name of the Father* and its consequences for collective and individual identity. In that sense, the use of Oedipus as a metaphor is interesting in its failure to accurately represent the contemporary human condition. The same applies to Ahab. To the extent that Theo is not exactly Ahab, the deployment of the literary figure draws attention to what does not fit the case.

In order to explain this double misalignment in Lacanian terms we need to focus on the socio-symbolic network of values, assumptions, and ideals that normally constitute the meaningful backdrop of our lives and confer consistency to our acts. Lacan calls this formation "the Other" (Evans, 1996). Among its aspects, the Other encompasses the symbolic Father as a figure of authority and guarantor of the Law; the desire to know (epistemophilic desire); and, along with the latter, our modern conviction that everything is potentially knowable, either through a journey that resembles the psychoanalytic excavation of the past or a scientific trajectory firmly grounded in reason. In line with the Lacanian perspective, I shall argue that *Flashforward* is notable for the way it articulates the desire for knowledge but also the opposite, a desire for ignorance and a return to normality.

As noted in the introduction, Deleuzian theory argues against the Oedipus myth and critiques Freudian psychoanalysis for its alignment with dominant bourgeois-capitalist values and for the propagation of fixed explanatory schemata (Deleuze & Guattari, 1972, 1980). Deleuze and Guattari propose a different kind of collective and individual becoming which is based on breaking away from psychoanalytic formations, emphasising movement over structure, randomness over fate, co-causality and unpredictable synergy of multiple forces over a fixed parental desire, and flight-escape in new directions over compulsive return to pathogenic trauma. They challenge the centrality of man, consciousness, and knowledge in contemporary thought, and often advocate loss of direction and failure as more interesting ways of becoming. As one of their emblematic heroes, Deleuze and Guattari's Ahab is not a counterpart to Oedipus but an example of a man venturing outside the fully charted social-symbolic realm, merging with the animal-whale and representing an altogether unfamiliar experience of becoming.

From a Deleuzian perspective, therefore, we should focus on those parts of the novel that support becoming via constant movement and flight or escape, resisting the moments when action stagnates or reverts to predetermined (psychoanalytic) patterns. Apart from Ahab, Deleuze and Guattari (1980) provide us with another likely matrix for understanding the role of the individual scientist at the frontier of the unknown. This is the figure of the sorcerer, the man who lives at the borders of the group and communes with humans, animals, and nature alike. As in the case of Oedipus, the distance between Ahab and the much more life-affirmative sorcerer raises questions about the persistent deployment of the former. In line with the Deleuzian reading, I shall argue that although a fluid, adventurous becoming which harmonises the individual with the group in unpredictable manners is inherent in human nature, and indeed palpable in the novel, it is systematically undermined by more traditional and stratified approaches to subjectivity and knowledge.

* * *

In Lacanian terms, fate is activated when the subject gets to know about it. Oedipus is told that he will kill his father. The prophecy, claims Žižek, comes true by virtue of being communicated to the person concerned and his attempt to elude it (Žižek, 1991). Another example is the servant in Somerset Maugham's *Sheppey*, who tries to avoid meeting Death in Baghdad. He escapes to Samara, where Death awaits him (ibid., p. 201). This subjective trip into the future and back, adds Žižek, exhibits the properties of a figure eight in which the subject tries to overtake himself. The illusion lies not simply in thinking that we overtake ourselves but "is rather an internal condition, an internal constituent of the so-called 'objective' process itself. It is always through this additional detour that the past itself, the 'objective' state of things, becomes retroactively what it always was" (ibid., p. 200). The future, too, appears open to potentially multiple outcomes. Žižek notes:

> These multiple futures are not the direct outcome of some radical indeterminacy or "ontological openness" inscribed in the fabric of reality; the alternate path of future reality is, rather, generated when the agent whose future acts are foretold gets to know about them; that is to say, its source is the self-referentiality of knowledge. (Ibid., p. 208)

The figure-eight movement of the past and the future and the relativity of both is, of course, nothing new. As discussed above, some cases prove the flashforward to be accurate and some don't. What is important, however, is the fact that clear knowledge of this randomness is generally silenced because it produces uncertainty and anxiety. In that sense, the flashforward shows that we always desire the opposite, the closeness and certainty of fate.

The relativisation of the outcome of fate on the level of the individual has as equivalent the collapse of certainty in the public domain. After the flashforward, all social, public, and financial institutions are dealt a blow. Trust at all levels is eroded, with people trying to profit from the situation, each using their little bit of knowledge. The Other in its symbolic, paternal dimension is compromised. If the role of the traditional Father–Other was to be that of the guarantor of Law and order (Žižek, 1999), this function is now impaired. The Father–Other ceases to operate as the incontrovertible authority that regulates the system. Thus, the once robust, seamless system emerges as a series of vulnerable institutions, bereft of authority and open to private exploitation.

Lacanian psychoanalysis highlights the fact that the Other is always inconsistent, vulnerable and patchy. However, assuming the existence of, or believing in, a consistent, robust Other is a necessary condition for an ideology and a semblance of order to be preserved (see Žižek, 2009, p. 31). Dealing with the inconsistency of the Other is an important step in Lacanian psychoanalysis. When analysands come to terms with it—that is, with the fact that no one really pulls the strings of their existence (Žižek, 1992, p. 58)—they approach the end of analysis, in the sense that they cease to attribute their troubles to powers outside themselves. In the public domain, the inconsistency of the Other is much harder to come to terms with, and this is the properly traumatic and horrible piece of knowledge that needs to be veiled and harnessed under a semblance of order. Thus, despite the obvious advantages of knowing something of the future, the flashforward leaves people in limbo, as it exposes the vulnerability of the symbolic system. It comes as no surprise, therefore, that already on the day following the traumatic event the first efforts are made to shore up the Other by rebuilding the world as it was, with a semblance of normality and order.

The collective illumination of the inconsistency of the Other and the private pursuit of fate bring to our attention the concept of "knowledge". Psychoanalytic knowledge is always knowledge of things that have occurred in the past. Yet, psychoanalysis is not a capricious excavation of the past and the unconscious for the sake of the past but a process necessitated by an affliction or a disturbance (symptom) in the present (see Žižek, 1991). In Lacanian theory the knowledge and truth of the unconscious are differentiated from the knowledge and truth of the drive. The latter is understood as a constant force with its own trajectory and aims, and harks back to the Freudian "instinct" (Lacan, 1977, pp. 174–186). The distinction between the knowledge of the unconscious and the drive as well as its importance for the present case are elucidated below with reference to Theo's pursuit of fate and his attempt to replicate the experiment.

The desire to replicate the experiment chimes with the efforts to re-institute order, to repair the radical indeterminacy of the Other and with it the trauma of excessive knowledge which intrudes in individual and collective life. Repetition produces knowledge that enlightens by way of a symbolic appropriation of the traumatic event (see Žižek, 1991, p. 205). The failure to replicate the experiment, however, leads to more uncertainty and illuminates the failure of the analytic process itself, of repetition as working-through an experience and facilitating interpretation (ibid.). The implication therefore is that humanity is unable to heal itself. At the same time, science as an objective, controllable and experimentally verifiable form of knowledge fails to close the gap of ignorance. What this move further illustrates becomes more apparent in Theo's individual case. For him, the obsessive pursuit of knowledge (getting to know the particulars of his imminent death) amounts to a failed repetition which does not bring him exactly to where he was supposed to be in his flashforward but to an understanding of the difference between "knowledge" and "the pursuit of knowledge"; in other words, between the (unconscious) knowledge and the drive. What Theo attains at the end of his journey, therefore, is a glimpse of the impossible, excessive and disturbing "kernel" of his being (Žižek, 1991, p. 211), the very fact that the course of his life had been sustained by a blind pursuit rather than by a rational mode of thinking.

For the individual who pursues his own death in order to avoid it, there is only one conclusion; that he invests himself in his own story and creates the paradox of freedom and fate:

> The question of freedom is, at its most radical, the question of how this closed circle of fate can be broken. The answer, of course, is that it can be broken not because "it is not truly closed" because there are cracks in its texture but, on the contrary, because it is overclosed, that is, because the subject's very endeavour to break out of it is included in advance … the only real way to escape fate is to renounce these attempts, to accept fate as inexorable. (Žižek, 1999, p. 207)

Travelling on the curvy sides of the "figure eight" of fate, Theo—and along with him humanity—must find a way to veil the inconsistency of the Father–Other and the separation of knowledge from the pursuit of knowledge. A new mythical veil needs to be drawn over the gap. By similarity and analogy, the small-scale personal story (Theo's story) substitutes the large-scale story of the global humanity, transcends itself and represents the human. Resonating with Oedipus and Ahab but being neither exactly, Theo's reference to myth veils the openness of meaning and the absence of absolute, secure knowledge. Thus Theo in his ordinariness, the man who, unlike Oedipus and Ahab, always returns to the fold despite the (extra) ordinariness of his pursuit, is raised to a "sinthome",[1] a typical nobody rather than an exceptional individual, who obliquely represents humanity to humanity itself, along with the hope for a new kind of balance after the event.

* * *

For Deleuze and Guattari the challenge for both individuals and communities is not fate but becoming, a process I shall endeavour to sketch below. Deleuze and Guattari never provide definitions for their key concepts, but allow the readers to formulate their own understanding by familiarising themselves with different aspects of a concept. The news of Theo's death uproots him from his ordinary life. The challenge for him therefore is not the pursuit of fate/death but another form of effacement, of himself as the arrogant, self-centred individual—a dimension which emerges in Theo's thoughts. It would not be an exaggeration to say that the Deleuzian logic of becoming is tragic; not as inescapable oedipal fate but as shuttering of the self, venturing beyond the limits of predictable identity and becoming diffuse—effaced in the moves, acts, and causes of others.

In their polemic against Freudian psychoanalysis, Deleuze and Guattari argue for a becoming which is involutionary, involuntary and creative (Deleuze & Guattari, 1980, p. 263). They envisage it as "merging-with" the collective, typical examples of which include the pack (of animals) that roam the land joined by mutual benefit but without a fixed internal hierarchy. Their membership changes as "packs form, develop, and are transformed by *contagion*" (ibid., p. 267, emphasis added). Another example is the universe which "does not function by filiation" (ibid., p. 267), that is, by forming internal and external alliances as human communities do, but by "multiplicities" of heterogeneous, co-functioning elements. When it comes to group identities, Deleuze and Guattari also advocate multiplicities, as well as forming "assemblages" (rather than internally structured alliances), held together not by strict internal rules but by the mobility of their elements, by relations of exteriority and by the setting of all their forces into a temporary balance (De Landa, 2006, pp. 10–11).

Contagion is the way of the *Mosaic*, a web of non-hierarchical participation, an assemblage which grows in unpredictable directions and is, strictly speaking, ungovernable. The important insight from a Deleuzian perspective is not that the *Mosaic* could happen, but that it has happened—in the remit of the book at least. Thus, the possibility of a Deleuzian becoming is inherent in groups/societies but goes largely un-acknowledged or is usually overwhelmed by the forces of the State which are forces of control and regulation (Deleuze & Guattari, 1980). By the same token, it is not the failure of science to replicate the fatal experiment to which we should be paying attention but the already existing knowledge of the multiple possible outcomes of the future and the ways of the universe. A CERN scientist in *Flashforward* echoes theories of a multi-dimensional becoming in space and time which are subject to random disruptions:

> "As you can see, the light made by Minkowski's movements forms a trail through time. He starts down here near the bottom in Lithuania, moves about Germany and Switzerland, and finally dies up here in Gottingen". The maps were stacked one atop another, forming a cube … "And, of course, you can map other people's path into the same cube". (Sawyer, 1999, pp. 130–131)

And also:

> "Well, Franco, if the visions weren't our future, then what did they portray?" "An alternative timeline, of course. That's completely reasonable …" The many-worlds interpretation of quantum physics says that every time an event can go two ways, instead of one or the other way happening, both happen in a separate universe. (Ibid., p. 147)

With the above examples I do not wish to imply that Deleuze and Guattari concur with popular science. I am only drawing attention to the fact that there exists, in popular imagination as well as in philosophy and science, an understanding of people's lives as trajectories, crosscutting maps and paths, and elements of an assemblage rather than discrete vectors of knowledge and drive (see Deleuze & Guattari, 1980, p. 266). In the same vein, Deleuze and Guattari emphasise that there are no other drives than the assemblages themselves (ibid., p. 286).

From a Deleuzian perspective, becoming for the individual is a form of experimentation (Deleuze & Guattari, 1980, p. 277), a valid pursuit as long as it involves "lines of flight" for escaping from the organised and stratified realm, seeking multiplicity and symbiosis (ibid., p. 275). Life is to be sought not in moments of arrival at predetermined ends, illuminations and tragic grandeur but "in the meantime", in interstices and intermezzos (Deleuze & Guattari, 1980). If Oedipus asked "who am I?", Deleuze and Guattari would reply that "[t]he self is only a threshold, a door, a becoming between two multiplicities … the error we must guard against is to believe that there is some kind of logical order to this string, these crossings and transformations" (ibid., p. 275). With regards to lines of flight: "No one can say where the line will pass: Will it let itself be bogged down and fall back to the Oedipal animal … or will it succumb to another danger, for example, turning into a line of abolition, annihilation, self-destruction, Ahab, Ahab …?" (ibid., p. 276).

Oedipus and Ahab: victims of their own excess of predetermination and freedom respectively. Thus, and despite appearing anarchic, Deleuze and Guattari's theory seems to advise caution and navigating prudently but with robust imagination between the two extremes, towards a becoming characterised by expansion. In that sense, Theo does not have to live as Oedipus or Ahab but indeed as what he already is: the scientist at the cross-roads between the known and the unknown, the present world and others, the organised social milieu and the unpredictable universe.

Alongside Ahab, Deleuze and Guattari discuss the figure of the sorcerer, to whom the scientist of *Flashforward* bears a resemblance. In *A Thousand Plateaus* (1980) the figure of the sorcerer is a privileged one, especially since the authors identify themselves as sorcerers by virtue of their non-hierarchical ways of seeking knowledge (Deleuze & Guattari, 1980, p. 276). The sorcerer is an exceptional individual in any multiplicity and harks back to the Loner and the Demon. He occupies an "anomalous" position in the pack, constituting a "phenomenon of bordering" rather than a distinct individual or a species (ibid., p. 270). What matters, therefore, is not the person itself but the position one occupies: "Sorcerers have always held the anomalous position, at the edge of the fields or woods. They haunt the fringes. They are at the borderline of the village or between villages" (ibid., p. 271). Sorcerers are in a special relationship to the community (the alliance) and its internal mode of organisation (filiation): "The important thing is their affinity with alliance, with the pact, which gives them a status opposed to that of filiation … The sorcerer has a relation of alliance with the demon as the power of the anomalous" (ibid., p. 271).

By virtue of his position, we can understand the sorcerer's function:

> It is evident that the Anomalous, the Outsider, has several functions: not only does it border each multiplicity, of which it determines the temporary or local stability … not only is it the precondition for the alliance necessary to becoming, but it also carries the

> transformations of becoming or crossing of multiplicities always farther down the line of flight. Moby-Dick is the white Wall bordering the pack; he is also the demonic Term of Alliance; finally, he is the terrible Fishing Line with nothing on the other end, the line that crosses the wall and drags the captain ... where? Into the void .... (Deleuze & Guattari, 1980, p. 275)

The scientist at the edges of the community, the anomalous element of the pack, could be the modern day sorcerer. It is his position between worlds rather than his fate that gives him his exceptional status. He lives between cross-cutting domains, the meeting point of multiplicities. In pre-modern times he stood between villages, today between worlds. He is not the exemplary sinner and does not live in order to solve riddles but in communion between multiplicities, just like the philosopher. In that sense, and following Deleuze and Guattari's choice of Moby Dick as an example, he is a white whale as much as the whaler. Thus, in *Flashforward*, the reference to Ahab points at the appropriate myth but not at the appropriate approach. The very obsessive element for which Ahab has been etched into popular memory obscures the alternative view of the multiplicities and his exceptional becoming.

There is one more significant aspect of becoming I would like to draw attention to and which returns Theo-the-scientist to the community like another figure eight but with no reference to individual fate. Deleuze and Guattari refer to it as "becoming everybody/everything":

> The *becoming everybody/everything* is another affair, one that brings into play the cosmos with its molecular components. Becoming everybody/everything (*tout le monde*) is to world (*faire monde*), to make a world (*faire un monde*). By process of elimination, one is no longer anything more than an abstract line, or a piece of a puzzle, that is itself abstract. (Deleuze & Guattari, 1980, p. 308)

The *Mosaic* is perhaps one such puzzle by virtue of being an aggregate of narratives. Is it not perhaps possible to see it also as a way of rethinking the world? Further, Theo's case illustrates that the challenge of becoming has nothing to do with becoming important, famous or acclaimed (Theo wins the Nobel Prize at a young age but does not seem to take pride in that achievement) but only with "becoming everybody/

everything" in engendering possible worlds. The scientist/new sorcerer's challenge is how to belong to the multiplicity of worlds that one is discovering without resisting them under the pretext of death.

* * *

Popular fiction registers the changes and shifts that eventually culminate in new cultural structures. Contemporary modernity, like any other epoch, is characterised by its own predominant moral and ethical dilemmas and hones its own tragic figures to represent them. In this context, *Flashforward* is interesting because it illuminates current concerns about the separation of knowledge from the pursuit of knowledge, the production of certainty, the erosion of faith in the traditional abstract symbolic forces (Father–Other) which guarantee the socio-political order, its effect on the individual and the group and, as a result, the relevance of traditional mythical-literary figures in representing the contemporary human condition. The line from Oedipus to Ahab and their contemporary incarnation, Theo, is not therefore one of affirmation of the universality of the Oedipus complex or of the validity of literary figures. It stands for an open search for the contemporary symbolic representative that will eventually and retrospectively join the line of past symbolic figures—a task all the more complicated for the demise of the heroic ethos (Featherstone, 2000), the rise of the ordinary man and the rise of popular culture at the expense of high literature.

From a psychoanalytic perspective, it is interesting to note that when traditional mythic-symbolic figures subside, the subjective structures are exposed and laid bare: in the present case, the structure of the Other and its inherent inconsistency, the drift between knowledge and the drive, the price to be paid for excessive knowledge and disillusionment. Attempting to interpret this exposure of structures, I should like to highlight two opposing tendencies—the pursuit of ignorance and the pursuit of knowledge—and the tension between them.

With the pursuit of ignorance we find ourselves in the realm of the postmodern reflexive individual who can think and reflect but not necessarily interpret (Žižek, 1999, p. 346), forever mired in reflexive (in) efficiency. For theorists of various persuasions (Barthes, 1957; Parker, 2010; Žižek, 1999) a return to myth in that context would chime with a process of re-mystification/re-mythification and resurrection of the shuttered Father–Other. Žižek warns that the demise of the symbolic efficiency of the Father–Other makes room for his return from the realm of the Real. Thus the unseen forces or individuals that are supposed to know and run our lives materialise once again when displaced on nature and moved to the borders of the organised world. This self-willed blindness would concern a more general de-politicization of culture. Thus, the deployment of the Oedipus myth as inescapable fate is an attempt to reinstate a limit, a central blindness, which draws not upon the symbolic richness of the myth but upon its emblematic-evocative potency. In that sense, the oedipal pursuit of knowledge which turns into a wider crisis of knowledge and is displaced upon nature, substitutes and veils the crisis of political ideology and the attempt to re-institute ignorance/fate at the heart of human subjectivity. This displacement is a defensive move against excessive knowledge and the very openness of experience as represented in the novel.

Of course, the radical message from a Lacanian perspective does not concern knowing and thinking per se but coming to terms with certain forms of knowledge and experience, such as castration in its cultural dimension, that is, powerlessness and impotence. Along these lines, Jacques-Alain Miller argues that the end of analysis transforms "powerlessness"—neurotic dependence on the Other's desire—into "impossibility" (Miller, 2009, p. 13). Thus, the real pursuit of knowledge is a settlement, a sinthome or solution/conclusion that takes the above impossibility/inconsistency into account. For that purpose, any viable figure of re-inscription, not necessarily the mythic Oedipus, will suffice to register and ground this development. This very function of "the average man" (Theo) emerges as one of the most important insights of the novel. In my view it points towards a potential collective maturity which remains just beneath the surface. The tension between the pursuit of ignorance and the pursuit of knowledge is therefore the contemporary manifestation of the fear of freedom, of learning to live with the knowledge of indeterminacy and impossibility. If it has to be expressed via traditional-mythical symbols, it is the richness of the tale in which they are embedded rather than their popularised (psychoanalytic) potency that needs to be exploited.

For Deleuzians, indeterminacy and lack of predictability, the very opposite of the qualities of Oedipus, are to be celebrated. In a quote echoing Oedipus' choices and his arrival at the crossroads, Deleuzian theorist Brian Massumi describes experience as a conjoining of the individual and the group: "One thing does not lead to another as a full cause to a simple effect. To begin with, there are two full causes (attractor states). Their line of co-causality then joined in co-causality with another line—constituted by chance. The supermolecular subject-group lies *at the double co-causal crossroads of chance and determinacy"* (Massumi, 1996, p. 63, emphasis added). Thus, according to Massumi, complete predictive knowledge is a fallacy, usually concerning our own or collective history. All we can do, notes Massumi, is "experimentally perturb [history]" as we walk our life's path (ibid., p. 68). Thus the new hero is a man walking the path of life, not an Oedipus at the crossroads, but a scientist. And blindness—oedipal blindness perhaps—pertains to the certainty of one's impact upon the world. The sorcerer already knows about his insignificance because he lives in harmony with the universe(s).

Popular culture points toward something we habitually call "crisis", an oscillation between past masters (like the Father or mythical figures) and the knowledge of their demise. The difficulty of disengaging from traditional modes of thinking produces a vacuum, a lack of referents, which is a historical fact more than anything else. We therefore remain in the grip of a repeated motion, a fort/da[2] between "breaking into the future/breaking-down", the latter subtended by an eternal return of the same and a nostalgic desire for order. In her polemic against Deleuze and Guattari, Jerry Aline Flieger argues in favour of the diachronic value of Oedipus and updates the latter by transforming him into a twenty-first century voyager, an "internaut" who travels in all directions departing and returning to a stable point of reference. The stable pattern of departure and return is characterised by her as a fort/da that strikes a balance between the achievement and deferral of pleasure (Flieger, 1999, p. 237). It is supposed to counter-balance the Deleuzian call for indeterminacy and openness. But the conditions of desire, Massumi (1996) reminds us, can never be predictable or stable and new causalities cannot be inferred from old ones just by looking back.

Popular culture both articulates the loss of faith in law, technology, knowledge, authority, and restores it after the (tragic) event by drawing a veil over it. It indulges in pondering that one is always duped by a faulty logic; that nothing is what it seems but one chooses to adhere to the principles of proportion, similarity, and metaphor which ensure the smoothness of everyday life and ultimately cover up one failure with another. The constant see-saw between willed knowledge and wilful blindness, Deleuzian becoming and Freudian "oedipalisation", is the ultimate fort/da of contemporary culture. It reflects the abject maturity of a society that knows too much and can pursue alternative ways of becoming but is always unable to break away from the traditional structures of power and knowledge. From Oedipus to Ahab and back (fort/da), the journey of knowledge and the pursuit of truth are superseded by an interminable oscillation. The mythologisation-veiling of this process needs to take place but the schism persists and the metaphorisation of the human condition is split between two myths. But neither of them can describe or represent without the other. What knowledge is to drive, Oedipus is to Ahab. So it is a new kind of fate that unites the two men, this time in the realm of contemporary popular culture until a third mythical figure (a new sorcerer?) brings the system to a temporary balance.

## *Notes*

1. In Lacanian psychoanalysis, the subject (individual) is discussed with reference to the Symbolic order (the order of organised-symbolic institutions and social structures mediated by language); the Imaginary order (which mostly consists of the formations of the ego) and the Real (the order of the unrepresented, e.g., traumatic events, or the unrepresentable, e.g., the primordial union with the mother). The sinthome is the unique way in which one is attached to the world and the three orders. Visualising the sinthome and its relation to the three orders, Evans (1996, pp. 188–190) characterises it as the "fourth ring" which keeps the other three together. In a recent article, Žižek (2009) discusses Josephine, Kafka's heroine in the short story *Josephine the Singer of the Mouse Folk* as a sinthome for her community, the one who reminds them of their humanity.
2. In Freud's *Beyond the Pleasure Principle* (1920g), fort/da represents a little boy's first attempt at representing his mother's absence through play and language. The boy throws away and retrieves a ball of wool while pronouncing "o" and "a" which Freud decodes as "fort/da", signifying "gone and there (back)". Freud discusses the fort/da in the immediate context of the child's attempt to grapple with loss (here, of the mother) through repetition. The more general context of the essay is Freud's discussion of the death instinct as manifested in a compulsive repetition of traumatic events. It is beyond the scope of this article to critique Flieger's deployment of fort/da alongside the Oedipus figure. Suffice it to say that their union provides a rather compulsive and death-instinct-oriented basis for contemporary culture.

## References


Barthes, R. (1957). *Mythologies*. London: Paladin Press, 1973.

De Landa, M. (2006). *A New Philosophy of Society, Assemblage Theory and Social Complexity*. London: Continuum Books.

Deleuze, G. & Guattari, F. (1972). *Anti-Oedipus, Capitalism and Schizophrenia*. London: Athlone Press, 2000.

Deleuze, G. & Guattari, F. (1980). *A Thousand Plateaus: Capitalism and Schizophrenia*. London: Continuum Press, 2008.

Evans, D. (1996). *An Introductory Dictionary of Lacanian Psychoanalysis*. London: Routledge.

Featherstone, M. (2000). *Undoing Culture: Globalisation, Postmodernism and Identity*. London: Sage Press.

Flieger, J. A. (1999). Overdetermined Oedipus: Mommy, Daddy, and me as desiring-machine. In: I. Buchanan (Ed.), *A Deleuzian Century?* (pp. 219–240). Durham, NC: Duke University Press.

Freud, S. (1920g). Beyond the pleasure principle. *S. E., 18*: 1–64. London: Hogarth.

Grigg, R. (2006). Beyond the Oedipus complex. In: J. Clements & R. Grigg. (Eds.), *Jacques Lacan and the Other Side of Psychoanalysis* (pp. 50–68). Durham: Duke University Press.

Lacan, J. (1977). *The Four Fundamental Concepts of Psychoanalysis*. London: Penguin Books, 1991.

Massumi, B. (1996). *A User's Guide to Capitalism and Schizophrenia: Deviations from Deleuze and Guattari*. Cambridge, MA: MIT Press.

Melville, H. (1851). *Moby-Dick*. London: Penguin Classics, 2003.

Miller, J. A. (2009). The logic of the cure of little Hans according to Lacan. *Lacanian Ink, 33*: 8–35.

Parker, I. (2010). *Psychoanalytic Mythologies*. London: Anthem Press.

Sawyer, R. J. (1999). *Flashforward*. London: Orion Books.

Žižek, S. (1991). The truth arises from misrecognition. In: E. Ragland-Sullivan & M. Bracher (Eds.), *Lacan and the Subject of Language* (pp. 188–225). London: Routledge.

Žižek, S. (1992). *Enjoy Your Symptom: Jacques Lacan in Hollywood and Out*. New York: Routledge.

Žižek, S. (1999). *The Ticklish Subject*. London: Verso Press.

Žižek, S. (2009). Josephine le sinthome. *Lacanian Ink, 33*: 157–163.

# PART III

## THEORISING MYTH AND THE UNCONSCIOUS

CHAPTER SIX

# Freudian and Jungian approaches to myth: the similarities

*Robert A. Segal*

For both Freud and Jung, modernity is distinctive in its decisive separation of the outer from the inner, which, oversimplified, means of the physical from the psychological. Previously, the demarcation had been blurry. There had been the projection of the inner onto the outer and even the reduction of the outer to the inner.

For example, in Marlowe's *Doctor Faustus* Mephistopheles famously describes hell as a sheer state of mind:

> Hell hath no limits, nor is circumscribed
> In any one self place; for where we are is hell,
> And where hell is, there must we ever be.
> (Marlowe, 1604 ed., I.553–555)

For Mephistopheles, whether or not for Marlowe himself, the world is the mind. Jung often cites Goethe's Mephistopheles but not Marlowe's and therefore not these lines.

In an even more famous case the outer is reduced to the inner yet still retained as outer. In *Paradise Lost* (1667) Milton somehow combines riveting descriptions of hell and paradise as places "out there" in the world with characterisations of them as sheer states of mind. Rather than reducing hell and paradise to states of mind, he makes them at once physical places and states of mind, though he never works out how they can be both. Jung cites *Paradise Lost*, most of all in analysing the Miller fantasies, but he considers different issues from this one (see Jung, 1911–12/1952, pars. 60–84 passim; see also Jung, 1952, pars. 468–473).

On the one hand for Milton hell, into which Satan and his retinue land after their fall from heaven, is a lake of fire, the light from which only makes the place darker. The beach is itself on fire and so offers no relief from the heat:

> At once as far as Angels' ken he [Satan] views
> The dismal Situation waste and wild,
> A Dungeon horrible, on all sides round
> As one great Furnace flam'd, yet from those flames
> No light, but rather darkness visible
> Serv'd only to discover sights of woe,
> Regions of sorrow, doleful shades, where peace
> And rest can never dwell, hope never comes
> That comes to all; but torture without end
> Still urges, and a fiery Deluge, fed
> With ever-burning Sulphur unconsum'd: (Milton, 1667, I.59–69)

On the other hand for Milton hell is a state of mind. Satan, upon awakening in hell, actually boasts that both heaven and hell are the product of mind and can therefore be established anywhere at will:

> The mind is its own place, and in itself
> Can make a Heav'n of Hell, a Hell of Heav'n. (I.254–55)

Later, Satan says the same, but now in self-doubt rather than arrogance, as he recognises what he has lost and recognises that, as himself evil, he turns everything into hell:

> Me miserable! which way shall I fly
> Infinite wrath, and infinite despair?
> Which way I fly is Hell; myself am Hell; (IV.73–75)

It is not just Satan the character who makes hell and paradise into mental states. As author, Milton writes of Satan that

> Horror and doubt distract
> His troubled thoughts, and from the bottom stir
> The Hell within him, for within him Hell
> He brings, and round about him, nor from Hell
> One step no more than from himself can fly
> By change of place. (IV.18–21)

What for Milton is true of hell is also true of paradise. On the one hand it is a place "out there", lovingly and lushly described:

> Thus was this place,
> A happy rural seat of various view:
> Groves whose rich Trees wept odorous Gums and Balm,
> Others whose fruit burnisht with Golden Rind
> Hung amiable, Hesperian Fables true,
> If true, here only, and of delicious taste. (IV.246–51)

On the other hand the archangel Michael, having consoled Adam with knowledge of the virtues that human beings can acquire only in the wake of the fall—Faith, Patience, Temperance, Love, and Charity—concludes:

> then wilt thou not be loath
> To leave this Paradise, but shalt possess
> A paradise within thee, happier far. (XII.586–87)

For Freud and Jung alike, there is no simultaneous retention of the supernatural outer world and translation of it into the inner world. The outer world, while remaining, is "de-supernaturalised". The modern psychologising of the world has not meant the reduction of the world to the mind, as in idealism, in Marlowe's Mephistopheles, and in one side of Milton. Nor has it meant the reduction of the world to a human creation, as in social constructionism. On the contrary, psychologising has meant the differentiation of the world "out there"—a world independent of humans—from the imposition upon it of elements belonging instead to humans. Projections onto the outer world, which had taken the form of gods, have by now largely been withdrawn. The outer world has come to be recognised as a natural rather than a supernatural domain, to be explained by impersonal scientific laws rather than by the decisions of gods.

Freud and Jung's position differs from Milton's. For Milton, there is no projection and therefore no conflation of mind with world. Rather, there is at once the reduction of the world to the mind, as in idealism, and the retention of an independent world "out there", as in realism.

For Freud and Jung alike, the modern rise of science has spelled the fall of religion. Writes Freud in *The Future of an Illusion*:

> Let us consider the unmistakable situation as it is to-day. We have heard the admission that religion no longer has the same influence on people that it used to ... Let us admit that the reason—though perhaps not the only reason—for this change is the increase of the scientific spirit in the higher strata of human society. Criticism has whittled away the evidential value of religious documents, natural science has shown up the errors in them. (Freud, 1927c, p. 38)

Writes Jung in "The philosophical tree":

> They [alchemists] did not find a solution, nor was this possible so long as their conceptual language was not freed from projection into matter and did not become psychological. Only in the following centuries, with the growth of natural science, was the projection withdrawn from matter and entirely abolished together with the psyche. This development of consciousness has still not reached its end. Nobody, it is true, any longer endows matter with mythological properties. This form of projection has become obsolete. (Jung, 1945/1954, par. 395)

For Jung, and also for Freud, the "development of consciousness" is not yet finished because projections remain, but they are "now confined to personal and social relationships"—that is, to other persons and peoples, but not to animals, plants, and stones (ibid.).

For the Freud of *Totem and Taboo*, religion not only incorrectly explains the physical world but, worse, harms adherents psychologically by aggravating rather than alleviating the guilt felt over sexual and aggressive drives. Freud therefore rejoices in the demise of religion. By contrast, Jung laments that the loss of religion as an explanation of the world—itself an advance—has consequently meant the loss of an effective means of tending to the unconscious. Alternative venues must therefore be found. But Jung does not thereby propose the rejection of science as the explanation of the world.

Yet for neither Jung nor Freud does the surrender of religion to science mean the surrender of myth. Even though for both Freud and Jung myth has traditionally been part of religion, they are able to decouple myth from religion and thereby save it from science. While Freud clearly cares less about saving myth than Jung does—if only because for Freud myth perpetuates rather than cures neurosis—he, too, makes myth possible in the modern age by extricating it from religion. Freud and Jung save myth both by widening the range of myth to include secular myths and, more, by interpreting myth as other than an explanation of events in the physical world. Their preservation of myth in the face of science exemplifies the twentieth-century approach to myth—and is the opposite of the nineteenth-century one.

## *The nineteenth-century approach to myth*

If one can generalise, the nineteenth century saw myth as really, not just seemingly, about the physical world. The most famous nineteenth-century theorists were the English anthropologist E. B. Tylor, whose chief work, *Primitive Culture,* first appeared in 1871, and the Scottish classicist and anthropologist J. G. Frazer, the first edition of whose main opus, *The Golden Bough,* was published in 1890. Both Tylor and Frazer take for granted that myth is part of religion and, as such, serves to explain physical events. For Tylor, the explanation is always a decision by a god. For example, a myth says that it rains because a god decides to send rain, with the myth often explaining how the god became responsible for rain and how the god exercises that responsibility. For Frazer, the explanation is not a decision by a god but the physical state of a god. For Frazer, the chief god is of vegetation. If that god is weak or dead, the crops wither or die. If the god is alive and healthy, so are the crops.

For Tylor, myth provides knowledge of the physical world as an end in itself. For Frazer, the knowledge that myth provides is a means to control over the physical world. For both, myth is the "primitive" counterpart to science, which is wholly modern. "Modern myth" is a contradiction in terms. By science is meant natural science, not social science. The events explained by myth are primarily external ones like the falling of rain and the rising of the sun, though also human events like birth and death. Myths about customs, laws, institutions, and other social phenomena are regarded as secondary.

For Tylor and Frazer alike, myth and science are identical in function. Both serve to account for all events in the physical world. Yet it is not simply that myth is no longer needed once science arises—the way horses were no longer needed once cars had been invented. It is that myth is no longer possible. For both myth and science offer direct accounts of events. According to myth, the rain god, let us suppose, collects rain in buckets and then, for whatever reason, chooses to empty the buckets on some spot below. According to science, meteorological processes cause rain. One cannot reconcile the accounts by stacking a mythological account atop a scientific account, for the rain god acts directly rather than through natural processes. Myth may presuppose tacit natural laws, which explain how rain accumulates in the buckets and how it goes to its intended destination. But the emphasis is on the action by the rain god. Taking for granted that science is true, Tylor and Frazer unhesitatingly pronounce myth false.

For Frazer, magic puts myth into practice in the form of ritual, which is an attempt to gain control over the physical world, especially over crops. Myth still explains the state of the crops, as for Tylor, but for the purpose of reviving them, not just for the purpose of explaining their revival. For Frazer, myth is the "primitive" counterpart to applied science rather than, as for Tylor, the "primitive" counterpart to theoretical science. Myth is even more blatantly false for Frazer than for Tylor because it fails to deliver the goods.

## *The twentieth-century approach to myth*

In the twentieth century Tylor's and Frazer's theories have been spurned by fellow theorists of myth on many grounds: for pitting myth against science and thereby precluding both traditional myths and modern ones, for subsuming myth under religion and thereby precluding secular myths, for deeming the function of myth explanatory or magical, for deeming the subject matter of myth the physical world, and for deeming myth false.

The overarching twentieth-century rejoinder to Tylor and Frazer has been the denial that myth must go when science comes. Twentieth-century theories have defiantly sought to preserve myth in the face of science. Yet they have not done so by challenging science as the reigning explanation of the physical world. They have not taken any of the easy routes: "relativising" science, "sociologising" science, or "mythicising" science. Rather, they have recharacterised myth as other than a literal explanation of the physical world. Myth for them is compatible with science because of their reconfiguration of myth, not because of any reassessment of science.

Freud and Jung are best seen as kindred twentieth-century theorists of myth. They may debate each other, but more deeply they are debating nineteenth-century theorists. For both Freud and Jung, the subject matter of myth is as far removed from that of nineteenth-century theorists as possible: the subject matter is the human mind, which projects, but thereby falsely projects, itself onto the physical world. For both Freud and Jung, myth is about a state of mind—not a conscious state, as for Marlowe's Mephistopheles and for Milton, but an unconscious one. For both Freud and Jung, the function of myth is neither to explain nor to manipulate the unconscious but to help encounter it. For neither Freud nor Jung does myth make the unconscious conscious. On the contrary, myth ordinarily operates unconsciously and, at least for Freud, must operate unconsciously.

Undeniably, Freud and Jung differ fundamentally over the nature of the unconscious and in turn over the reason that myth is needed to express it. Because the Freudian unconscious is composed of repressed, antisocial drives, myth releases those drives in a disguised way, so that neither the myth maker nor the reader of the myth ever confronts its meaning and thereby the myth maker's or the reader's own true nature. Myth, like other aspects of culture, serves at once to reveal and to hide its unconscious contents. Myth is a "compromise formation".

The classical Freudian approach to myth takes myth as wish fulfilment. Focusing on myths of male heroes, Freud's one-time disciple Otto Rank, in *The Myth of the Birth of the Hero* (1914), sees the myths as providing a partial fulfilment of, above all, oedipal drives. By unconsciously identifying oneself with the named hero, one gains a vicarious, mental fulfilment of one's own lingering desires. Myths serve neurotic adults fixated at their oedipal stage. The real hero of the myth is not the named hero but the myth maker or reader. At heart, myth is not biography but autobiography.

Spurred by the emergence of ego psychology, which has broadened psychoanalysis from a theory of abnormal personality to a theory of normal personality, contemporary Freudians see myth as contributing to psychological development and not just to neurosis. For them, myth helps one grow up rather than, like Peter Pan, remain a child. Myth abets adjustment to society and the physical world rather than childish flight from them. Myth may still serve to release repressed drives, but it serves even more to sublimate them and to integrate them. It serves the ego and the superego, not merely the id. Moreover, myth serves everyone, not only neurotics. To quote Jacob Arlow:

> Psychoanalysis has a greater contribution to make to the study of mythology than [merely] demonstrating, in myths, wishes often encountered in the unconscious thinking of patients. The myth is a particular kind of communal experience. It is a special form of shared fantasy, and it serves to bring the individual into relationship with members of his cultural group on the basis of certain common needs. Accordingly, the myth can be studied from the point of view of its function in psychic integration—how it plays a role in warding off feelings of guilt and anxiety, how it constitutes a form of adaptation to reality and to the group in which the individual lives, and how it influences the crystallization of the individual identity and the formation of the superego. (Arlow, 1961, p. 375)

In *The Uses of Enchantment* (1976) Bruno Bettelheim asserts much the same, but insistently asserts it of fairy tales rather than of myths, which he continues to interpret in a classical Freudian way.

The telling phrase from Arlow is "adaptation to reality". For contemporary Freudians, no less than for classical ones, myth presupposes a divide between the individual's fantasies and reality. Where myth for classical Freudians functions to satisfy in the mind what cannot be satisfied in reality, myth for contemporary Freudians functions to help one accept the inability to be satisfied in reality. Still, for both varieties of Freudians, myth is not, as for Tylor and Frazer, about reality—that is, the external world. It is about the individual, who comes smack up against reality. It is about the clash between fantasy and reality. Myth either shields the individual from reality (the classical view) or foments acceptance of reality (the contemporary view). Rather than explaining reality, myth takes reality for granted and responds to it, either negatively (classical view) or positively (contemporary view). To explain reality, one turns to natural science. Myth taken literally is incompatible with science, and for the same reason that it is for Tylor and Frazer. Myth psychologised is compatible with science because it is no longer about reality—this antithetically to Tylor and Frazer.

For neither Tylor nor Frazer does myth arise from any confrontation between the individual and reality. It arises from the experience of reality, which the individual wants either to explain (Tylor) or to manipulate (Frazer). Whatever role the individual plays in creating myth, the subject matter of myth is still the world, not the individual. Even though, especially for Tylor, mythic explanations stem from the analogy that "primitives" hypothesise between the behaviour of humans and that of the world, myth is still about the world, not about humans. Myth arises not from the unconscious projection of human personality onto the world but from the conscious application of the explanation of human behaviour to the world. Tylor is not even intrigued by the subsequent kinship between human behaviour and that of a deified world. Frazer, for his part, does attribute myth, as part of religion, to the experience of the failure to control the world through impersonal magic. That experience leads to the assumption that the world operates instead at the behest of gods. But myth is still not about how the world is experienced. It is about the world itself.

For Freudians, myths project human nature onto the world in the form of gods—for Freud himself, largely father-like gods. To understand the world is to withdraw those projections. The world really operates according to mechanical laws rather than according to the wills of a divine family. There is no symmetry between humans and the world. There is a disjunction. Even myths about heroes, who can be either human or divine, involve projection: the plot of hero myths is the fantasised expression of family relations, with the named hero playing the role of the idealised myth maker or reader. There are no comic-book heroes in the real world. There are only human beings, some better than others.

For Jungians as well as for Freudians, myths project human nature onto the world in the form of gods and of heroes, who, similarly, can be either human or divine. To understand the world is, similarly, to withdraw those projections and to recognise the world as it really is. Jungian projections are more elusive than Freudian ones because they cover a far wider range of the personality. After all, there are an endless number of sides of the personality, or archetypes. Almost anything in the world can be archetypal—that is, can provide a hook for the projection of an archetype.

Unlike Freudians, Jungians have taken myth positively from the outset. For them, the unconscious expressed in myth is not a repository of repressed, antisocial drives but a storehouse of innately unconscious archetypes that have simply never had an opportunity at realisation. Myth is one means of encountering this unconscious. The function of myth is less that of release, as for classical Freudians, than that of growth, as for contemporary ones. But where even contemporary Freudians see myth as a means of adjustment to the demands of the outer world, Jungians see myth as a means of the cultivation of the inner world. The payoff is not adjustment but self-realisation. Myth is a circuitous, if nevertheless useful, means of self-realisation precisely because it involves projection: one encounters oneself through the world.

The journey that the hero makes in Joseph Campbell's largely Jungian *Hero with a Thousand Faces* (1949) is only literally outward. The real journey is inward. It is "tripping". It is a journey to the strange, new, divine-like world of the collective unconscious, from which, in the course of establishing ordinary consciousness, one has ineluctably become severed. For Campbell, successful heroism requires not merely reaching the new world but also returning from it, with ordinary consciousness thereby harmonised with the unconscious to form the self. For Campbell, as for Rank, the real hero is not the named hero, such as Odysseus or Aeneas, but whoever created the myth or is entranced by it.

Both Freudians and Jungians bypass the power of myth at the conscious, usually literal, level. While both appreciate the need to be moved by the life of the named hero or protagonist, that figure can be fictional. One does not have to accept the historicity of Oedipus to be moved by his saga. The named figure is a mere peg onto which to hang the autobiography. As Freud writes, "Oedipus' destiny moves us only because it might have been ours—because the oracle laid the same curse [i.e., the Oedipus complex] upon us before our birth as upon him" (Freud, 1900a, p. 262). Jung would concur. For both, a story that can never be imagined as happening to oneself will not work. In short, myth for Freudians and Jungians alike never takes one outside oneself. No theory of myth is more solipsistic than theirs.

## *Freudians and Jungians against the nineteenth-century approach to myth*

It is conventionally assumed that Jung, on myth as in general, is arguing against Freud. It is also commonly assumed that Freud or Freudians on myth are arguing against Jung and Jungians. But in fact both are arguing even more against nineteenth-century theorists like Tylor and Frazer. Freudians and Jungians alike must first show that myth is not about the physical world before they can debate each other over what psychologically myth is about.

In "The theme of the three caskets" Freud comments snippily on an interpretation made by one E. Stucken of the choice of the caskets in *The Merchant of Venice*:

> He [Stucken] writes: "The identity of Portia's three suitors is clear from their choice: the Prince of Morocco chooses the gold casket—he is the sun; the Prince of Arragon chooses the silver casket—he is the moon; Bassanio chooses the leaden casket—he is the star youth".
>
> Thus our little problem has led us to an astral myth! The only pity is that with this explanation we are not at the end of the matter. The question is not exhausted, for we do not share the belief of some investigators that myths were read in the heavens and brought down to earth; we are more inclined to judge with Otto Rank that they were projected on to the heavens after having arisen elsewhere under purely human conditions. It is in this human content that our interest lies. (Freud, 1913f, pp. 291–292)

Rather than originating in the experience of the natural world, as for Tylor and Frazer, myth for Freud originates in the experience of the family and is then projected onto the world.

Along with Rank's *The Myth of the Birth of the Hero*, to which Freud is referring, the other classic Freudian analysis of myth is Karl Abraham's *Dreams and Myths* (1913). Like Freud, both Abraham and Rank dismiss those theorists, called nature mythologists, who either take myth to be about the physical world rather than about the human mind or, worse, turn myths about humans into myths about the physical world. Rank is especially disdainful of those who, for example, turn the life of Oedipus into a symbol of the daily course of the sun:

> as given by a representative of the natural mythological mode of interpretation, Oedipus, who kills his father, marries his mother, and dies old and blind, is the solar hero who murders his procreator, the darkness; shares his couch with the mother, the gloaming, from whose lap, the dawn, he has been born, and dies blinded, as the setting sun. (Rank, 1914, pp. 9–10)

Here myth is not a literal explanation of the course of the sun, as it would be for Tylor, but a symbolic description of the course of the sun. Still, myth is about the sun, not a family.

At times both Rank and Abraham, rather than dismissing the view that myth is a depiction of the natural world, accept it but attribute it to projection from the human world. Writes Rank: "We also hope to demonstrate that myths are ... structures of the human faculty of imagination which may be secondarily transferred to the heavenly bodies with their baffling phenomena" (Rank, 2003, p. 9). Writes Abraham: "Creation is nothing but procreation divested of the sexual" (Abraham, 1913, p. 41). Rank goes beyond Abraham to attribute the failure of nature mythologists to acknowledge the true subject or source of nature myths to, in stereotypically Freudian fashion, resistance (see Rank, 1914, pp. 8–9; on nature mythologists, see also Rank, 1992, pp. 224–25; Rank & Sachs, 1916, pp. 37–42).

Toward nature mythologists, Jung is at least as dismissive as Rank. Campbell's contempt is for what he idiosyncratically assumes is the literal interpretation of myth by religion, especially Western religion. Jung's criticism of Tylor, who is cited only occasionally, is not wholly clear. Apparently, Tylor, and Frazer as well, are guilty of mischaracterising "primitive" religious beliefs. They deem the key belief that of individual souls, or spirits, in natural phenomena—the notion of "animism"—rather than that of an underlying universal spirituality. This criticism is not specifically psychological and was regularly made by fellow anthropologists, who contended that "primitives" believe in a divine power, often called *mana*, which only in turn is divided into distinct spirits.

Jung's psychological criticism of both Tylor and Frazer is that they misconstrue the source of this power, which comes not, as they assume, from conscious reflection but from the unconscious. Jung combines both criticisms as follows:

> [T]he idea of energy and its conservation must be a primordial image that was dormant in the collective unconscious ... [T]he most primitive religions in the most widely separated parts of the earth are founded upon this image. These are the so-called dynamistic religions whose sole and determining thought is that there exists a universal magical power [i.e., *mana*] about which everything revolves. Tylor, the well-known English investigator, and Frazer

> likewise, misunderstood this idea as animism. In reality primitives do not mean, by their power-concept, souls or spirits at all, but something which the American investigator Lovejoy has appropriately termed "primitive energetics" ... So this idea has been stamped on the human brain for aeons. That is why it lies ready to hand in the unconscious of every man. Only, certain conditions are needed to cause it to appear. (Jung, 1917/1926/1943, pars. 108–109)

The experience of the external world provides the "condition" for the appearance of the unconscious: the awesome grandeur of the external world provides an ideal peg onto which to project the unconscious, which is always experienced as extraordinary rather than ordinary, as magical rather than natural, and as divine rather than human.

Like many others, Jung often turns to Frazer for example after example of myths worldwide, but he always psychologises whatever examples he uses. Above all, he cites examples of Frazer's own key myth, that of the death and rebirth of the god of vegetation. Unlike Tylor, who stalwartly reads myth literally, Frazer, like Rank's nature mythologists, reads the myth as symbolic of the course of vegetation itself:

> the story that Adonis spent half, or according to others a third, of the year in the lower world and the rest of it in the upper world, is explained most simply and naturally by supposing that he represented vegetation, especially the corn, which lies buried in the earth half the year and reappears above ground the other half. (Frazer, 1922, p. 392)

True, Frazer, like Tylor, assumes that "primitives" themselves take their myths literally and must do so for those myths to explain events in the world. But Frazer breaks with Tylor in asserting that myths about either the decisions or the actions of gods are in fact, albeit unrecognised, symbolic descriptions of natural processes themselves.

Against Frazer, Jung offers his own symbolic rendition of these myths: the myth of the death and rebirth of a god symbolises a process occurring not in the world but in the mind. That process is the return of the ego to the unconscious—a kind of temporary death of the ego—and its re-emergence, or rebirth, from the unconscious:

> I need only mention the whole mythological complex of the dying and resurgent god and its primitive precursors all the way down

> to the re-charging of fetishes and churingas with magical force. It expresses a transformation of attitude by means of which a new potential, a new manifestation of life, a new fruitfulness, is created. (Jung, 1921, par. 325)

Jung does not deny that the psychological process of the death and rebirth of the ego parallels the physical process of the death and rebirth of vegetation. Like Freud, Rank, and Abraham, he denies that the physical process explains the psychological one, let alone for the mythic one. For Frazer, as for Tylor, the leap from vegetation to god is the product of reasoning: "primitives" observe the course of vegetation and hypothesise the existence of a god to account for it—even if, again, for Frazer himself the god is a mere symbol of vegetation.

For Jung, the leap is too great for the human mind to make. Humans generally, not merely "primitives", lack the creativity required to concoct consciously the notion of the sacred out of the profane. They can only transform the profane into a sacred that already exists for them. Humans must already have the idea of god within them and can only be projecting that idea onto vegetation and the other natural phenomena that they observe:

> This latter analogy [between god and natural phenomenon] explains the well-attested connection between the renewal of the god and seasonal and vegetational phenomena. One is naturally inclined to assume that seasonal, vegetational, lunar, and solar myths underlie these analogies. But that is to forget that a myth, like everything psychic, cannot be solely conditioned by external events. Anything psychic brings its own internal conditions with it, so that one might assert with equal right that the myth is purely psychological and uses meteorological or astronomical events merely as a means of expression. The whimsicality and absurdity of many primitive myths often makes the latter explanation seem far more appropriate than any other. (Jung, 1921, par. 325)

Even early Jung, who was prepared to give more weight to experience than later Jung, distinguishes between the experience of the sun itself and the experience of the sun as a god. The experience of the sun provides the occasion for the manifestation of the sun archetype but does not cause that archetype:

> I have often been asked where the archetypes or primordial images come from. It seems to me that their origin can only be explained by assuming them to be deposits of the constantly repeated experiences of humanity. One of the commonest and at the same time most impressive experiences is the apparent movement of the sun every day. We certainly cannot discover anything of the kind in the unconscious, so far as the known physical process is concerned. What we do find, on the other hand, is the myth of the sun-hero in all its countless variations. It is this myth, and not the physical process, that forms the sun archetype ... The archetype is a kind of readiness to produce over and over again the same or similar mythical ideas. (Jung, 1917/1926/1943, par. 109)

It is not only allegories of physical processes that Jung rejects as the real subject matter of myth. It is also literal interpretations of myth like Tylor's, which still make the subject matter outer rather than inner. For Tylor, myths are actual explanations of natural phenomena and not merely, as for Frazer, colourful descriptions of them.

Jung conflates Tylor's theory with Frazer's in declaring that "People are very loath to give up the idea that the myth is some kind of explanatory allegory of astronomical, meteorological, or vegetative processes" (Jung, 1928, par. 71). The phrase "explanatory allegory" equates Tylor's theory—myth as explanation—with Frazer's—myth as allegory. Jung asks rhetorically "why", if myth is really about the sun, "the sun and its apparent motions do not appear direct and undisguised as a content of the myths" (1921, par. 748). But the question is rhetorical only for Frazer's theory. For Tylor, a myth describes the sun god and not merely the sun because the myth is about the sun god and not merely about the sun. Yet even if Jung were to distinguish Tylor's view from Frazer's, he would still invoke his fundamental claim that human beings are incapable of consciously inventing gods and can only cast onto the world gods already in their minds.

For Jung, myth is no more about gods than about the physical world. It is about the human mind. Myth must be read symbolically, as for Frazer, and the symbolised subject is a process, as likewise for Frazer, but the process is an inner rather than outer one. If on the one hand Jung would doubtless prefer Frazer's symbolic reading of myth to Tylor's literal reading, on the other hand he would surely prefer

Tylor's appreciation of the divine referent of myth to Frazer's reduction of it to something natural, or the reduction of the unconscious to consciousness.

Jung takes as projections not only nature myths but all other kinds of myths as well. He states that "in fact, the whole of mythology could be taken as a sort of projection of the collective unconscious ... Just as the constellations were projected into the heavens, similar figures were projected into legends and fairytales or upon historical persons" (Jung, 1927/1931, par. 325). One might suggest that once Jung uncouples myth from the natural world, he is free to look for myths elsewhere. No longer confined to myths that at face value are about the external world—creation myths, flood myths, myths of the seasons, myths of paradise, and myths of the end of the world—he can now fix his psychological gaze on myths that at face value are about human beings—for example, children, old persons, kings and queens.

Hero myths, of which Jungians are especially enamoured, are projections onto mere human beings of a quasi-divine status: "the hero myth is an unconscious drama seen only in projection, like the happenings in Plato's parable of the cave. The hero himself appears as a being of more than human stature" (Jung, 1911–12/1952, par. 612). Moderns, even while often professed atheists, still create myths by projecting onto their fellow human beings exaggerated qualities that turn them into superhuman figures—not only into heroes but also into saints and demons:

> [T]he archetypes usually appear in projection; and, because projections are unconscious, they appear on persons in the immediate environment, mostly in the form of abnormal over- or under-evaluations which provoke misunderstandings, quarrels, fanaticisms, and follies of every description. Thus we say, "He makes a god of so-and-so", or, 'so-and-so is Mr. X's *bête noire*". In this way, too, there grow up modern myth-formations, i.e., fantastic rumours, suspicions, prejudices. (Jung, 1917/1926/1943, par. 152)

For Jung, traditional myths—those focused on by nature mythologists—have been religious myths. They have been either about gods acting in the world (Tylor) or about the world as symbolised by gods (Frazer). The decline of religion in the wake of science has obliged moderns to seek secular myths, such as myths about heroes, who, if superhuman, are still not quite gods.

The decline of religion has also spurred moderns to forge their own private myths. Jung had the creativity to forge—or to find—his own myth, and he announces at the outset of *Memories, Dreams, Reflections* that he will proceed to "tell my personal myth" (Jung, 1963, p. 3), which refers either to the course of his whole life or, less likely, to his speculations about life after death. Far from an inferior alternative to a group myth, under which would fall all religious myths, a personal myth for Jung is the ideal, for it alone is geared to the unique contour of one's personality. A personal myth seeks to nurture unrealised aspects of one's personality. At times, Jung even defines myth as personal: "Myth is more individual and expresses life more precisely than does science. Science works with concepts of averages which are far too general to do justice to the subjective variety of an individual life" (ibid., p. 3).

Seemingly, a passage like this undoes my claim that for Jung science rules and that myth must accommodate itself to science, just as religion must be abandoned because it cannot be accommodated to science. Jung even writes that "In itself any scientific theory, no matter how subtle, has, I think, less value from the standpoint of psychological truth than religious dogma" (Jung, 1938/1940, par. 81). But he is referring to psychological value—that is, to the value in understanding human beings. To explain the physical world he, no less than Freud, turns to natural science, to which religion must defer.

Whatever the superiority of a personal myth or even of a group myth to science, Jung still employs science—psychology—to decipher myth. If Jung's personal myth led him to his psychology, his psychology is not itself his myth. Rather, it is the key to his and every other myth. In short, no more than any of the other twentieth-century respondents to Tylor and Frazer is Jung turning science into myth. The accomplishment of twentieth-century theorists of myth, not least that of Jung himself, lies in re-characterising myth to accommodate science, not in subsuming science under myth. It cheapens both science and myth to fuse them.

Freud and Jung are far more akin to each other than opposed because they, more relentlessly than even their fellow twentieth-century theorists of myth, remove myth from the sphere of natural science. Myth is about human nature rather than about the nature of the physical world. (I do not want to consider here, as I have done elsewhere, the supposed return of myth to the physical world through Jung's concept of synchronicity: see Segal, 2008). Myth is about the mind rather than the body—whatever the relationship between the one and the other—and it is about the unconscious rather than the conscious side of the mind. Finally, the function of myth is neither to explain nor to control the unconscious but to abet the experience of the unconscious. Only once Freudians and Jungians have established that myth is a psychological phenomenon can they begin debating each other over the nature of that psychological phenomenon.

## *References*

Abraham, K. (1913). *Dreams and Myths*. W. A. White (Trans.). New York: Journal of Nervous and Mental Disease Publishing.

Arlow, J. (1961). Ego psychology and the study of mythology. *Journal of the American Psychoanalytic Association, 9*: 371–393.

Bettelheim, B. (1976). *The Uses of Enchantment*. New York: Knopf.

Campbell, J. (1949). *The Hero with a Thousand Faces*. 1st ed. New York: Bollingen.

Frazer, J. G. (1922). *The Golden Bough*. Abridged ed. London: Macmillan [1st unabridged ed. 1890].

Freud, S. (1900a). *The Interpretation of Dreams*. *S. E., 4, 5*. London: Hogarth.

Freud, S. (1913f). The theme of the three caskets. *S. E., 12*: 289–301. London: Hogarth.

Freud, S. (1927c). *The Future of an Illusion*. *S. E., 21*: 1–56. London: Hogarth.

Jung, C. G. (1911–12/1952). *Symbols of Transformation*. *The Collected Works of C. G. Jung*. H. Read, M. Fordham, & G. Adler (Eds.). W. McGuire (Executive Ed.). R. F. C. Hull et al. (Trans.). [Hereafter *C. W.*,] *5* (2nd ed.). Princeton, NJ: Princeton University Press, 1967.

Jung, C. G. (1917/1926/1943). On the psychology of the unconscious. In: *C. W., 7* (2nd ed.): pp. 1–119/pars. 1–201. Princeton, NJ: Princeton University Press, 1966.

Jung, C. G. (1921). *Psychological Types*. *C. W., 6*. Princeton, NJ: Princeton University Press, 1971.

Jung, C. G. (1927/1931). The structure of the psyche. In: *C. W., 8* (2nd ed.): pp. 139–158/pars. 283–342. Princeton, NJ: Princeton University Press, 1969.

Jung, C. G. (1928). On psychic energy. In: *C. W., 8* (2nd ed.): pp. 3–66/pars. 1–130. Princeton, NJ: Princeton University Press, 1969.

Jung, C. G. (1938/1940). Psychology and religion. In: *C. W., 11* (2nd ed.): pp. 3–105/pars. 1–168. Princeton, NJ: Princeton University Press, 1969.

Jung, C. G. (1945/1954). The philosophical tree. In: *C. W., 13*: pp. 251–349/pars. 304–482. Princeton, NJ: Princeton University Press, 1968.

Jung. C. G. (1952). Foreword to Werblowsky's *Lucifer and Prometheus*. In: *C. W., 11* (2nd ed.): pp. 311–315/pars. 468–473. Princeton, NJ: Princeton University Press, 1969.

Jung, C. G. (1963). *Memories, Dreams, Reflections*. A. Jaffé (Ed.). R. & C. Winston (Trans.). New York: Vintage Books.

Rank, O. (1914). *The Myth of the Birth of the Hero*. 1st ed. F. Robbins & S. E. Jelliffe (Trans.). New York: Journal of Nervous and Mental Disease Publishing.

Rank, O. (1992). *The Incest Theme in Literature and Legend*. 1st ed. G. C. Richter (Trans.). Baltimore: Johns Hopkins University Press.

Rank, O. (2003). *The Myth of the Birth of the Hero*. 2nd ed. E. J. Lieberman & G. C. Richter (Trans.). Baltimore: Johns Hopkins University Press.

Rank, O. & Sachs, H. (1916). *The Significance of Psychoanalysis for the Mental Sciences*. C. R. Payne (Trans.). New York: Nervous and Mental Disease Publishing.

Segal, R. A. (2008). Bringing myth back to the world: the future of myth in Jungian studies. In: L. Huskinson (Ed.), *Dreaming the Myth Onwards* (pp. 91–105). London: Routledge.

Tylor, E. B. (1871). *Primitive Culture*. 2 vols. 1st ed. London: Murray.

CHAPTER SEVEN

# The boy who had dreams in his mouth

*Eric Rhode*

Jaan Puhvel (1987, p. 1) introduces his readers to a survey of comparative mythology by considering the derivation of the word myth. He claims that the original derivation of the word myth is unclear—"most probably it is based on the interjection (mu) mu". He thinks that "word, speech, talk" is the original sense of myth. Homer, he says, juxtaposes the word myth to *epos*, meaning speech—and to *ergon*, meaning deed. In the Greek tragedians, as well as in Homer, myth can mean "tale, story, narrative", without any reference to truth. Puhvel relates myth to implausibilities and tall tales. He opposes it to logos, which he thinks of as truth-centred. I do not want to follow him down this fascinating path. My concern is with myth as sacred telling, myth as mouth-making—the ways in which mouth can be thought to be a site for the sacred. My concern is with myth as (mu) mu, myth as linking mouth to a mother.

The psychologist Jean Piaget once asked a little boy where he dreamt; and the boy answered, in my mouth (Lewin, 1946, cited in Arlow, 1973, p. 92).[1] You may think that the little boy is talking nonsense. Or you may think that he is in touch with some likeness between the act of dreaming and the act of being nourished by food. It is as though food, in particular a mother's milk, were a concrete equivalence for the ability to dream.

Perhaps each of us carries this concrete equivalence somewhere in our minds. Dreaming by means of a mouth is an archaic mode of awareness. Evidence for it is to be valued because most people, I would think, lose direct touch with it fairly early on. If I extend the idea, I come to the view that the umbilical cord prior to its severance performs the same service for a foetus. The nourishment that passes by way of the umbilical cord is identified with the capacity to dream. (However, making a connection between dreaming and mouth cuts out an important factor in nurture: that the one who nurtures the infant does so by means of a gaze, as well as by food. I conjecture that it is the gaze, when loving, that is of paramount importance in the process of being so nourished).

The notion of dreaming in the mouth is informative about the nature of aesthetics. It might be possible to write about aesthetics in terms of an appetite that can be satisfied, at least temporarily, by the contemplation of a work of art. The pleasure in this contemplation may elude direct definition. But it does appear to involve phantom sensations of oral incorporation. Dreaming in the mouth may be an analogue for the archaic supposition that when I enjoy a work of art it is as though I were in the process of eating it: in so being related to oral discrimination, it is reasonably assumed to be an object of taste.

In his *Studies in Extended Metapsychology* (1986), Donald Meltzer has written hauntingly about a twenty-six year old man whose "equipment of thought is still somewhat fixed in a buccal (or mouth) phase, so that the theatre of thought has not yet become located in his dream life but is still in his mouth during waking hours" (Meltzer, 1986, p. 180). He goes on to say, "If the buccal cavity (or mouth) is his theatre of thought, anything happening in his mouth might be expected to have the same impact on his view of the self and world as we are accustomed for dreams to have" (ibid.).[2] So here the idea of dreaming in the mouth is related to thought process in general and to an idea of the theatre in particular.

Mouth has an intriguing place in the evolution of our awareness, since so far as sensation is concerned it appears to take on being without a history. The umbilical cord, I presume, does not offer the foetus an experience that defines satisfaction by means of its contrary, which is dissatisfaction. There is no experience of a feeding object in the mouth that actually provides spiritual as well as physical nourishment. There is no possible correlation of a mouth with a possibly loving gaze. Nonetheless, perhaps the experience of mouth as an aperture, whose shape one can explore by the movement of tongue, precedes the class of experience that comes into being with the loss of the umbilical cord. It is an experience without precedent; and it is for this reason that it lends itself to the speculations of those who are attracted to thinking by way of myths. The tongue is a prototype of the feeding object; it is an equivalence of the nipple or teat in the mouth of the foetus. There is a temptation to project the terrifying notion of an external circumstance on which one totally depends as a newborn into, or onto, a part of one's own body, so that one can think to appropriate that on which one depends; in this way I may come to think that the nipple or teat that feeds me, or fails to feed me, has become my tongue. I may believe then that I can control the vagaries of an object that is outside me and on which I depend for my existence.

Does the boy who dreams in his mouth think of the dreams as gifts from afar, like the nourishment he receives, or does he think of his mouth as a site whose surfaces magically generate dreams? Obviously I don't know; but if I assume the second case, I may be doing the Piaget boy an injustice. He may experience the dream words in his mouth as an inspiration and as a gift from afar. On the other hand, if I assume the second case as a possibility and assume my mouth to be womblike and my tongue to be a magician that creates the cosmos, I would find myself in a state of extreme delusion. In correspondence with the conception of the mouth as a cave whose walls emanate dreams, or words, or babies, is the conception of mouth as an interior within the earth or mountain, say, in which the dead and the unborn exist in a netherworld and yearn for a tongue-magician to bring them to life. The mouth that claims to make its own dreams can take the form of a prison, working a scapegoat system, with the tongue as its victim. There is an idiom that catches exactly the feeling of this system. I could have bitten my tongue—meaning I should have choked back my ill-considered thought, I must punish myself—better to punish myself than bite the hand that feeds me. The prison system may be idealised as a church in which profanity—fragmented bits of nourishment, aftertastes, obscenities—are consecrated by rite: food, sounds, speech then return to their rightful condition, which is to be holy as well as wholesome. The mouth thinks to have recaptured the creative process; it once more thinks itself to be the site in which dreams generate symbols.

The relation of the feeding object and the mouth that feeds from it, or the exchange of glances between feeder and fed, are intimately connected. The nourishing effects of food are similar to the belief that insight or dream can be ingested, often in the form of a radiance associated with the loving quality in a gaze. Someone once told me about taking his daughter to a surgeon who was a consultant in speech difficulties. The surgeon gently drew the daughter's tongue out of her mouth by tying a piece of material about it. He warmed a mirror on a spirit lamp. He then placed a torch on his forehead and looked into the child's mouth. Light fell on her vocal cords. I don't know whether it was then claimed that she was cured or not! Someone else told me about a strange locum doctor who, when asked to look into a patient's mouth, directed the torch into his own mouth. It is possible to see these two anecdotes as being unusual slants on the nature of insight, with the light of the lamp or torch being equivalences in meaning to the relation of a gaze to the ingestion of food. John Milton's denunciation in *Lycidas* of the English bishops as "blind mouths" is relevant; it is also poignant. Milton's mother had just died; presumably the concept of a nipple-gaze was dimmed within him. Later, in *Paradise Lost*, he was to proclaim the need for a poet to ingest spiritual light.[3]

Lewin alludes to Isakower's proposal that infants in general are unable to appreciate the distinction between their own skin and their own mouths and the skin on their mother's breast. (Whether this fascinating idea is true in observation, I do not know.) He writes, following Otto Isakower (1936): "The baby does not know what it is eating: it may be eating something on the breast or in the breast, or something that belongs to itself" (Lewin, 1946, p. 428). He mentions dreams and phantasies in which skin lesions are comparable to mouths, or oral devourings, projected onto or into skin. This is like the markings on the skin-like surfaces of Oceanic art. Presumably the skin projected into by these mouth-thoughts is skin denied the curatorship of a nipple; it is cloud-like, enclosing the mouth, a pale extension of the infant's own mouth, an ectoplasm or ghost tongue, a dream screen that exudes as breath does in a sub-zero temperature. This is not as fantastic as it may sound: the novelist Proust imagined a whole world to take on being from a taste in his mouth. An infant who experiences its mother's skin as an extension of its own reveries presumably will confuse her skin with its own skin and imagine the skin that swaddles its body as being an extension of its mother's cradlings of it.

In *The Arunta*, first published in 1927, Bernard Spencer and Francis Gillen described the initiation rite by means of which a member of the Arunta tribe could become a medicine man. The initiate had to sleep by the mouth of a cave in a range of hills fourteen miles south of Alice Springs. The cave was a disquieting place. People who entered it were thought to disappear. Its interior appeared to realise some idea of the afterlife. The initiate believed that ancestral spirits inhabited the cave: presumably he lay outside the cave in a state of terror. At the break of day, state Spencer and Gillen, a spirit from within the cave, finding the sleeper outside it, "threw an invisible lance at him, which pierced his neck from behind and passed through the tongue, making a large hole in the tongue. It then came out of his mouth" (Spencer & Gillen, 1927, p. 392; see also 1899, pp. 523–524). A second lance pierces the man from ear to ear. He dies, and the spirits carry him into the cave—a place of perpetual sunshine and running waters. The spirits remove the man's internal organs and replace them with another set of internal organs. They also place magic stones inside him, which are intended to combat the forces of evil. When he awakes from sleep, the initiate is out of his mind. But then the state of insanity diminishes, and he may be thought to be fit to be elected as a medicine man.

I mentioned this incident to the eminent child psychotherapist Frances Tustin, who said that she thought that the hole that appears in the initiate's mouth on a concrete level was a nipple in negation and had the significance of being a black hole on the mouth. In many rites, an initiate must pass through states akin to death in order to be born into a more meaningful life. The Arunta sees the place of transformation as a mouth, being the site of death (equally being the loss of the feeding object), and also as a cave, a homologue to mouth that is associated with the redemptive power of the ancestral spirits.

If the loss of the feeding object can be acknowledged, and a little mourned, then a weaning process will be under way. The ancient Egyptians thought that the cave of the netherworld was perpetually brilliant (Blackman, 1916). The Arunta similarly thought of the cave of resurrection as a place of perpetual sunshine. Might this not be a reflection of the belief that a mouth can be irradiated by the power of a loving gaze? The sun at night travels royally through the netherworld as a king in progress to reincarnation. Here lives the alter ego twin of the pharaoh, whom the pharaoh was thought to placate throughout his life by venerating his own umbilical cord as a sacred image of his dead counterpart (Blackman, 1916).

In *Themis*, first published in 1912, the classical scholar Jane Harrison related the Arunta initiation rite (which she had taken from an earlier Spencer and Gillen publication) to Epimenides of Crete, whom she thought to be a "typical medicine man of antiquity". Epimenides was a member of a select band of initiates known as the Bacchoi. He was "beloved of the gods", according to Plutarch, and "an adept in religious matters dealing with the lore of initiation rites". Epimenides had acquired his religious skills by means of dreaming. Once he was lying at midday in the cave of the Diktaean Zeus when a deep sleep lasting many years overcame him, and he dreamt of meeting with the gods and with Justice and Truth. When he awoke he thought that only a short time had passed (Harrison, 1912, pp. 52–53). If Epimenides is compared to the tongue in a dreamer's mouth, then his long sleep in the cave is analogous to the pre-verbal period that each of us passes through while in the womb and in infancy.

Asclepius, the first Greek physician, a legendary figure thought to be in part divine, was reputed to have practised dream therapy as a means to affect physical cures. He would arrange for his patients to dream in cave-like spaces. Incubation was a form of therapy. Beliefs in the curative powers of group dreaming had a spatial congruence with the founding of a theatre. The dream sanatorium of Asclepius at Epidaurus stood close by a theatre dedicated to Dionysus, one of the gods of death and resurrection, and from this fact I assume that the power of the drama to bring about catharsis was similar in meaning to the power of dreaming in a mouthlike cave to bring about a cure. There was also another dimension. At the place known as Kos, a dream sanatorium by the river Lethe was associated with rite-of-passage crossings into the netherworld, as David Napier has described in a study on masks:

> Asclepius' celebrated ability to heal through dream analysis depended on an environment whose symbolism reiterated mythic structure. It included subterranean chambers and tunnels and sacred springs as representations for rite of passage. The curing centres may originally have been associated with the worship of netherworld daemons. Cure arrived by contact with the netherworld. (Napier, 1986, p. 234n.)

Passages beneath the earth, like labyrinthine tree roots, effectively represent the confused states that passing through the liminal phase of rite of passage might entail.

In a footnote in a collection of papers published under the title of *A View from Afar*, Claude Lévi-Strauss alludes to an article by Tristan Platt on mirror symmetry, in which lightning as a fork of light is identified with the idea of binary division. Some of the Macha peoples of Bolivia at one time believed that the occurrence of lightning was synonymous with the appearance of harelips and the making of twins. It is as though the fork of lightning were to split an aperture that is equally a mouth or womb. Platt writes:

> It is … said that if a pregnant woman is frightened by thunder and lightning, the child in her belly divides in two. I was recently told that twins are sometimes born with lips split vertically down the middle; this, too, is attributed to the fear caused by thunder and lightning. (Platt, 1978, p. 1097, quoted in Lévi-Strauss, 1985, p. 209)

In at least one African tribe a mother is called "Sky", if she is the mother of twins. The fork of lightning that divides the heavens into parts that mirror each other is an example of what Lévi-Strauss elsewhere has called split representation. The iconography of the forked lightning is identical to the iconography of the split lip and other forms of binary representation. I imagine the tongue that is split to be like the forked tongue of the devil. But why should fire be associated with the mouth? Separation can take the form of a wrench in the mouth, as though a tongue had been pulled out. The pain may be confused with acts of biting or being bitten, or with ulceration, and other types of fiery pain in the mouth.

Myth is sacred speech. The infant's mouth says mu. Adoration imbues a certain space. A mouth in communion with a glance, as well as a feeding object, can take on an atmosphere of love. The great scholar F. M Cornford, in Harrison's *Themis* (1912, p. 329), refers to a native American, a member of a tribe of Indians situated in Iowa, who said to the anthropologist J. O. Dorsey: "There are sacred things, and I do not like to speak of them, and it is not our custom to do so, except when we make a feast and collect the people and use the sacred pipe" (Dorsey, 1889–1890, p. 430).

I owe my final reference to Charles Malamoud's commentary on a certain passage in the *Bhagavata Purana* (Malamoud, 2005, pp. 83–85). The siblings of baby Krishna, who is an avatar of Vishnu, report to his mother Yashoda that they have seen him eating cow dung. When challenged, the baby denies any such act and invites its mother to look into his mouth. There his mother beholds the entire cosmos

> of mobiles and immobiles, the ethereal dome, the cardinal points, the sphere of the earth along with the mountains, continents and oceans, the wind, the fire of lightning, the moon, the stars, the whole of the planetary system, the elements of water, fire, wind and the sky, the presiding deities of the senses and the mind, the subtle elements and the three gunas. (Bhagavata Purana X. 8. 37–38, in Tagare, 1978. p. 1303)

You can see this legend as an example of an interaction between two beings who are crazy. Or you can see it as a legend that invites prolonged contemplation about the mother–infant relationship.

## *Notes*

1. "Usually the children told Piaget that their dream was in the room or in their eyes, although one little boy said, inexplicably in terms of Piaget's method, that he dreamt in his mouth. To have followed this up would have gone beyond Piaget's fixed questionnaire and spoiled his tabulations". (Lewin, 1946, in Arlow, 1973, p. 92)
2. In this chapter of his book, Donald Meltzer quotes from a paper written by Maria Rhode on oral phantasies concerning hard and soft in speech, consonants and vowels. I wish to acknowledge my debt to both these authors.
3. I owe the linking of Lycidas to the death of the poet's mother to a beautiful essay on this subject by Meg Harris Williams.

## *References*

Arlow, J. A. (Ed.) (1973). *Selected Writings of Bertram D. Lewin*. New York: Psychoanalytic Quarterly.

Blackman, A. M. (1916). The pharaoh's placenta and the moon god Khons. *Journal of Egyptian Archaeology, 3*: 235–249.

Dorsey, J. O. (1889–90). A study of Siouan cults. *11th annual report of the Bureau of Ethnology*, Washington: 351–544.

Harrison, J. (1912). *Themis*. Cambridge: Cambridge University Press.

Isakower, O. (1938). A contribution to the psychopathology of phenomena associated with falling asleep. *International Journal of Psycho-Analysis, 19*: 331–345. [Original work published 1936.]

Lévi-Strauss, C. (1985). *The View from Afar*. J. Neugroschel & P. Hoss (Trans.). Oxford: Blackwell.

Lewin, B. (1946). Sleep, the mouth and the dream screen. *Psychoanalytic Quarterly, 15*: 419–434.

Malamoud, C. (2005). *La danse des pierres: études sur la scène sacrificielle dans l'Inde ancienne*. Paris: Éditions du Seuil.

Meltzer, D. (1986). *Studies in Extended Metapsychology: Clinical Applications of Bion's Ideas*. Perthshire, Scotland: Clunie Press.

Napier, A. D. (1986). *Masks, Transformation, and Paradox*. Berkeley: University of California Press.

Piaget, J. (1926). *La représentation du monde chez enfant*. Paris: Alcan.

Platt, T. (1978). Symétries en miroir: le concept de yanatin chez les Macha de Bolivie. *Annales 33*: 1081–1107.

Puhvel, J. (1987). *Comparative Mythology*. Baltimore: John Hopkins Press.

Spencer, B. & Gillen, F. J. (1899). *The Native Tribes of Central Australia*. London: Macmillan.

Spencer, B. & Gillen, F. J. (1927). *The Arunta*. London: Macmillan.

Tagare, G. V. (1978). *The Bhagavata Purana*. Part 4. Delhi: Motilal Banarsidass.

CHAPTER EIGHT

# Myth, synchronicity, and re-enchantment*

*Roderick Main*

## *The disenchantment of the world*

Max Weber (1864–1920) described modern culture as characterised by capitalism, rationalisation, disenchantment, subjectivist culture, and democratisation (Scaff, 2000, pp. 103–107). These features of modernity are intimately interlinked in Weber's thought, and any one of them gives access to the overall problem of modernity as he saw it. In this chapter I shall focus on the feature of disenchantment (Entzauberung, "de-magification"), described by Weber as a condition in which "there are no mysterious incalculable forces that come into play, but rather … one can in principle, master all things by calculation", and in which, therefore, "[o]ne need no longer have recourse to magical means in order to master or implore the spirits" (Weber, 1918, p. 139). The Weberian scholar Lawrence Scaff neatly elaborates:

> The *disenchantment thesis* holds that modernity represents a loss of the sacred sense of wholeness and reconciliation between self and

*This is a revised and updated version of a paper previously published as 'Ruptured time and the re-enchantment of modernity' in Casement, 2007, pp. 19–38.

> world provided by myth, magic, tradition, religion, or immanent nature. It ushers in the disruptive sense of disengagement, abstraction, alienation, homelessness, and the "problem of meaning" that begins to gnaw at the vital core of modern experience and social philosophy. (Scaff, 2000, p. 105)

In what follows I shall explore one influential attempt, of a kind foretold and observed by Weber, to re-enchant modernity: the psychological model and related theory of myth of the Swiss psychiatrist C. G. Jung (1875–1961). Although this attempt occurs primarily at a conceptual level, I shall show that the re-enchanting process also informs the language, imagery, and narrative structures through which Jung's conceptual argument is elaborated.

Scattered throughout Jung's voluminous work can be found an analysis of modernity broadly matching Weber's. Though decidedly less articulate than Weber on the subjects of capitalism and democratisation, Jung does write about these as well as, more extensively and with the same general emphases as Weber, about rationalisation, subjectivist culture, and disenchantment. For example, in relation to capitalism, Jung writes about the dangers of unbridled materialism, as well as about the effects of urbanisation, industrialisation, and the specialisation of work (e.g., 1896–9, pars. 11–66; 1945/1948, par. 393; 1912, par. 428; see also Main, 2004, pp. 119–121). In relation to democratisation, he writes about the problems of mass-mindedness, collectivisation, and the delegation of responsibility (e.g., 1957, pars. 488–504; see also Main, 2004, pp. 136–138). In relation to rationalisation, he writes frequently and at length about the perilous one-sidedness of scientific rationalism and overly rational approaches to religion (e.g., 1957, pars. 488–504; 1952b, pars. 821, 904; 1896–9, pars. 243–291; see also Main, 2004, pp. 123–129). With regard to subjectivist culture, Jung was both a contributor to this, with his focus on personal experience and the value of the non-rational, and an insightful critic of it, commenting on the dangers of as much as the need for the subjective turn in modern culture (e.g., 1957; see also Main, 2004, pp. 117–143; Main, 2008). Lastly, and most pertinently for the present paper, on the topic of disenchantment and its consequences, he writes about spiritual confusion, loss of tradition, loss of myth, and alienation from nature, and about the sense of uprootedness, disorientation, meaninglessness, and profound uncertainty to which these conditions give rise (e.g., 1933/1934, par. 313; 1938/1940, pars. 140–141; 1963, pp. 142, 165–166, 306; 1945, pars. 1360–1368; 1934, par. 815; 1928/1931, par. 155; see also Main, 2004, p. 120).

### *Jung and the re-mythologisation of modernity*

Where Weber described and explained the disenchantment of the modern world, Jung actively sought to remedy it through bringing about a re-enchantment, and one of the principal ways in which he tried to do this was through his theory of myth. His theory interprets myths positively as means by which the unconscious, specifically the collective unconscious, can reveal itself to consciousness. Thus the myth of the hero, discussed at length in Jung's *Symbols of Transformation* (1911–12/1952), reveals unconscious structures and processes of the psyche. As Robert Segal summarises:

> the myth of the hero symbolizes at once an archetype and, even more, the psychological life cycle. The birth, childhood, and adolescence of the hero symbolize the emergence and development of the ego and ego consciousness, which is consciousness of the difference between oneself and the external world. The adulthood and death of the hero symbolize the return of the ego to the unconscious and its reintegration with the unconscious to form the self. (Segal, 1998, p. 145)

Attending to myths and mythic motifs, whether in poetry, novels, films, and art, or in dreams and other forms of personal fantasy, enables one to integrate into consciousness the revealed contents of the collective unconscious, including the instinctual energy bound up in these contents, thereby both animating the psyche and furthering the process of self-realisation that Jung terms individuation (ibid., pp. 17–19). In this way the enchanting world of myth bestows meaning and can again be taken seriously by modern individuals.

Myths, therefore, are of the utmost importance from a psychological point of view. However, as Segal notes, Jung's theory of myth—better, as we shall see, his early theory of myth—falls short of a re-enchantment of the world. For in this process of psychic revelation the external world acts only as a screen onto which the collective unconscious contents are projected. The inner psychological meaning of myths is appreciated precisely because these outer projections are withdrawn, that is, to the extent that one realises the myths refer not to the outer physical world but to the inner psychic world. As Segal summarises the implication of Jung's theory of myth:

> Myths for moderns do not function to connect the inner world with the outer world, which remains impersonal and mechanical. Instead, modern myths function to connect—better, to reconnect—moderns to the inner world. Modern myths still provide meaning, but that meaning now lies entirely within humans rather than also within the world. (Ibid., p. 19)

Segal suggests that for Jung the world serves only as a middleman, which could be happily dispensed with if the contents of the collective unconscious could be revealed and encountered more directly, as arguably they can through the analysis of dreams or by the process of waking fantasy that Jung called "active imagination". Such an approach to myth might restore inner meaning but not the "sacred sense of wholeness and reconciliation between self and world". Jung's strategy for a fuller sense of re-enchantment and re-mythologisation of the world depends on a feature of his psychological model that he did not develop in detail until late in his life: his theory of synchronicity.

### *Synchronicity*

Briefly, synchronicity describes and theorises coincidences in which, for example, a person's dream or thought is matched by something that happens in the outer world, without it being possible that either event could have caused the other. Such coincidences can be experienced as especially meaningful and prompt one to wonder whether something more than mere chance may be involved. Jung defined synchronicity in a variety of ways. Most succinctly, he defined it as "meaningful coincidence" (Jung, 1952b, par. 827), as "acausal parallelism" (Jung, 1963, p. 342), or as "an acausal connecting principle" (Jung, 1952b). More fully, he defined it as "the simultaneous occurrence of a certain psychic state with one or more external events which appear as meaningful parallels to the momentary subjective state" (ibid., par. 850).

I would like to look in detail at an episode of synchronicity which Jung says "is meant only as a paradigm of the innumerable cases of meaningful coincidence that have been observed not only by me but by many others, and recorded in large collections" (Jung, 1951, par. 983). Famous though this incident is, I believe its full significance for Jung's theory of synchronicity and his attempt to re-mythologise and re-enchant the modern world has been insufficiently appreciated. The account is from Jung's lecture "On Synchronicity" delivered at an Eranos conference in Ascona in 1951. Writes Jung:

> My example concerns a young woman patient who, in spite of efforts made on both sides, proved to be psychologically inaccessible. The difficulty lay in the fact that she always knew better about everything. Her excellent education had provided her with a weapon ideally suited to this purpose, namely a highly polished Cartesian rationalism with an impeccably "geometrical" idea of reality. After several fruitless attempts to sweeten her rationalism with a somewhat more human understanding, I had to confine myself to the hope that something unexpected and irrational would turn up, something that would burst the intellectual retort into which she had sealed herself. Well, I was sitting opposite her one day, with my back to the window, listening to her flow of rhetoric. She had had an impressive dream the night before, in which someone had given her a golden scarab—a costly piece of jewellery. While she was still telling me this dream, I heard something behind me gently tapping on the window. I turned round and saw that it was a fairly large flying insect that was knocking against the window-pane in the obvious effort to get into the dark room. This seemed to me very strange. I opened the window immediately and caught the insect in the air as it flew in. It was a scarabaeid beetle, or common rose-chafer (*Cetonia aurata*), whose gold-green colour most nearly resembles that of a golden scarab. I handed the beetle to my patient with the words, "Here is your scarab". This experience punctured the desired hole in her rationalism and broke the ice of her intellectual resistance. The treatment could now be continued with satisfactory results. (Jung, 1951, par. 982)

Jung related a shorter version of the same incident the following year in his essay "Synchronicity: An Acausal Connecting Principle" (Jung, 1952b, pars. 843, 845). The only major addition this later account provides is an amplification of the symbolic meaning of the scarab beetle:

> There … seems to be an archetypal foundation to [this] case…. Any essential change of attitude signifies a psychic renewal which is

> usually accompanied by symbols of rebirth in the patient's dreams and fantasies. The scarab is a classic example of a rebirth symbol. The ancient Egyptian Book of What Is in the Netherworld describes how the dead sun-god changes himself at the tenth station into Khepri, the scarab, and then, at the twelfth station, mounts the barge which carries the rejuvenated sun-god into the morning sky. (Ibid., par. 845)

Jung states that his purpose in recounting this episode is "simply to give some indication of how meaningful coincidences usually present themselves in practical life" (Jung, 1952b, par. 845). The incident shows, for Jung, that psychic and physical events can parallel one another acausally but meaningfully, and that the imagery that provides the focus of the coincidence can be archetypal, that is, it can express a part of the mind that "is identical in all individuals"—what Jung refers to as the "collective unconscious" (ibid., par. 840). However, there is a lot more going on in his presentation of this episode than Jung declares. In particular, the episode plays a crucial role, in several ways, in his attempt to re-enchant the modern world. I shall look first at some general implications of the principle of synchronicity that the incident illustrates, then at the actual content of the incident, and finally at the narrative through which it is presented.

### *Synchronicity and re-sacralisation*

In an interview with Mircea Eliade (1907–1986), Jung connected synchronicity to numinous and religious experience:

> Religious experience is *numinous*, as Rudolf Otto calls it, and for me, as a psychologist, this experience differs from all others in the way it transcends the ordinary categories of space, time, and causality. Recently I have put a great deal of study into synchronicity (briefly, the "rupture of time"), and I have established that it closely resembles numinous experiences where space, time, and causality are abolished. (McGuire & Hull, 1978, p. 230)

In this statement, religious experience is characterised as numinous, and what is distinctive about numinous experiences is said to be that they transcend the ordinary categories of space, time, and causality. Synchronicity, as the technical term that Jung developed to articulate this transcendence of space, time, and causality, thus implicitly describes what for Jung is the kernel of numinous or religious experience. His view of the social and cultural significance of this emerges from an assertion he made later in the same interview: "The modern world", he states, "is desacralized, that is why it is in a crisis. Modern man must rediscover a deeper source of his own spiritual life" (ibid.). Jung's concept of synchronicity can therefore be seen as part of his strategy for rediscovering a deeper source of spirituality in order to re-sacralise the modern world and thereby address the crisis of modernity.

## *Myth beyond projection*

This was confirmed by the scholar of Gnosticism, Gilles Quispel (1916–2006), who was present at the 1951 Eranos lecture where Jung first formally presented his theory of synchronicity, including the example of the scarab beetle. Quispel reports that, after the lecture,

> even Jung himself seemed quite relieved and unusually good humoured. All his life he had rummaged in the collective unconscious, but now he had forced a breakthrough from the soul to the cosmos. He beamed when he told me: "*Es geht um die Erfahrung der Fülle des Seins*"; it is the experience of the fullness, the pleroma, of Being that matters. And he said to me on another occasion that now the concept of projection should be revised completely. (Quispel, 1995, p. 19)

In his earlier theory of myth, Jung, like Sigmund Freud (1856–1939), considered myths to be the projection of the contents of the unconscious psyche onto the world. He differed from Freud in believing that these projected contents stemmed from a collective rather than personal stratum of the psyche. But for both thinkers the world onto which the unconscious contents were projected was in itself impersonal and mechanical, the world revealed and investigated by the hard sciences. Indeed, the psychological concept of projection had in its way contributed to the disenchantment of the world, for the concept implies that the meanings we perceive in the world are not there in reality but are being foisted onto the world by the human mind. However, when his theory of myth is supplemented by his theory of synchronicity, Jung can argue that the outer world may not after all be totally alienated from human purposes but, at least on occasion, can be intimately involved with them. Thus, the real scarab beetle in his example behaved in a way that seemed mysteriously connected with the patient's inner psychic world. As Jung later remarked to a correspondent: "at the moment my patient was telling me her dream a real 'scarab' tried to get into the room, *as if it had understood that it must play its mythological role as a symbol of rebirth*" (Jung, 1976, p. 541, emphasis added). Jung goes further: "Even inanimate objects", he writes, "behave occasionally in the same way—meteorological phenomena, for instance" (ibid.).

## *Myth and history*

As well as providing a resource for Jung to re-enchant or re-mythologise modernity, this revised theory enables him to reconsider the relationship between myth and history—modernity's view of the past. Specifically, synchronicity provides a new perspective on one of the issues that had undermined the religious view of the world—historical criticism of the Bible. Jung had lectured on this topic to his student fraternity, the Zofingia Society, in 1899, arguing against a rationalistic, historicising interpretation of Christ (1896–9, pars. 237–291). Now he can approach such problems from a new angle. With his theory of synchronicity, the mythic character of a story does not for Jung necessarily imply a lack of historical truth, since the archetypal motifs informing the myth, and giving it the vitality to persist as a gripping story, can express themselves as much outwardly as inwardly. In his book *Answer to Job* (1952a), published in the same year as his major essay on synchronicity, Jung applies this principle to stories about Christ:

> The fact that the life of Christ is largely myth does absolutely nothing to disprove its factual truth—quite the contrary. I would even go so far as to say that the mythical character of a life is just what expresses its universal human validity. It is perfectly possible, psychologically, for the unconscious or an archetype to take complete possession of a man and to determine his fate down to the smallest detail. At the same time objective, non-psychic parallel phenomena can occur which also represent the archetype. It not only seems so, it simply is so, that the archetype fulfils itself not only psychically in the individual, but objectively outside the individual. My own conjecture is that Christ was such a personality. (Jung, 1952a, par. 648)

## *A living myth*

When we turn to the content of Jung's paradigmatic synchronicity, we find that the narrative through which the incident is presented and, even more, the mythic image at its core are doing much more than just illustrating his theory. They are also conveying symbolically a whole cluster of personal and cultural meanings that actively contribute to Jung's argument and its emotional charge.

### *The scarab incident as a synchronicity for Jung*

Not mentioned by Jung but surely important is that there are at least two senses in which the incident involving the scarab beetle was a synchronicity not only for the patient but also for Jung. First, if we recall Jung's description of synchronicity as "the simultaneous occurrence of a certain psychic state with one or more external events which appear as meaningful parallels to the momentary subjective state" (Jung, 1952b, par. 850), we can find this definition fulfilled by Jung's psychic state of "hope that something unexpected and irrational would turn up" (1951, par. 982) and the physical event of "something unexpected and irrational" actually occurring with the "very strange" (ibid.) appearance of the scarab "at this particular moment" (1952b, par. 843). Second, the image of the scarab beetle already had considerable significance for Jung, and in view of this the occurrence in his consulting room of the patient's synchronicity with the scarab beetle will have formed part of a synchronicity with Jung's own vivid interest in the symbol. The sources of the possible significance of the symbol of the scarab for Jung are worth exploring in detail.

### *Jung's 1913 vision of an Egyptian scarab*

Most importantly, Jung himself had had a vision of an Egyptian scarab during the period of intense psychic turmoil in his life referred to in his memoirs as his "confrontation with the unconscious" (Bishop, 2000, pp. 17, 24–25). The relevant part of this vision is that Jung, finding himself in an underground cavern, sees a corpse float by in some running water: "a youth with blond hair and a wound in the head. He was followed by a gigantic black scarab and then by a red, newborn sun, rising up out of the depths of the water" (Jung, 1963, p. 203; see also 2009,

p. 237). Drawing on his knowledge of mythology, Jung "realised … that it was a hero and solar myth, a drama of death and renewal, the rebirth symbolized by the Egyptian scarab" (1963, p. 204). In the light of the events occurring in his own life at the time of the vision—his break with Freud and the beginnings of his own model of analytical psychology—the ideas of death and renewal are singularly appropriate.

### *The scarab as symbol of living a myth*

In another visionary episode, made available with the publication of Jung's *Red Book* (2009), Jung imagines himself in a desert landscape where he sees a scarab beetle and is prompted to the following musings:

> Over there a small dark beetle is crawling along, pushing a ball in front of it—a scarab. You dear little animal, are you still toiling away in order to live your beautiful myth? How seriously and undiscouraged it works! If only you had a notion that you are performing an old myth, you would probably renounce your fantasies as we men have also given up playing at mythology….
>
> Dear beetle, where have you gone? I can no longer see you—Oh, you're already over there with your mythical ball. These little animals stick to things, quite unlike us—no doubt, no change of mind, no hesitation. Is this so because they live their myth? (Jung, 2009, p. 271; see also images on folio iii [verso] and p. 22)

Here the scarab beetle provides the focus for Jung to reflect on the value of living a myth: myths can be beautiful and can foster seriousness, courage, and tenacity. But myths are of the past (the scarab lives "an old myth"). As soon as we become conscious of myth as myth, the magic departs, we "renounce [our] fantasies", give up "playing at mythology", and enter a state of uncertainty and indecisiveness. It is apt that the scarab, which here symbolises a condition of continuing enchantment in which it is still possible to live within myth, should later in Jung's paradigmatic synchronicity play precisely the role of re-enchanter of the world—the patient's world, Jung's world, and, as we shall see later, the modern world generally.

### *Freud's collection of antiquities*

It is worth bearing in mind one of the places where Jung, prior to these visions, almost certainly would have seen actual Egyptian antiquities in the form of scarabs: Freud's study. As can be confirmed from a visit to the Freud Museum in London, where Freud's study was reconstructed as closely as possible to how it had been in Vienna, Freud was a great collector of antiquities, and within his collection are several scarab amulets (Rizzuto, 1998, pp. 120–121, 123). Such amulets were used in ancient Egypt as general good luck charms and, more importantly, for magical protection of the soul on its underworld journey through death—associations pertinent to the themes of synchronicity, re-enchantment, and Jung's "underworld journey" following his break with Freud. Freud had begun to build up his collection of antiquities in 1896 following the death of his father. Ana-Maria Rizzuto (1998) has revealed its fascinating significance for understanding Freud's relationship to religion, noting that many of the antiquities Freud collected are of mythological and religious figures represented in the Philippson Bible which Freud's father had given to his son on his thirty-fifth birthday in the hope that he would become more religiously observant. On page 340 of volume one of the Philippson Bible is an image of a colossal scarab (ibid., p. 123). Also in Freud's study, among other books on Egyptology, is the classic work by Isaac Myer entitled *Scarabs* (1894) (E. Freud et al. 1978, p. 235). Intriguing, too, are the anecdotes about Freud's engaging in imaginal dialogues with figures from his collection of antiquities (Noll, 1992, p. 80).

That Jung would have been interested in these antiquities and, if he saw it, Myer's book is clear from his own early and enduring interest in archaeology (Squyres, 1999). In one of the chapters he himself wrote for *Memories, Dreams, Reflections*, Jung tells how, as he was approaching the age to go to university, his interests drew him in different directions: on the one hand towards science, and on the other hand towards the humanities including "Greco-Roman, Egyptian, and prehistoric archaeology" (Jung, 1963, p. 91). It is noteworthy that, much later, in his principal essay on synchronicity, which was specifically written to combat the one-sidedness of contemporary science, Jung should give central importance to an experience involving a representative image (the ancient Egyptian scarab) from the other side of his divided interests—an image, moreover, that consciously or unconsciously he might have suspected of being bound up with the problem of religion and enchantment for Freud.

It is interesting, too, that Jung dates his fascination with the problem of synchronicity to "the middle twenties" (1952b, par. 843), for this dating coincides with the explosion of popular interest in Egyptology following the discovery in 1922 of the tomb of Tutankhamen. The royal cartouche of Tutankhamen includes the hieroglyph of the scarab, so that this image appears on many of the treasures recovered from the tomb, as well as being the central image of several exquisite jewels (pectorals and pendants) that would have been widely described, if not reproduced, and may have been the direct or indirect source of Jung's patient's dream (see plates II, XII, XVIII, and XX–XXIII in Desroches-Noblecourt, 1972). (There are, however, no clues in Jung's published writings as to when exactly the synchronicity with the scarab occurred.) The association of the scarab with the discovery of a fabulous treasure in the desert is pertinent both to the effect of the synchronicity in suddenly opening Jung's patient to the hidden riches of her unconscious and to Jung's own excitement, as related by Quispel, at how the concept of synchronicity "forced a breakthrough from the soul to the cosmos".

### *Scarabs and alchemy*

Aside from its possible associations with his confrontation with the unconscious and with Freud, the mythic image of the scarab may have been further charged for Jung, especially in relation to synchronicity and re-enchantment, by his encounters with it in alchemical contexts. These encounters were few—by Jung's account, "[t]he scarab is seldom mentioned in alchemical literature" (Jung, 1944, par. 531). But where such references do occur, they are suggestive.

One reference to the scarab occurs in the first few pages of the Taoist alchemical text *The Secret of the Golden Flower*, to which Jung contributed a psychological commentary. In a section of the text titled "The primal spirit and the conscious spirit", the author discusses how by a meditative process called "circulation of the light" one can return to "the light that is the Creative" and produce one's immortal body. The text then has recourse to the following simile:

> The scarabaeus rolls his ball and in the ball there develops life as the result of the undivided effort of his spiritual concentration. If now an embryo can grow in manure, and shed its shells, why should not the dwelling place of our heavenly heart also be able to create a body if we concentrate the spirit upon it? (Wilhelm & Jung, 1931, pp. 26–28)

Although Jung's commentary does not pick up on this image, he will certainly have read it, and that alone may have created in his mind an association between the mythic image of the scarab and synchronicity.

For his timely receipt of this text from Richard Wilhelm was specifically registered by Jung as a synchronicity (Jung, 1963, p. 223; 2009, pp. 163, 320). Furthermore, the association of the scarab with the ability to create living bodies by spiritual concentration once more connects the mythic image with the theme of re-enchantment.

Another reference to scarabs occurs in *Psychology and Alchemy*, in a sub-section on "The one-horned scarabaeus" (Jung, 1944, pars. 530–531). There Jung argues that, like other real and imagined one-horned creatures ("unicorns"), the one-horned scarab is a symbol of the alchemical figure of Mercurius, who in turn is a symbol of the self. Among the properties attributed to this scarab in the alchemical literature, Jung notes its being "only-begotten", "a creature born of itself", "*increatum* [uncreated]", "bisexual, capable of self-fertilization and self-parturition", and its undergoing beheading and dismemberment (ibid., par. 530). These references show Jung's awareness that in Egyptian mythology the scarab is not only a symbol of rebirth but also just as much a symbol of creation. The latter meaning stems from two sources. On the one hand, the word for beetle in ancient Egyptian (at least its Heliopolitan form) was pronounced like the word Khoprer, "the Becoming One", "He Who Comes into Existence", one of the deities of creation (Clark, 1959, p. 40). On the other hand, the scarab beetle "has the habit of pushing its eggs out of the sand enclosed in a ball of its own dung. The beetle therefore became the symbol of God as he came into existence and of the rising sun, the daily recapitulation of creation" (ibid.).

This association of the scarab with creativity and autogenesis is again interesting in relation to synchronicity. For, as acausal events, synchronicities precisely do not have antecedent causes but emerge spontaneously; they are, for Jung, "creative acts" (Jung, 1952b, par. 967). The concept of the autonomous psyche—that is, the ability of the psyche to generate contents that do not stem from interaction with other people or the environment—is of the greatest importance in Jung's psychological thinking and is one of the features that distinguish his model from those of other depth psychologists. One could even argue that his theory of synchronicity is in part an attempt to provide an underpinning framework for this notion (Main, 2004, p. 133). It therefore adds to the charge of the synchronistic experience related by Jung that its central image of the scarab symbolises such autonomous emergence.

In addition to these references, there is a surprising "non-reference" to the scarab in Jung's writings. It concerns the work of the seventeenth-century polymath Athanasius Kircher (1602–82). On page 415 of volume two, part one, of his work *Oedipus Aegyptiacus* [*Oedipus the Egyptian*] (1652–54), Kircher presents the symbol or hieroglyph of the scarab as the key to the alchemical art and elaborates on various facets of its meaning, including its role in the spiritualisation of matter (Bonnefoy, 1991, pp. 709–710). Jung refers to Kircher's works several times (see *General Index* to Jung's *Collected Works*), and even three times cites *Oedipus Aegyptiacus*. It may be that he simply overlooked this alchemical reference to the scarab or felt he had no specific reason to note it. But in view of the significance of Oedipus and indeed Egypt for Freud, and the connection we have found between the scarab and Freud, it is tempting to see here a complex of associations that may have further contributed, however unconsciously, to the charge Jung experienced in the synchronicity with the scarab.

## *Overcoming Cartesian rationalism*

In addition to these possible personal and scholarly resonances for Jung, the synchronicity with the scarab beetle also enacts, with Jung's patient, what the theory of synchronicity is intended to achieve for culture. It is not just the patient's "animus" (Jung, 1952b, par. 845) or "highly polished Cartesian rationalism" with its "impeccably 'geometrical' idea of reality" (Jung, 1951, par. 982) that needs to be broken down but, as Paul Bishop notes, "Cartesian philosophy, with its 'geometrical method', and rationalism in general" (Bishop, 2000, p. 17). The patient's problem stands for the problem of the culture as a whole, and Jung's success with the patient is the success he hopes his essay will have with culture. On 24 January 1955, Jung wrote to Michael Fordham about what he hoped would be "the impact of synchronicity upon the fanatical one-sidedness of scientific philosophy" (Jung, 1976, p. 216), and on the same day he reported to R. F. C. Hull: "The latest comment about 'Synchronicity' is that it cannot be accepted because it shakes the security of our scientific foundations, as if this were not exactly the goal I am aiming at" (ibid., p. 217). Weber famously described the rationalised forms of modernity as an "iron cage" (Weber, 1904, p. 123). Jung's language in describing the synchronicity with the scarab evokes something similar. His patient is "inaccessible" (Jung, 1951, par. 982), "rigid" (Jung, 1952b, par. 845), "sealed" in an "intellectual retort", in the "ice of her intellectual resistance" (Jung, 1951, par. 982), in the "armour of her animus possession" (Jung, 1952b, par. 945). Jung hopes for and then witnesses an event that will enable her to escape from—"burst" (ibid.), "puncture", "break" (Jung, 1951, par. 982)—this imprisoning condition.

### *Hidden heroics in the scarab synchronicity*

Jung commented that his 1913 vision was "a hero and solar myth, a drama of death and renewal, the rebirth symbolized by the Egyptian scarab". The hero myth there was indicated by the floating corpse of the "youth with blond hair and a wound in the head". The significance of this became clearer for Jung after a subsequent dream in which he participated in the killing of the hero Siegfried, which led him to reflect that "the attitude embodied by Siegfried, the hero, no longer suited me. Therefore it had to be killed" (Jung, 1963, pp. 204–205). In his amplification of the scarab symbol in his patient's synchronicity, Jung explains its status only as a symbol of rebirth. However, here too it may be possible to detect the latent presence of, if not a hero myth as such, at least the kind of heroic exploits one finds in fairy tales.

Jung's "young woman patient" sealed in the "intellectual retort" of her rationalistic attitude might be compared to a maiden imprisoned in a tower. The string of doctors who have failed to cure her suggests a series of suitors or champions who have failed to rescue the maiden. Jung's eventual success thanks to the synchronicity reflects the motif of the improbable suitor who eventually succeeds thanks to supernatural aid. As the scarab entered through the window, so in the stories the rescuer or the rescuer's supernatural accomplice sometimes reaches or contacts the maiden through a window. As Jung's patient is at first inaccessible, rigid, sealed up, icy, and resistant, and his efforts to free her are "fruitless", but later she is sweetened and her natural being bursts forth when Jung "punctured the desired hole", so the hero typically not only rescues the maiden but also wins her as his consort. Finally, just as Jung closes his anecdote with a vague but optimistic "[t]he treatment could now be continued with satisfactory results", so the story of a hero rescuing an imprisoned maiden typically ends with them "living happily ever after" (see, e.g., Thompson, 1958, H310, L100, L160, N530, N640, R110, R121.1, T68.1, T381 [alphanumeric references are to the system of classifying folk-motifs in Thompson's work]). A Jungian interpretation of such an episode in a myth or fairy tale would doubtless revolve around the task of awakening and entering into relationship with the anima or soul. In embedding this motif in his account of the synchronistic event, Jung implies that, with his theory of synchronicity, he is heroically attempting to rescue the anima or soul of Western culture. Such heroics may not contradict his earlier repudiation of the heroic attitude, since what they now involve is not asserting his will but respectfully co-operating with non-rational manifestations of the autonomous psyche.

## Conclusion

To summarise and conclude, Jung's writings on myth can be seen as part of his attempt to re-enchant the modern world. However, the success of his attempt was limited so long as he saw myth solely in terms of the projection of intrapsychic, albeit archetypal, contents. With the theory of synchronicity, developed late in his life, Jung felt able to postulate a parallelism and acausal connectedness between inner and outer events that allowed him to find mythic motifs not only intrapsychically but also, non-projectively, in external situations and events, thus enabling a more far-reaching re-enchantment (see Main, 2011, for further discussion of the extent to which synchronicity may be able to effect re-enchantment). I have suggested, further, that in his choice of example to illustrate synchronicity Jung was drawing on a hypothesised feature of the unconscious psyche, its autonomous mythopoeic power, to present an image so richly charged with personal and cultural associations that it not only illustrated his argument but actively contributed to it and its emotional appeal. This was not simply a rhetorical ploy, in the sense that Jung consciously assembled the charged cluster of associations. It would better fit with his outlook to view the synchronicity with the scarab as an instance of the transpersonal psyche "staging its own manifestations spontaneously" (Jung, 1945/1948, par. 395), presenting Jung with a compelling incident of whose full symbolic and mythological resonance he may not have been aware even as he intuited that it was absolutely the right example to use.

## References

Bishop, P. (2000). *Synchronicity and Intellectual Intuition in Kant, Swedenborg, and Jung*. Lampeter: Edwin Mellen.

Bonnefoy, Y. (1991). *Mythologies*. 2 vols. J. Honegsblum et al. (Trans.). Chicago: University of Chicago Press.

Clark, R. (1959). *Myth and Symbol in Ancient Egypt*. London: Thames and Hudson, 1991.

Desroches-Noblecourt, C. (1972). *Tutankhamen*. Harmondsworth: Penguin.

Freud, E., Freud, L., & Grubrich-Simitis, I. (Eds.) (1978). *Sigmund Freud: His Life in Pictures and Words*. London: André Deutsch.

Homans, P. (1979/1995). *Jung in Context: Modernity and the Making of a Psychology*. Chicago: University of Chicago Press.

Jung, C. G. (1896–9). *The Zofingia Lectures. The Collected Works of C. G. Jung*. H. Read, M. Fordham, & G. Adler (Eds.). W. McGuire (Executive Ed.). R. F. C. Hull et al. (Trans.). [Hereafter *C. W.*] *A*. London: Routledge, 1984.

Jung, C. G. (1911–12/1952). *Symbols of Transformation. C. W., 5* (2nd ed.). London: Routledge & Kegan Paul, 1967.

Jung, C. G. (1912). New paths in psychology. In: *C. W., 7* (2nd ed.): pp. 245–268/pars. 407–441. London: Routledge & Kegan Paul, 1966.

Jung, C. G. (1933/1934). The meaning of psychology for modern man. In: *C.W., 10* (2nd ed.): pp. 134–156/pars. 276–332. London: Routledge & Kegan Paul, 1970.

Jung, C. G. (1934). A review of the complex theory. In: *C. W., 8* (2nd ed.): pp. 92–104/pars. 194–219. London: Routledge & Kegan Paul, 1969.

Jung, C. G. (1938/1940). Psychology and religion. In: *C. W., 11* (2nd ed.): pp. 3–105/pars. 1–168. London: Routledge & Kegan Paul, 1969.

Jung, C. G. (1944). *Psychology and Alchemy. C. W., 12* (2nd ed.). London: Routledge & Kegan Paul, 1968.

Jung, C. G. (1945). Marginalia on contemporary events. In: *C. W., 18*: pp. 591–603/pars. 1360–1383. London: Routledge & Kegan Paul, 1976.

Jung, C. G. (1945/1948). The phenomenology of the spirit in fairytales. In: *C. W., 9i* (2nd ed.): pp. 207–254/pars. 384–455. London: Routledge & Kegan Paul, 1968.

Jung, C. G. (1951). On synchronicity. In: *C. W., 8* (2nd ed.): pp. 520–531/pars. 969–997. London: Routledge & Kegan Paul, 1969.

Jung, C. G. (1952a). Answer to Job. In: *C. W., 11* (2nd ed.): pp. 355–470/pars. 553–758. London: Routledge & Kegan Paul, 1969.

Jung, C. G. (1952b). Synchronicity: an acausal connecting principle. In: *C. W., 8* (2nd ed.): pp. 417–519/pars. 816–968. London: Routledge & Kegan Paul, 1969.

Jung, C. G. (1957). The undiscovered self (present and future). In: *C. W., 10* (2d ed.): pp. 245–305/pars. 488–588. London: Routledge & Kegan Paul, 1970.

Jung, C. G. (1963). *Memories, Dreams, Reflections*. A. Jaffé (Ed.). R. & C. Winston (Trans.). London: Collins and Routledge & Kegan Paul.

Jung, C. G. (1973). *Letters 1: 1906—1950*. G. Adler & A. Jaffé (Eds.). R. F. C. Hull (Trans.). London: Routledge & Kegan Paul.

Jung, C. G. (1976). *Letters 2: 1951-1961*. G. Adler & A. Jaffé (Eds.). R. F. C. Hull (Trans.). London: Routledge & Kegan Paul.

Jung, C. G. (2009). *The Red Book—Liber Novus*. S. Shamdasani (Ed.). New York: W. W. Norton.

Main, R. (2004). *The Rupture of Time: Synchronicity and Jung's Critique of Modern Western Culture*. Hove, UK: Brunner-Routledge.

Main, R. (2007). Ruptured time and the re-enchantment of modernity. In: A. Casement (Ed.), *Who Owns Jung?* (pp. 19–38). London: Karnac.

Main, R. (2008). Secularisation and the "holistic milieu": social and psychological perspectives. *Religion Compass, 2*: 365–384.

Main, R. (2011). Synchronicity and the limits of re-enchantment. *International Journal of Jungian Studies, 3*: 144–158.

McGuire, W. (Ed.) (1991). *The Freud/Jung Letters: The Correspondence between Sigmund Freud and C. G. Jung*. R. Manheim & R. F. C. Hull (Trans.). Abridged by A. McGlashan. London: Penguin Books.

McGuire, W. & Hull, R. F. C. (Eds.) (1978). *C. G. Jung Speaking: Interviews and Encounters*. London: Thames and Hudson.

Myer, I. (1894). *Scarabs*. London: D. Nutt.

Noll, R. (1992). Jung the *leontocephalus*. In: P. Bishop (Ed.), *Jung in Contexts: A Reader* (pp. 51–91). London: Routledge, 1999.

Quispel, G. (1995). Gnosis and psychology. In: R. Segal, J. Singer, & M. Stein (Eds.), *The Allure of Gnosticism: The Gnostic Experience in Jungian Psychology and Contemporary Culture* (pp. 10–25). Chicago, IL: Open Court.

Rizzuto, A. -M. (1998). *Why Did Freud Reject God? A Psychodynamic Interpretation*. New Haven, CT: Yale University Press.

Scaff, L. (2000). Weber on the cultural situation of the modern age. In: S. Turner (Ed.), *The Cambridge Companion to Weber* (pp. 99–116). Cambridge: Cambridge University Press.

Segal, R. (Ed.) (1998). *Jung on Mythology*. Princeton, NJ: Princeton University Press.

Squyres, E. (1999). C. G. Jung and archaeology: Exploration of a guiding image. *Harvest: Journal for Jungian Studies, 45*: 122–143.

Thompson, S. (1958). *Motif-Index of Folk-Literature: A Classification of Narrative Elements in Folktales, Ballads, Myths, Fables, Medieval Romances, Exempla, Fabliaux, Jest Books, and Local Legends*. Revised and enlarged edition, 6 vols. Bloomington, IN: Indiana University Press.

Weber, M. (1904). *The Protestant Ethic and the Spirit of Capitalism*. T. Parsons (Trans.). London: Routledge, 2001.

Weber, M. (1918). Science as a vocation. In: H. Gerth & C. Wright Mills (Trans. & Eds.) *From Max Weber: Essays in Sociology* (pp. 129–156). New York: Oxford University Press, 1946.

Wilhelm, R. & Jung, C. G. (1931). *The Secret of the Golden Flower: A Chinese Book of Life*. London: Routledge & Kegan Paul, 1975.

# PART IV

## READINGS IN MYTH AND THE IMAGINARY

CHAPTER NINE

# The confrontation with the anima in Akinari Ueda's story "Jasei no in" ("A serpent's lust", 1776)

*Janet A. Walker*

In 1776 the Japanese writer Akinari Ueda (1734–1809) published "Jasei no in", one of nine stories in the genre of the *kaidan*, or narration of the "strange or anomalous" (Ueda, 2007, p. 13), that were compiled under the title *Ugetsu monogatari* (*Tales of Moonlight and Rain*). (In this chapter I shall refer to the author in the customary way, as Akinari, but I shall refer to the original version of his story, and the translation of it from which I quote, under his family name, Ueda.) The story, consisting of twenty-four pages in the Japanese edition, depicts the encounter of the youthful male character, Toyoo, with an alluring woman who turns out to be a serpent—an encounter that leads him into his first experience of love, then into unethical behaviour, then into a dangerous situation in which not only he himself but others stand to lose their lives if he does not act, and finally, through the help of a Buddhist priest mentor figure, into a state of maturation. The story of a male confronting an alluring but malevolent serpent-woman goes back at least to Tang-dynasty China (618–907), according to Wilt L. Idema (2009). Akinari modelled his story on a later version of it in *Jingshi tongyuan* (*Stories to Caution the World*, 1624), by Feng Menglong (1547–1646), which has been translated by Diana Yu (1978). Feng shaped the story into a conversion narrative, wherein the weak hero, freed from his possession by a white serpent woman by a Buddhist priest, becomes a monk. The japanologist Leon Zolbrod follows this interpretation in considering Akinari's story as depicting Toyoo's "quest for enlightenment" (Zolbrod, 1974, p. 58), whereas the Akinari scholar Blake Morgan Young interprets the story as a Confucian morality tale that emphasises Toyoo's overcoming of "lax behavior", "disciplining himself and confronting his problem head on" (Young, 1982, pp. 61, 63).

Though both of these interpretations have value, I propose a third one, which uses the Jungian process of male individuation through confrontation with the anima as a way to illuminate the particular nature of Toyoo's development. Jung argued in his "Commentary on *The Secret of the Golden Flower*" that modern European man suffered from a "one-sided belief in the power of consciousness" (Jung, 1929, par. 62). In his essay "Relations between the ego and the unconscious" he argued that this resulted in his separation from "the world of spirits" (Jung, 1928, par. 322). In order to achieve the union of the outer world, the world of the persona, and the inner world, that of the anima (the world of spirits), he must "objectivate the effects of the anima and then try to understand what contents underlie those effects" (ibid., par. 327). By contrast, Jung argued: "In the Eastern view the concept of the anima … is lacking, and, so logically, is the concept of the persona" (ibid., par. 304). In his view, "the Chinese … never succeeded in forcing the opposites in man's nature so far apart that all conscious connection between them was lost" (Jung, 1929, par. 15). Thus, Jung felt that for Eastern man there was no need to regain this connection through a confrontation with the anima. Similarly, the doyen of Jungian studies in Japan, the late Hayao Kawai, argued that "For most Japanese men, the Mother axis is too strong to allow for a relationship on the anima axis" (Kawai, 1992, p. 169)—though he noted that his comments "leave much room for refinement and revision" (ibid., p. 140).

It is significant that both Jung and Kawai drew their conclusions about Eastern or Japanese man in relation to the anima on the basis of premodern texts: Jung's Daoist text in its written form dated from the seventeenth century though it was based on oral traditions dating back to the eighth century and even earlier (Wilhelm, 1962, p. 5), and Kawai's text was the dream records of a monk of the thirteenth century (Kawai, 1992). To my knowledge, neither Jung nor Kawai attempted to chart the operations of the "Eastern"—to be more specific, East Asian—psyche in later narratives, in which one can discern the development of a more individualised personality. In what follows I argue that Akinari's text, written during what is known as Japan's early modern period, demonstrates a crucial sign of modernity in its emphasis on how a "quasi-scientific examination of the external world" (Nosco, 1984, p. 6) threatens to undermine the respect for the spirit world—Eastern man's unity with "the world of spirits", in Jung's phrasing—that had characterised earlier Japanese culture. I argue that Akinari's text treats an early modern individual suffering from a separation from the world of the spirits and needing to regain a balance between the external world (the persona) and the spirit world (the anima). In "Jasei no in", Akinari reinterprets the East Asian serpent woman myth as the spirit world repressed from cultural consciousness and stages Toyoo's confrontation with the serpent woman, the unintegrated anima, as a psychologically enriching encounter with the world of the spirits. I interpret Toyoo's subduing of the serpent woman, with the help of a mentor figure, in Jungian terms: as the hero's objectivation of the anima. The Japanese author continues the practice of earlier tellers of the serpent woman story in interweaving realism with the strange, but, in the manner of the European *Bildungsroman*, he also constructs an "allegory of the inner life" of the hero through his depiction of the hero's struggle in the world of "practical reality" (Swales, 1978, p. 29). The interest and charm of the Japanese story lie, I argue, in its depiction of this psychic battle, which involves Toyoo in mystery, ecstasy, danger, and death, and from which he emerges by the skin of his teeth.

The focus of Akinari's story is the youngest child of a prosperous fish merchant in Miwa, on the Kii peninsula. Unlike his older brother, a man of an "unaffected, honest nature" who manages his father's business, Toyoo is described as a "gentle boy … [who] favoured the courtly, refined ways of the capital and had no heart for making a living" (Ueda, 2007, p. 160). The story is set in the Heian period (795–1185), a time when a great literature dominated by women writers and focusing extensively on love emerged at the imperial court in Heian-kyō (present-day Kyoto). Jung wrote that "the growing youth must be able to free himself from the anima fascination of his mother" (Jung, 1936/1954, par. 146). Toyoo's mother is not mentioned at all in the story, but I would argue that the author constructs the Heian court here as a world of surrogate literary mothers, and Toyoo as immersed in a kind of "anima fascination" with this feminine world. I would also suggest that Akinari chose the Heian period for the location of this story, because he wished to foreground historically the feminised nature of Toyoo and to contextualise the nature of the anima that his youthful hero needed to objectivate in order to develop psychologically. The father, accepting Toyoo's feminised nature, has decided to rear him to be a "scholar or a monk" and make him dependent on his older brother (Ueda, 2007, p. 160). At this point one can view Toyoo, in Jungian terms, as not yet having constructed a "collectively suitable persona" (Jung, 1928, par. 306). His persona is constructed out of the literary discourse of a social world to which he does not belong. There are no "demands coming from without" (ibid., par. 311), such as the need to work and to marry, and Toyoo is therefore still living in the feminised realm of the mother: adept at the Heian discourse of love, involved with his books, and possessing the moral and psychological status of an innocent child. A sign that he is ripe for psychological development beyond the world of the mother, however, is that he has established regular contact with a male mentor figure at a nearby temple.

Significantly, it is on the way back from a lesson with this priest teacher that Toyoo, taking refuge from a sudden rainstorm in the hut of one of his father's fishermen, meets the female figure that will instigate his psychological development. She is a woman of about twenty, who, drenched to the skin, also takes refuge in the hut. I consider this woman as an anima figure, in the form of "the glamorous, possessive, moody, and sentimental seductress in a man" (Jung, 1951, par. 422). As Jung writes: "the archetypes have, when they appear, a distinctly numinous character which can only be described as 'spiritual', if 'magical' is too strong a word" (Jung, 1947/1954, par. 405). Thus, Toyoo views the woman as possessing unearthly beauty and his "heart leaped at her elegance" (Ueda, 2007, p. 161). Sure that she must be from the capital, he initiates a conversation with the woman, Manago, using the discourse of love of Heian literature. Up to this point in his life, Toyoo has had no love interest, the feminine in his nature being represented solely by the Heian literary mothers. As a beautiful and elegant woman, Manago conforms to Toyoo's idea of the feminine formed from Heian literature, and thus he is able to project his anima onto her. As a real woman, however, Manago is in need of an umbrella in order to return to her home in the rain, so Toyoo offers to lend her one. She tells him to look for "Manago's house" when he comes later to pick it up, thus confirming Jung's theory that the anima, as an "autonomous complex", is "a personality, and this is why she is so easily projected upon a woman" (Jung, 1928, par. 314). Manago functions as an anima figure that constellates Toyoo's inner woman; she opens his gate to the unconscious by precipitating a dream he has early the next morning after a sleepless night, in which he visits her in a mansion with an "imposing gate" (Ueda, 2007, p. 162), and, after being fed by her, consummates a sexual union with her.

After waking from the dream he leaves home without having breakfast, a sign of his removal from practical reality, and, while searching several hours for her house, does not question why no one knows her name or where she lives. Miraculously her servant, a fourteen- or fifteen-year-old girl named Maroya, finds him and brings him to Manago's house, which is just like the house in his dream of the night before. What Westerners would call the supernatural enters the story for the first time here, yet Toyoo insists on the reality of the events: he felt that he was "dreaming again and must awaken", but "that everything was real made it all the more wonderful for him" (Ueda, 2007, p. 163). Akinari follows the conventions of the *kaidan* genre here in weaving supernatural events into the fabric of real life without attempting to rationalise them. But I interpret this strategy as the weaving into the fabric of real life the life of the psyche, which consists of dreams, projections, and imaginings. Following Jung, the life of the psyche is just as real as "real" life. In that case, Manago is an anima figure, who exists both as a real human being and as a figure upon whom Toyoo has projected internal psychic contents.

Manago welcomes Toyoo into her house and, when he says that he will pick up the umbrella another time now that he knows where she lives, she tells her servant: "Maroya, do not allow him to leave" (Ueda, 2007, p. 163). As Jung writes, the anima has "the power to wield … enchantment" and acts with "tendencies" and purposes of her own (Jung, 1928, pars. 320–321). Jung wrote that "Most men, probably, who have any psychological insight at all will know what Rider Haggard means by "She-who-must-be-obeyed" (ibid., par. 298)—referring to the powerful anima heroine of Haggard's novel *She* (1887). Toyoo yields to the influence of the wine and food served by Manago as well as to the power of her bewitching beauty. When both of them are feeling the effects of the sake they have drunk, Manago, in a lengthy speech that is designed to move the young man through its elegance and passion, tells him of the loss of her husband and, swearing her devotion to him, asks him to take her under his care. Since this was just what Toyoo wanted to do, he "felt his heart leap with joy, like a bird soaring from its roost" (Ueda, 2007, p. 164).

Yet, even in the same sentence, Toyoo recalls that he will need to ask the permission of his father and older brother to marry. Jung writes that the ego needs to distinguish between "what *I* want and what the unconscious thrusts upon me", for the ego stands between "demands coming from without and from within" (Jung, 1928, par. 311). Here Toyoo's ego at first seems strong enough to mediate between "outside" [the demand that he ask permission to marry] and "inside" [the demand of the anima to unite with her]. When Manago looks forlorn, however, and apologises for having asked him this favour, he gives in, swearing that he will stand by her. Manago then relents and merely asks that he come to see her from time to time. She gives him a jewelled sword that she says had belonged to her deceased husband, and asks him to wear it always (Ueda, 2007, p. 164). Toyoo accepts the gift but, when Manago presses him to stay the night, tells her that his father would punish him if he stayed away from home at night but that he will make some excuse and come the following night. He then goes home, where he again lies awake until dawn, unable to sleep for thoughts of Manago. In giving Toyoo the phallic sword, Manago invites him to enter a relationship with her. According to Jung, in confronting the anima, "the more personally she is taken the better". Thus, Toyoo's acceptance of her plea that he enter into a relationship with her is a step toward "objectivation of the anima" or "recognizing the anima as a personality" (Jung, 1928, par. 321).

Manago seems to be inviting Toyoo to assume the adult role of husband, a role that he shows himself ready to assume in promising to marry her. Yet her invitation can also be seen, in Jungian terms, as the anima's attempt to "enforce a separation" (Jung, 1928, par. 320) between Toyoo and society. When the sword she gave him turns out to have been one of the treasures stolen from a temple, her giving him the stolen sword can be viewed as Manago's plan to lure Toyoo not into marriage but into her realm of the anima, regardless of how that would injure his status as son and social being. Jung writes that "the mother protects … [her son] against the dangers that threaten from the darkness of his psyche" (ibid., par. 315). But, lacking a mother, and trapped in his literarily constructed persona, Toyoo is now delivered over to this darkness, which is constructed socially as crime and morally as evil. Thus, the anima forces Toyoo out of the childlike innocence that he had enjoyed and into the adult world, where his actions have moral consequences.

Toyoo is arrested for having stolen the sword given him by Manago. When he pleads his innocence, urging the governor's deputy to go with him to Manago's house and talk to her (Ueda, 2007, p. 167), he is ordered to go, accompanied by ten warriors assigned to the case, to the house where he had met Manago. A strange but real element intrudes here, as an "elderly blacksmith" living in the neighbourhood explains that no one has lived in the house, which now appears broken-down and deserted, for three years, but that yesterday Toyoo had stayed in the house for quite a while. When the warriors enter the house and open the shutters leading to the main hall, they are overcome by a foul stench. The boldest of the warriors charges forward defiantly into the inner part of the house, intending to arrest its occupant, but he finds only a "blossom-like woman" sitting alone "amid the rat droppings, beside an old curtain stand" (ibid., p. 168). The juxtaposition of Manago, the beautiful and refined lady, with stench and ruins here reveals the dual potentiality of the anima, who, as Jung describes her, is "… now a good fairy, now a witch; now a saint, now a whore" (Jung, 1941, par. 356). On one hand, the anima has a "disintegrating effect", taking on "an independence which threatens the coherence of the psyche as a whole", but, on the other hand, she has "the potentiality to be integrated within the whole self, to be explored and exploited on the road towards individuation" (Clarke, 1994, p. 86).

When the bold warrior tries to take hold of her, Manago responds by creating "a clap of thunder as violent as though the ground itself were splitting open". The ten warriors and Toyoo, unable to escape in time, are thrown to the ground. When they "finally look up, the woman had vanished without a trace", leaving a heap of treasures stolen from the temple (Ueda, 2007, pp. 168–69). When the two highest-level male authority figures, the vice governor and the head priest of the temple from which the items had been stolen, view the retrieved items, "recognizing the work of an evil spirit, [they] relaxed their investigation of Toyoo" (ibid., p. 169). That the officials approach the situation in a matter-of-fact way suggests that they regard what has happened as natural, and for this reason they exculpate Toyoo of some of the burden of his crime. As figures of legal and religious authority, they naturally consider the spirit as in some way causing problems; but while Anthony Chambers, the translator of the story into English, uses the term "evil spirit" to refer to the perpetrator of the action, Yukihiko Nakamura, the editor of the Japanese text, points out that the Japanese term, *mononoke*, is, more neutrally, "a general designation for an apparition of a living person (*ikiryō*), an apparition of a dead person (*shiryō*), or something strange that involves change or disguise (*ka'i*)" (Ueda, 1968, p. 90 n. 22). The term can also indicate a being on the border between "one category and another" (Campany, 1996, p. 250). Thus, the term does not possess a moral meaning, and I would argue that, in the psychological world of Akinari's story, the term indicates a liminal being that straddles practical reality and psychic reality.

Toyoo is imprisoned for having committed a crime, but his family succeeds in getting him released after 100 days (Ueda, 2007, p. 169). After this, ashamed to be seen in his own town, he visits his older sister in the market town of Tsubaichi. One day Manago and Maroya appear in the marketplace and, when Toyoo sees them, he calls out to people: "That demon has followed me here", and tries to escape (ibid.). Again, Nakamura translates the term "demon" (kano oni), not in a moral way but more neutrally, as supernatural being (Ueda, 1968, p. 110 n. 4). In front of all the people, Manago defends herself, denying that she is a supernatural being (Akinari uses the term *ayashiki mono*; ibid., p. 110) and insisting that she is a real person. His suspicions somewhat dampened, Toyoo nevertheless refers to Manago as not a real human being, giving as evidence that she had been living in "the kind of dwelling that a supernatural being would live in", and also that she had "disappeared without a trace" after causing "a clear sky suddenly to shake with thunder". Then he asserts: "All of this I saw with my own eyes" (Ueda, 2007, p. 170). He asks why she has followed him and requests her to go away at once. Manago begins to weep at the harshness of his words but answers by rationalising the supernatural events, on the one hand, and ensuring him tearfully of her undying love, on the other. At this point, Manago is the anima who, in Jung's words, "intensifies, exaggerates, falsifies, and mythologizes all emotional relations" (Jung, 1936/1954, par. 144). After hearing her out, "Now suspicious, now sympathetic, Toyoo could find nothing more to say" (Ueda, 2007, p. 171).

From a Jungian point of view, Toyoo is in a state of mind similar to that state which Jung described as ideal for the practice of active imagination, where "rational judgment" is suspended "as far as possible, allowing images and fantasies to emerge and unfold" (Clarke, 1994, p. 86). Thus, the play of Manago, the anima figure, will continue to the point where Toyoo can "bring unconscious material into conscious awareness and … integrate it into the whole personality" (ibid.). Toyoo's sister and her husband aid Manago in carrying out her intention to stay with him. Though they were terrified by his account, they demonstrate their adherence to the confidence in the "quasi-scientific" practices of examining the external world (Nosco, 1984, p. 6) that were increasingly influential in the early modern period: they actively discourage him from believing what he says he saw, saying "surely such things could not occur in this day and age" (Ueda, 2007, p. 171). After Manago ingratiates herself with them for a few days, they urge Toyoo to consummate his marriage with her. After the wedding, his "heart melted day by day"; he regretted "only that their reunion had been so long delayed" (ibid.).

Toyoo's conversation with Manago at this point in the story is an example of what Jung calls "dialectics with the anima", in which a man first listens to the anima, the affect, without criticism, but then criticises her "as conscientiously as though a real person closely connected with us were our interlocutor", until "a satisfactory end to the discussion is reached" (Jung, 1928, par. 323). Yet the coherence of Toyoo's psyche threatens to be overwhelmed by the anima, assuming a condition which, in the European context, "would be recognised in former times as a state of divine or diabolical possession" (Clarke, 1994, p. 86). Indeed, the danger that Toyoo is in is pointed out to him about a month later by an elderly holy man whom he, his family, and the two women encounter when, visiting the famous mountains of Yoshino to view the cherry blossoms, they are picnicking by a waterfall. The man first looks at the two women suspiciously but then he reacts: "Glaring at them, the old man mutters: 'Disgraceful. Demons. Why do you go on deceiving people?'" (Ueda, 2007, p. 172). He dares them to remain in his presence, after which Manago and Maroya leap into the waterfall and disappear. Then a heavy rain begins to fall "as though the clouds had overturned a pot of ink" (ibid.)—a strange but natural event that reveals the danger that Manago as an anima figure represents. Toyoo's psychic vulnerability lays him open not only to the influence of the anima, however, but also to the Jungian archetype of the Wise Old Man, in the form of a mentor figure who can strengthen the young man's ego to the point where he can deal with the anima.

The old man, clearly conversant with the world of the spirits, does not remove agency from Toyoo by exorcising the spirits but, instead, tells him that he can see by the young man's face that he is being tormented by spirits that hide their true nature. He warns Toyoo that, if he is not careful, he will surely lose his life, as they are tenacious (Ueda, 2007, p. 173). The old man's description enables the reader to link Manago with the "apparent man or woman", the *kakuregami*, who, in the Chinese anomaly tale that was one of the precursors of the *kaidan*, attempted "to seduce the opposite-sex protagonist of the tale, then transformed into his or her 'true form'—some species of animal" (Campany, 1996, p. 254). When Toyoo worshipfully asks the old man to help him keep his life, the latter describes the demon (ashiki kami) as a primeval giant snake or dragon (orochi) that from time immemorial has had a lustful inner nature, giving a list of abnormal couplings that the creature typically indulges in. After the old man has seen them all home, the next day Toyoo travels by himself to the village of Yamato, to the Shinto temple where the old man is serving, and offers gifts, asking this psychological-spiritual mentor figure respectfully to perform a purification ritual to protect him from Manago (Ueda, 2007, p. 173). Later, after distributing Toyoo's offerings among his disciples, the adept diagnoses the psychological-spiritual relationship between Toyoo and the *mononoke*, or monster: "The beast has attached itself to you out of lust for your beauty. You, for your part, have been bewitched by the shape it took and have lost your manly spirit" (ibid.).

Toyoo's sister and brother-in-law, dismissing the existence of the strange or supernatural, had only been able to see the human side of Manago. Toyoo has similarly only been able to discern Manago's human side, though part of him felt she was not a human being. The governor's deputy and the head priest of the temple, by contrast, with their greater experience of both the human and the spirit worlds, had been able to assume her duality as both human being and spirit, though they had not seen Manago. But the elderly priest here has the power granted him through his religious experience to see Manago and Maroya in their "true form" (Campany, 1996, p. 254): as serpents disguised as human beings. The dual nature of the anima figure is revealed even on the level of language, in his referring to her using the character for beast: "the kanji word *chiku* (a word used to speak contemptuously of beasts) is meant to be read *kare* (she)" (Takata, 1972, p. xxiv). Unlike Toyoo, however, he does not acknowledge her human side.

The elderly Shinto priest's identification of Manago as a serpent connects her to Jung's concept of the anima, who "has affinities with animals, which symbolize her characteristics. Thus she can appear as a snake or a tiger or a bird" (Jung, 1941, par. 358). In the Western tradition, the lamia is the closest figure to Akinari's serpent, and Keats' 1819 poem *Lamia* constructs the snake woman as an anima figure to the young hero, Lycius. Furthermore, the priest's description of Manago as *toshihetaru* or primeval (Ueda, 1968, p. 114)—as having through time attached herself to various beings (Ueda, 2007, p. 173)—links her to Jung's identification of the anima as one of those "archetypal components" of the unconscious that "never disintegrate but lie dormant, waiting to be re-activated" (Stevens, 1983, p. 123). As Jung argued, such archetypal components as the anima and animus "bring into our ephemeral consciousness an unknown psychic life belonging to a remote past. It is the mind of our unknown ancestors" (Jung, 1939, par. 518). By describing Manago as a primeval serpent, the priest roots Toyoo's psyche firmly in the realm of the archetypes.

The serpent woman who wishes to achieve union with a human being is an important East Asian archetype of the feminine, its importance to Chinese culture comparable to that of Faust and Don Juan for European culture (Lévy, 1971, p. 97). But the Japanese had constructed their own versions of the serpent woman tale in earlier literary texts: in a story about a monk of the Dōjōji Temple who had brought salvation to a pair of serpents, from the collection *Konjaku monogatarishū* (Tales of Former Times, compiled 1130–1140) and in the sixteenth-century Noh play *Dōjōji*. In telling his tale of a man's encounter with a serpent woman, Akinari paid homage to the serpent woman tale of his own tradition by having the Buddhist monk who helps Toyoo subdue Manago come from the Dōjōji Temple associated with both earlier Japanese versions.

After warning Toyoo about the tenacity of the beast, the elderly priest tells him: "If henceforth you summon your courage and calm your restless heart, you will not need to borrow an old man's powers to repel these demons" (Ueda, 2007, p. 173). Analogically to the Zen Ox-Herding pictures, which describe the process of a student's quieting and emptying his heart through the images of a herder becoming aware of, catching, and subduing an ox, the words of the Shinto priest can be read in two ways. In one reading, Manago is a liminal being straddling the boundary between human and animal, and Toyoo needs to quiet his heart so that he can deal with Manago as a beast/woman in the real world. To him, Manago is a liminal being, existing both in the form of a woman with whom he has a relationship, and internally, as a part of his inner life. Thus, Toyoo needs to quiet his heart so that he can deal with the female beast within—in Jungian terms, his anima. The old man stands by him here as a spiritual and psychological mentor figure and his words, spoken kindly, make Toyoo feel as if he has "awakened from a dream" (ibid.).

Nakamura argues that, at this moment, "Toyoo puts aside his spirit of *fūryū* and expresses the resolve to return to a moral spirit [*seishin*]" (Ueda, 1968, p. 115 n. 40). *Fūryū,* or living the elegant, aesthetic life, was used straightforwardly during the Heian period to describe the world of aristocrats whose writings Toyoo was so attracted to—but it is clear that the author at this point is criticising *fūryū* from the Confucian standpoint, arguing that it is not aesthetics and elegance that discipline the human being but rather that it is the "moral self-cultivation of the individual" that maintains "the delicate equilibrium at the heart of both man and the cosmos" (Nosco, 1984, pp. 7–8). In Jungian terms, Toyoo owes his awakening from the dream of living on the aesthetic plane and his decision to undertake a moral life to his relationship with Manago as both human being and anima figure, for Jung writes that "the anima gives relationship and relatedness to a man's consciousness" (Jung, 1951, par. 33). But his relationship with the elderly Shinto priest has given him a model of how to relate to the world ethically, and as an adult male, so that it is no accident that from here on he takes moral responsibility for his situation. Deciding to leave his sister and her husband, he soberly blames the trouble he has caused them on the "unrighteousness of my heart" (Ueda, 2007, p. 174) and expresses his gratitude for their kindness.

When Toyoo returns to his parents' home, they take pity on him and, reasoning that his unmarried state has made him attractive to the lustful supernatural being, arrange a marriage for him with a woman named Tomiko, the beautiful daughter of a steward from a nearby village, who had been in service at the emperor's court. Akinari's inclusion of this figure, a figure absent from all the earlier versions of the serpent woman legend, enables him to thicken the tension by introducing the theme of jealousy as a motive for Manago's increasing domination of Toyoo. But his insertion of Tomiko into the plot of the story permits a different interpretation: from a Jungian standpoint, Tomiko is an obstacle to Toyoo's psychological development, and Manago, just as she had earlier caused a separation between the young man and his family, now brings about a separation between Toyoo and his wife. This time, however, since Tomiko as the new object of Toyoo's love directly threatens her influence on him, Manago separates Toyoo from her by taking over her personality and, eventually, by eliminating her.

To return to the story, once married, and satisfied with Tomiko's beauty and aristocratic manners, Toyoo "could barely remember the giant snake that had been in love with him" (Ueda, 2007, p. 175). But things quickly turn dramatic. On the second night after his marriage, while inebriated, he is jokingly provoking Tomiko about the men she must have slept with while in the service of the emperor, when she suddenly begins to speak in the voice of Manago. She reproaches him for having forgotten his vows to her in having married another woman and adds that, if he believes what others say about her and avoids her, she will take revenge, killing him (ibid., pp. 174–75). Here Manago demonstrates the qualities that Jung, quoting from *The Secret of the Golden Flower*, describes as typical of the anima: "sensuous desires and impulses to anger" (Jung, 1929, par. 57). This is the threatening anima figure at her most powerful—but she is also beneficent. As the anima figure who promotes psychological growth, Manago views Tomiko as a threat to Toyoo's development. Whereas he had earlier been fascinated with the Heian aristocratic world in its literary form, now the former court lady Tomiko, a representative of that world in the flesh, threatens to keep him imprisoned in his anima fascination. When Toyoo jokes with Tomiko about her supposed affairs with many men while in service at court, Manago takes over the personality of Tomiko to command Toyoo to evolve beyond the playful aesthetic sphere of the court, remaining faithful only to her and to the path of psychological growth. That she now threatens him with death if he does not follow her demands makes Toyoo faint out of sheer fright, remaining "unconscious until dawn" (Ueda, 2007, p. 177).

When he wakes up, he tells his father-in-law what has happened, relying, for the second time in the story, on an older male mentor for help. This figure is, significantly, a member of the samurai class, the class motivated to courageous action, as warriors, and practicality, as administrators that toward the close of the Heian period ended the domination of the court aristocracy and ushered in military rule. He sends for a Buddhist monk renowned for his ability to exorcise, among other things, *mononoke*, which term Nakamura translates as "spirits of the dead and the living" (Ueda, 1968, p. 118). But the monk blanches when he sees, coming at him through the door of Toyoo's and Tomiko/Manago's room, a "giant snake" that "thrust out his head and confronted him", a head "gleaming whiter than a pile of snow, its eyes like mirrors, its horns like leafless trees, its gaping mouth three feet across with a crimson tongue protruding, … [that] seemed about to swallow him in a single furious gulp" (Ueda, 2007, p. 178). Possessing neither the humility nor the spiritual insight necessary to confront Manago in the form of the primeval serpent, the monk is killed by her/it.

This is the only place in the story where the snake appears as the white serpent of Chinese legend and literature: it is the anima at its most animalistic and most primeval, an archetypal force erupting from the depths of the unconscious. Though Toyoo himself does not look at the snake, he sees the power that the snake can exercise through its effects on the monk. In Jungian terms, it is here that Toyoo faces the archetype of the anima. Though everyone who witnessed the event is weeping in terror, he is calm, for he has been able to see his inner self through the intervention of the anima. Instead of escaping or fainting, he responds consciously and soberly to his situation. Aware now that he will not be able to avoid Manago, he tells Tomiko's parents that it is dishonest of him to involve others in his suffering, and that from now on he will face her alone (Ueda, 2007, p. 179). To their horror, he goes into the bedroom he shares with Tomiko/Manago, but all is quiet there, and Tomiko once again appears as a beautiful woman.

Toyoo and Tomiko, who has been possessed by Manago, then have a very interesting dialogue. She again threatens to kill him if he continues to treat her as an enemy, but this time adds that she will also "torment the people of this village" (Ueda, 2007, p. 179). As the maleficent anima that tries to come between a man and his family "like a jealous mistress" (Jung, 1928, par. 320), Manago has obliterated Toyoo's wife, but as beneficent anima, by destroying his relationship to Tomiko she forces him to look again at her, and respect her demand for psychological development. She asks Toyoo not to feel enmity toward her but rather to continue to relate to her—I would argue, because there is still more for him to learn.

By severing his connection to Tomiko, a former Heian court lady, Manago in her function as anima has cut Toyoo's childish bond with the mother-dominated, aesthetic Heian world while catalysing him to develop psychologically. That she has attained her goal is evident when Tomiko/Manago, in her seductive anima guise, "put[s] on coquettish airs" in speaking to him, and Toyoo is disgusted, no longer swept away by the coquettishness and beauty of women. Now, having depersonalised the anima, he responds to Manago with dispassion and a psychologically mature recognition of her dual nature. He accepts the fact that she, as a serpent, will naturally hurt a person; but he also realises that her love for him is no different from the love that humans feel. Through his encounter with Manago as anima giving "relationship and relatedness to a man's consciousness" (Jung, 1951, par. 33), Toyoo is able to face the inner world of the feminine that she represents, even knowing the destruction that she has wreaked and the danger that she still represents. He listens to her words and agrees to go away with her, even though this would mean living with a serpent woman and giving up wife and social status. Psychologically, Manago functions positively for Toyoo as a "bridge to the unconscious" (Jung, 1929, par. 62), but, in the real world, she does not heed his request that she spare Tomiko's life.

When Toyoo tells his father-in-law that he wishes to leave the house to avoid involving other people in his problems, and assures the steward that Tomiko's life will be spared, the steward, proud of his status as a samurai, rides off to ask the help of the very elderly priest Hōkai of Dōjōji Temple in Komatsubara. Toyoo subdues Manago in accordance with the directions of this priest. The monk from Kumano Temple had approached Manago with a self-important air and without the bridge of Eros, so she had appeared to him as a huge primeval serpent and killed him. Since Toyoo had honoured her love for him, Manago remains in her human form when he approaches her, telling her that they should be on their way. No longer lured by Manago's beauty or influenced by her feminine wiles, Toyoo resolutely pulls out the sacred stole given his father-in-law by the priest, throws it over Manago and presses down with all his strength. When she exhorts him to stop, as he is hurting her, this time he does not listen to her words (Ueda, 2007, p. 180). The priest Hōkai arrives, says prayers, and lifts the stole, revealing a "white serpent, more than three feet long", lying coiled and "perfectly motionless" on Tomiko's unconscious body (ibid.). He carefully places the serpent, and a smaller serpent (the servant Maroya) in an iron bowl, and, covering the bowl tightly with the stole, returns to Dōjōji Temple, where he buries it in a hole dug before the main hall and forbids the serpents "ever to appear in the world again" (ibid., p. 181).

In a Buddhist interpretation, which was valid for the Chinese and earlier Japanese versions of the serpent woman myth, the priest's exorcism transferred the two serpents from the worldly to the sacred sphere. But if Ueda's story is interpreted in Jungian terms, Toyoo has recognised the personal nature of the anima and can thus think of depersonalising it and objectivating it (Jung, 1928, par. 321). James Hillman argues that, "by returning the infusions, the beauty, the wiles, and vanities to their origins in the Goddesses, giving it all back to its background, … [a man] depersonalize[s] the entire compulsive, autonomous performance" (Hillman, 1985, p. 127). Toyoo's subduing of the serpent was, in Jungian terms, his objectivation of Manago as anima figure and his integration of the anima through recognition of "the relatively autonomous, personified nature of the archetype" (ibid., p. 119).

Manago, always both human and spirit and, in my reading, anima figure, was integrated into the consciousness of Toyoo and thus disappeared as both human being and spirit. Through being integrated, Manago, the anima, becomes "the Eros of consciousness" for Toyoo (Jung, 1951, par. 33), enabling him to go beyond a "one-sided belief in the power of consciousness" (Jung, 1929, par. 62)—to reach a state that Hillman refers to as "relativizing the ego", which involves a "sacrifice of our habitual consciousness, internalizing it within the embrace of the wider notion of psyche" (Hillman, 1985, p. 127). I would argue that what has happened psychologically in this Japanese story is that Toyoo's process of education at the hands of the anima has brought him an understanding of "the figures of the unconscious" as "real and effective factors". He has faced the eruption of the unconscious in the form of the anima figure and gained a sober recognition of "what is meant by psychic reality" (Jung, 1929, par. 62). The author indicates no future path for Toyoo, having brought him to the stage of confrontation with the anima. The narrator's terse words at the end of the story: "The steward's daughter eventually fell ill and died. Toyoo's life was spared" (Ueda, 2007, p. 181) communicate his sense that the hero had barely escaped with his life from this dangerous confrontation, and recall Jung's reflective comment on reading the ancient Chinese yogic text *The Secret of the Golden Flower*: "The way is not without danger. Everything good is costly, and the development of personality is one of the most costly of all things" (Jung, 1929, par. 24). In his story of Toyoo's confrontation with the serpent woman Akinari demonstrated a way for the early modern Japanese male to restore the balance between man and cosmos that threatened to be destroyed in the development of a quasi-scientific mentality that repressed the spirit world—or, in Jungian terms, to re-establish the link of the inner life to the collective unconscious. The story suggests that the Japanese author, in his portrayal of Toyoo's confrontation with the anima, might have agreed with Jung, who wrote that "self-culture" in the sense of confronting and objectivating the anima is "the most universal, the most legitimate fulfilment of the meaning of the individual's life" (Jung, 1928, par. 327).

## *References*

Campany, R. F. (1996). *Strange Writing: Anomaly Accounts in Early Medieval China*. Albany: State University of New York Press.

Clarke, J. J. (1994). *Jung and Eastern Thought: A Dialogue with the Orient*. London: Routledge.

Hillman, J. (1985). *Anima: An Anatomy of a Personified Notion*. With excerpts from the writings of C. G. Jung and original drawings by Mary Vernon. Dallas: Spring.

Idema, W. L. (2009). *The White Snake and Her Son: A Translation of "The Precious Scroll of Thunder Peak" with Related Texts*. Indianapolis: Hackett.

Jung, C. G. (1928). The relations between the ego and the unconscious. In: *The Collected Works of C. G. Jung*. H. Read, M. Fordham & G. Adler (Eds.). William McGuire (Executive Ed.). R. F. C. Hull et al. (Trans.). [Hereafter *C. W.*,] *7* (2nd ed.): pp. 121–241/pars. 202–406. Princeton, NJ: Princeton University Press, 1966.

Jung, C. G. (1929). Commentary on *The Secret of the Golden Flower*. In: *C. W., 13*: pp. 1–56/pars. 1–84. Princeton, NJ: Princeton University Press, 1967.

Jung, C. G. (1936/1954). Concerning the archetypes, with special reference to the anima concept. In: *C.W., 9i* (2nd ed.): pp. 54–72/pars. 111–147. Princeton, NJ: Princeton University Press, 1968.

Jung, C. G. (1939). Conscious, unconscious, and individuation. In: *C. W., 9i* (2nd ed.): pp. 275–289/pars. 489–524. Princeton, NJ: Princeton University Press, 1968.

Jung, C. G. (1941). The psychological aspects of the kore. In: *C. W., 9i* (2nd ed.): pp. 182–203/pars. 306–383. Princeton, NJ: Princeton University Press, 1968.

Jung, C. G. (1947/1954). On the nature of the psyche. In: *C. W., 8*: pp. 159–234/pars. 343–442. Princeton, NJ: Princeton University Press, 1960.

Jung, C. G. (1951). *Aion*. *C. W., 9ii* (2nd ed.). Princeton, NJ: Princeton University Press, 1968.

Kawai, H. (1992). *The Buddhist Priest Myōe: A Life of Dreams*. M. Unno (Trans. & Ed.). Venice, CA: Lapis.

Lévy, A. (1971). Le "serpent blanc" en Chine et au Japon: excursion à travers les variations d'un thème. In: *Études sur le conte et le roman chinois* (pp. 97–113). Paris: École Française d'Extrême-Orient.

Nosco, P. (1984). Introduction. In: *Confucianism and Tokugawa Culture* (pp. 3–26). Peter Nosco (Ed.). Princeton: Princeton University Press.

Stevens, A. (1983). *Archetypes: A Natural History of the Self*. New York: Quill.

Swales, M. (1978). *The German Bildungsroman from Wieland to Hesse*. Princeton: Princeton University Press.

Takata, M. (1972). *Ugetsu monogatari*: a critical interpretation. In: U. Akinari, *Tales of Moonlight and Rain: Japanese Gothic Tales* (pp. xxi–xxix). K. Hamada (Trans.). New York: Columbia University Press.

Ueda, A. (1968). *Jasei no in* [the lust of the serpent]. In: *Ueda Akinari shū* (pp. 98–121). Y. Nakamura (Ed.). Nihon kotenbungaku taikei 56. Tokyo: Iwanami Shoten.

Ueda, A. (2007). *Tales of Moonlight and Rain*. A study and translation by A. H. Chambers. New York: Columbia University Press.

Wilhelm, R. (1962). A discussion of the text. In: *The Secret of the Golden Flower: A Chinese Book of Life*. R. Wilhelm (Trans. from Chinese to German). C. F. Baynes (Trans. from German to English). With a commentary by C. G. Jung. San Diego: Harcourt Brace Jovanovich.

Young, B. M. (1982). *Ueda Akinari*. Vancouver: University of British Columbia Press.

Yu, D. (Trans). (1978). Eternal prisoner under the Thunder Peak Pagoda. In Y. W. Ma and J. S. M. Lau (Eds.), *Traditional Chinese Stories: Themes and Variations* (pp. 355–378). New York: Columbia University Press.

Zolbrod, L. (Trans. & Ed). (1974). *Ugetsu Monogatari: Tales of Moonlight and Rain: A Complete English Translation of the Eighteenth-Century Japanese Collection of Tales of the Supernatural*. Vancouver: University of British Columbia Press.

CHAPTER TEN

# Sorrow and surprise: a reading of Théophile Gautier's sphinx complex

*Leon Burnett*

In Freudian theory, the "Oedipus complex" refers to a psychosexual configuration the name of which is derived from, and alludes to, the plot of Sophocles' Theban tragedy of fate, *Oedipus Rex*. The focus is upon the outcome of a prophecy, initially predicted by the oracle before Oedipus was born, which reflected or, rather, exposed the allegedly hidden desires of the eponymous hero: that Oedipus, in Freud's words, "is destined to murder his father and take his mother in marriage" (Freud, 1900a, p. 261). Since the publication of *The Interpretation of Dreams* in 1899, Freud's theory has had both its enthusiastic advocates and its sceptical detractors. One of the more articulate—and more interesting—of the latter in recent years is Jean-Joseph Goux, who, in his book *Oedipus, Philosopher*, questions the basis of Freud's generalising interpretation of the myth. He takes issue with Freud's epistemological postulate that "the complex explained the myth" (Goux, 1993, p. 1) and offers a counter-proposition that "it is the Oedipus myth that explains the complex" (ibid., p. 2). "It is", he argues, "because the West is Oedipean that Freud discovered the 'Oedipus complex'" (ibid.). In contesting Freud's proposition, Goux grounds his argument in a structural analysis of the myth as anomalous. Fundamental to his thesis is the contention that "Oedipus is the prototypical figure of the philosopher, the one who challenges sacred enigmas in order to establish the perspective of man and self" (ibid., p. 3). While this orientation in no way diminishes the importance of the oracular pronouncement, it does bring into play the hero's encounter with the sphinx, which receives no more than a cursory mention in *The Interpretation of Dreams*, as an event of considerable significance, for the fabulous monster is the very incarnation of sacred enigma.

It is not my intention in this paper to revisit Goux's dismantling of Freud's reading of myth point by point, but rather to take the hint from the French critic that there are more ways of looking at the Theban myth than through the fate of Oedipus. Instead of the "Oedipus complex", then, I propose to examine the "sphinx complex" in Théophile Gautier (1811–1872) and to explore it from a literary, rather than a therapeutic, perspective. My conclusion will be that throughout the oeuvre of the nineteenth-century author, there is to be found, constellated in the figure of the sphinx, an emotional complex which may be described as an amalgamation of sorrow and surprise.

For Jung, complexes were "feeling-toned" structures, composed of ideas and images integrated (or constellated) by the psyche around a central theme or archetype. In his view, complexes belong to the personal unconscious—in contrast to archetypes, which inform the collective unconscious. Consistent with this distinction, the "sphinx complex" that I explore is unique to Gautier, although many of the symbolic and mythic aspects of the archetypal image may be, and indeed are, shared by others. In "A review of the complex theory" (1934), Jung defined a complex as "the image of a certain psychic situation which is strongly accentuated emotionally". In his review, he stated that "Everyone knows nowadays that people 'have complexes'. What is not so well known, though far more important theoretically, is that complexes can *have us*" (Jung, 1934, par. 200).

The phrasing of this formulation recalls Goux's riposte to Freud: that it is not the Oedipus complex that explains the myth but "the Oedipus myth that explains the complex". To combine these two reversed commonplaces into one schema is to create a hierarchy—or hegemony—of agency: it is myths which account for the complexes that control our being. The human consciousness becomes the passive recipient of the mythic imagination. Gautier, in one of the critical reviews discussed in this paper, "Théodore Chassériau", made use of the expression "retrospective assimilation" (*La Presse*, 25 May 1852). This expression, in effect, addresses the same process as the composite schema constructed from the amalgamation of the statements of Goux and Jung. It suggests that through a mythic or archetypal symbol we possess the facility to assimilate retrospectively a cluster of emotions into an aggregate, which itself may inform a work of art or literature in such a way as to invest it with an imaginative force that appeals to a wider community.

One such symbol is the sphinx. In Gautier's writing the sphinx repeatedly takes on the function of constellating a set of emotions to such a degree that it is possible to refer to a "sphinx complex" in his work. In what follows, I conduct a literary, rather than a psychoanalytic, investigation of the nature of that complex, that is to say, my focus is more upon the work than the man.

The first observation that needs to be made about Gautier's writing on the sphinx is that this figure is most prominent in works that are set in Egypt. This fact already distances the "sphinx complex" from the "Oedipus complex", at least in its genesis and initial frame of reference, for the Egyptian sphinx comes with its own set of connotations and nuances. Nevertheless, the application of a single word to name a mythological creature, which to the nineteenth-century European mind existed as a composite, stretching, as it were, from Thebes to Thebes, ensures that the shadow of Oedipus falls on the pages of the French writer's oeuvre, while it at the same time enables recourse to a richer and more extensive symbolism.

Of all Gautier's compositions *The Novel of the Mummy* (*Le Roman de la Momie*), which first appeared *en feuilleton* in *Le Moniteur universel*, from 11 March to 16 May 1857, and was subsequently published as a single volume by Hachette in 1858, presents the most substantial treatment of the writer's preoccupation with ancient Egypt. This dual exploration of the practices of nineteenth-century Egyptology and the world of Ancient Egypt, had the self-proclaimed aim, according to its dedication to M. Ernest Feydeau, of envisioning "a gigantic civilisation that had disappeared" (Gautier, 1858). (Feydeau had published *Histoire des usages funèbres et des sépultures des peuples anciens* in 1856.) This ancient civilisation had exercised the author's imagination from the start, although he was not to visit Egypt to see the sphinxes, pyramids and other vestiges of antiquity *in situ* for another decade, when he attended the official opening of the Suez Canal in 1869.

The heroine of Gautier's 1857 novel is Queen Tahoser, an Egyptian whose perfectly preserved remains are found by two Egyptologists,

Lord Evandale and Dr. Rumphius, in a secret underground chamber in the valley of Biban-el-Molouk where the mummified body had lain undisturbed for millennia. The main interest of the story is the personal account of the fictional queen, as revealed in a roll of papyrus discovered in her possession and subsequently translated, and Lord Evandale's fascination with his discovery. In keeping with the conventions of the genre, Gautier concludes his prologue with the announcement that he has turned the Latin translation of Doctor Rumphius into French.

The motifs of sorrow and surprise, which Gautier associated with the sphinx, were already well established in his oeuvre by the time he came to write *The Novel of the Mummy*. The present chapter addresses itself mainly to the author's earlier compositions in order to chart the genesis of his "sphinx complex" rather than offering a close reading of the image of the sphinx in the novel that Gautier had commenced working on in the autumn of 1856. Though much in evidence, the sphinxes in *The Novel of the Mummy* only serve a subsidiary function of embellishment to the main plot, to which the motifs of surprise and sorrow already established in Gautier's earlier works have been transferred.

In the same year as the appearance in print of the first edition of *The Novel of the Mummy*, Gautier set out on a Russian adventure. His abiding impression of the expedition, one of wonder and admiration, is recorded in the journalistic reports that he sent back to France at the time and which were published in the following decade as *Travels in Russia* (*Voyage en Russie*, 1867). Despite his recent fictional engagement with the civilisation of the past and the creation of a fictional heroine from that period, allusions to Egypt in the bulletins that Gautier wrote about his Russian travels, as one might expect, were few and far between. Nevertheless, they existed. The observation that the Cathedral of St Isaac's unbroken, granite staircase is "worthy of the Temple of Karnac" takes up an earlier reference, where mention is made of two sphinxes on the "colossal staircase" leading from the river Neva to the Academy of Fine Arts (Gautier, 1900–03, p. 145). In his best guidebook style, Gautier informs the reader:

> From the palace the river is reached by a colossal staircase adorned with two great human-headed Egyptian sphinxes, surprised at bearing upon their rose granite quarters housings of snow that make them shiver. The Roumiantzov Obelisk rises in the centre of the square. (Ibid.)

In this description, part of a verbal tour of the palaces and mansions that border the quay, one detail stands out as unlikely to grace the pages of a Baedeker: the sphinxes are "surprised at bearing upon their rose granite quarters housings of snow that make them shiver". Gautier is reluctant, as ever, to pass by the opportunity to entertain with a fanciful flourish: the "housings of snow"—or, more picturesquely in the French account, "caparaçons de frimas"—that have settled on the sphinxes acquaint them with their newly acquired northern identity. What is striking here is not the animation of the granite to the point of anthropomorphism (if indeed we consider surprise of this kind to be a uniquely human response), but rather the implied ability of the sphinxes to remember a previous incarnation in which there was no snow or, in the French version, no decorative dusting of frost.

In the chronology of these fabulous creatures, their awakening marks the end of a repose as lengthy as the "twenty centuries of stony sleep" that Yeats was later to attribute to the "rough beast" in his poem of "The Second Coming" (1919). The destiny of Gautier's Egyptian sphinxes, however, was not, as in Yeats's poem, to set out at a slouch towards a sacred site to be reborn. Moribund hybrids caught between the literary-historical cycles of Romanticism and Symbolism, they appeared poorly equipped for such an apocalypse. In the cold northern environment, they lacked the vitality, manifest in the nearby bronze statue of horse and rider—designed by Falconet and celebrated by Pushkin—that stood in Senate Square, to fire Russian modernity with the new mythology it sought. While Yeats's later "shape with lion body and head of a man" was "vexed to nightmare" by a premonition of its imminent revival in a strange, new age, but, on awakening, it was still able to move its "slow thighs" under a familiar desert sun (Yeats, 1965, pp. 210–211), Gautier's sphinxes of St Petersburg are roused from their slumbers by the sensation of coldness and they can only shiver in an alien wind that "comes straight from the Pole" (Gautier, 1900–03, p. 145).

It is to be doubted, however, that the surprise ascribed to them was spontaneous, at least on Gautier's part, for his observation recycles a motif that appears in a poem he had written earlier and included in his collection, *Enamels and Cameos* (*Émaux et camées*), which had first appeared in 1852. Gautier's "Parisian obelisk" was one of a pair of poems, the other being "Luxor obelisk", that made up the poetic composite "Nostalgias of obelisks", each obelisk yearning for what is unattainable for itself but accessible to the other. "Parisian obelisk" opens with the obelisk expressing a sense of ennui and loss, located, as it is, in the northern city, where "Snow, frost, mist, and rain / Freeze my already rusted flank" (Gautier, 1895, p. 63). The poem concludes, some seventeen stanzas later, with the obelisk's reminiscence of a sphinx sharpening its claws on the edges of its pedestal. The Luxor obelisk, in the companion piece, expresses a wish to be transported "like my brother" to Paris, concluding: "He is alive and I am dead" (ibid., p. 70).

Oscar Wilde alludes to Gautier's "Parisian obelisk" in *The Picture of Dorian Gray*, when the eponymous hero settles down in Chapter XIV of the novel with Charpentier's elegant 1881 edition of *Enamels and Cameos* to read of:

> the Obelisk in the Place de la Concorde that weeps tears of granite in its lonely sunless exile, and longs to be back by the hot, lotus-covered Nile, where there are Sphinxes, and rose-red ibises, and white vultures with gilded claws, and crocodiles, with small beryl eyes that crawl over the green steaming mud. (Wilde, 2007, p. 138)

As for Gautier, the presence of the nearby obelisk in the northern city of St Petersburg, may have stimulated a memory of the yearning monument in "Parisian obelisk" and prompted the conceit of the surprised sphinxes in *Travels in Russia*.

Although, in *Travels in Russia*, the two Egyptian sphinxes situated outside the Academy of Arts on the bank of the Neva receive no more than a fleeting mention for their part in the monumental ornamentation of St Petersburg, other sphinxes featured more prominently in Gautier's earlier poetry, fiction and critical writing, leading one commentator to remark that the intractable mystery of his universe is "recalled by numerous sphinxes" (Tennant, 1975, p. 112). It is from these references that we gather something of the symbolic import of the fabulous creatures in the French author's imagination.

Two decades before, in 1838, Gautier had composed a short story, "A night with Cleopatra" ("Une nuit de Cléopâtre"), which first appeared in *La Presse* (29 and 30 November, 1, 2, 4 and 6 December, 1838) and was subsequently included in a collection of his tales, *Nouvelles* (1845). In this story the sphinx acts as a mythological correlate to the mood of sadness that pervades the bleak atmosphere of the Egyptian desert:

> The banks were deserted; a deep and solemn gloom (*une tristesse immense et solennelle*) weighed on that land which was never aught

> else than a mighty tomb, a land whose living inhabitants seemed never to have had any other occupation but of embalming the dead. A sterile gloom (*tristesse aride*), dry as pumice stone, without melancholy, without reverie, having no pearl-grey cloud to gaze at on the horizon, no secret spring in which to bathe its dusty feet; the gloom of the sphinx (*tristesse de sphinx*) wearied with perpetually watching the desert, the sphinx who can never quit the granite pedestal on which it has sharpened its claws for twenty centuries. (Gautier, 1933, p. 32)

It is conceivable that the reference to "twenty centuries" present in Gautier's account may have caught the eye of Yeats, either in the original French (*depuis vingt siècles*) or in the translation by Lafcadio Hearn that was first published in 1882, and lodged in his mind to resurface as the span of time mentioned in "The Second Coming".

This sorrowful sphinx, however, was by no means the first to grace the pages of Gautier's fiction. Already in the first paragraph of "A feast in the Egyptian desert", his first fictional work to appear in print, albeit anonymously, sphinxes await the reader:

> The moon was sleeping on the sands. The great Thebes, covering the endless plain with its ruins, raised here and there its crumbling gates, its painted columns, its gods seated in sadness (*tristement*) on remote trunks that once surrounded the naves of temples now overturned, its sphinxes crouching in the shadows like nocturnal and fantastic monsters. ("Un repas au désert de l'Egypte", in *Le Gastronome*, 24 March 1831)

Sphinxes are frequently pressed into service in Gautier's critical writings on literature and art. In a review of the paintings of Théodore Chassériau, Gautier took the customary association of the sphinx with secrets and enigmas one stage further. Claiming that the disciple of Ingres was "born Etruscan, as others have become it by force of abstraction", Gautier proceeded to characterise the paintings belonging to Chassériau's "Greco-Asiatic cycle" in the following manner:

> To the pure beauty of Phidias, to Athenian elegance, he added a mysterious and disconsolate feeling (*un sentiment mystérieux et triste*), a certain wild grace, and an indefinable oriental languor. On

> these marble masks, he often placed the eyes of a sphinx full of enigmas and reverie, a profound gentleness (*une douceur profonde*), and a disturbing and serene fixedness; their mouths, slightly more drawn out than the classical mouths of statues, seemed to inhale the warm breath of the Orient, and a barbaric variation of style or some exotic jewellery indicated the vicinity of Asia and Egypt. One would have said a pupil of Apelles had followed Alexander in his conquest of India, and had mixed, on his return to Greece, memories of alien races with the pure types of his own country. (*La Presse*, 25 May 1852)

In this extract we find evidence of several motifs associated with the sphinx. In addition to the references, which seem mandatory for this period (and, indeed, for succeeding ones), to the exoticism of Egypt and the mysteriousness of enigma, the sphinx is endowed with a kind of composure that often accompanies reverie. The hybrid nature of the sphinx is attested to not only by an ambivalence of mood that combines gentleness with savagery, but also by the miscegenation, effected on Chassériau's palette, that comes, as the result of what Gautier called "retrospective assimilation", to engender the Greco-Asiatic type, in contrast to the pure art of Greece alluded to at the beginning and the end of the extract. The distinctive quality of Gautier's sphinx, however, is to be found in its sense of sadness, in its *tristesse*.

Retrospective assimilation produced, among Chassériau's most distinguished achievements in the Greco-Asiatic style, a painting of *Susanna Bathing* (1839), now exhibited in the Louvre and originally conceived, in Gautier's opinion, from the point of view of the ancient Orient:

> The beauty of the Israelite, ennobled by the art of Greece, had perhaps never been so happily realised: a kind of biblical modesty has cloaked the chaste nakedness of this beautiful body spied upon by obscene old men crouching in the shadows like tawny beasts ready to pounce on their prey. This perfect torso, which the Venus de Milo would not have spurned, is allied through the sharper contour of the breast and through the more hollow slenderness of the side to the forms of the Orient and it recalls vaguely the priestesses of India, the custodians of pagodas, who, at Benares, descend to the Ganges by white marble steps. (*La Presse*, 25 May 1852)

Although the sphinx is not invoked directly in the passage above, its ambivalence of aspect spills over, as it were, into the critique of *Susanna Bathing*. The main subject of Chassériau's painting is sphinx-like in the mystery of her unimpeachable womanhood. Her "beautiful body" is exposed to a prurient gaze, yet it remains "cloaked" chastely in a "biblical modesty", a modesty that, however, does not prevent Gautier, the secondary onlooker, from taking in the erotic and the exotic with the eye of a connoisseur, as the allusions to the Venus de Milo and the Benares priestesses indicate. In the course of this appreciation, Israel and Greece yield dominion to the Orient and India, so that, by the end of the passage, Shiva is as much a presence in the world of antiquity as Yahweh, while the attention to the detail of the ghat (the "white marble steps") gestures towards an interior narrative that remains untold. Gautier's "custodians of pagodas" makes a discreet reference to the devadasis, who gave up their lives to the caretaking of Hindu temples. Benares (now Varanasi) was an important centre of Hindu worship and the presence of the devadasis an integral part of the temple life. Over time, the devadasis came to be seen as prostitutes and were subject to exploitation by priests and worshippers.

If we turn to the primary onlookers, we note that the elders of the actual biblical story (in Daniel 13) have been stripped of their status in Gautier's blunt depiction of them as "obscene old men". Behind this characterisation, however, there is another, hidden, one. If Susanna's torso recalls obscurely the custodians of the pagoda, then the phraseology selected to describe the elders' demeanour invokes no less the sphinxes in Gautier's early story, "A feast in the Egyptian desert". The old men "crouching in the shadows like tawny beasts ready to pounce on their prey" ("accroupis dans l'ombre comme des bêtes fauves prêtes à sauter d'un bond sur leur proie") adopt the same posture—and inhabit the same phraseology—as the sphinxes "crouching in the shadows like nocturnal and fantastic monsters" ("accroupis dans l'ombre comme des monstres nocturnes et fantastiques") of the tale that marked Gautier's début. The simile of the "tawny beasts", chosen here to designate the lustful threat of the voyeurs, reinforces the covert association with a creature that is half-man and half-lion. In "A feast in the Egyptian desert", the main character in the story, a French traveller, alone in the dark among the ruins of the vast solitude, "believed, at each moment, that he saw emerging from behind the motionless head of one sphinx or another the pointed snout of a hyena, or the enormous head of a desert lion" (*Le Gastronome*, 24 March 1831).

Gautier draws his readers' attention to one further aspect of Chassériau's representation of Susanna: her sorrow. Her face, he writes, has "a melancholy, disdainful mien, a languorous and virginal expression, the memory of which haunts you" (*La Presse*, 25 May 1852). The sense of oppression that lies beneath Susanna's impenetrable mask of sorrow is shared by other female figures in Chassériau's Greco-Asiatic cycle of paintings. Gautier mentions three other works, drawn from the same source, which provide evidence of a replenished mythology. These are *Andromeda Exposed* (*Andromède attachée au rocher par les Néréides*, 1840), *Diana Surprised* (*Diane surprise par Actéon*, 1840), and *Apollo in Pursuit of Daphne* (*Apollon et Daphné*, before 1846). (The translated titles are based on Gautier's ascriptions.)

While it would be reasonable to assign Andromeda and Daphne to the category of the persecuted maiden, as discussed in *The Romantic Agony* (Praz, 1933), the situation is rather different for Diana (or Artemis), whose bathing is observed by Actaeon. The voyeuristic motif here is the one already encountered in the painting of Susanna spied on by the elders. The focus in the portrayal of Diana, however, is not so much upon proud melancholy or oppressive trespass, each with its tacit acknowledgement of the moral superiority of the woman observed, but more, as the title of the painting suggests, upon surprise. Diana, of course, in keeping with her status as a Greco-Roman divinity, takes terrible revenge upon the onlooker for his ocular ambush. She becomes the pursuer, unlike Susanna, the chaste Israelite, who of necessity has to suffer the false charge of adulterous conduct until absolved by Daniel's timely intervention.

The explicit reference to surprise in the title of Chassériau's painting of the Roman goddess Diana alerts us to the fact that such a reaction is also a latent motif in Susanna's narrative. Chassériau's *Susanna Bathing* and *Diana Surprised* are both paintings of surprise, and, as indicated earlier in this paper, Gautier associates surprise (and, we may assume, a rather melancholic disposition following the realisation of their translocation) with the awakening of the sphinxes of St Petersburg. The Orient, or its counterpart, is not simply a source of exotic wonder and amazement for Gautier: a sense of surprise, attendant upon the revelation of hiddenness, is a central constituent of Gautier's sphinx complex.

As we have seen, for Gautier, the sphinx often stands metonymically for the area with which it is identified, whether it be Egypt, as in his prose narratives, the Middle East, as depicted in the paintings that belong to the Greco-Asiatic cycle of Chassériau, or even, as he travelled to the extremity of Europe, Russia. It was, however, with the lost civilization of the pharaohs that Gautier identified the sphinx most frequently and it was with one of the pharaohs in particular that he associated the mythological hybrid.

Gautier regarded the Greco-Egyptian queen, Cleopatra VII, as a universal type whose appeal lay squarely in the prestige that antiquity bestowed upon her. Though Greek by descent, she belonged to the Egyptian past and shared with its architectural wonders the attributes of monumentality and power. "A night with Cleopatra" offers to its readers a larger-than-life rendering of antiquity centred on a heroine whose very existence confirmed Gautier's contention that beauty, glory, and power may all be combined in one woman. "She was", we are told, "the most complete woman who had ever lived, a type of wonder to whom the poets can add nothing, and whom dreamers find forever at the end of their dreams" (Gautier, 1933, p. 34). Cleopatra is presented as a product of her time, the "personification of the common thought"; she carries symbolically the life and aspirations of the people. She is "one of these meteoric names which blaze inextinguishably in the night of the ages" and whose prodigious existence proved to be the diurnal realisation "of the dream that all of us dream at night" (ibid., p. 56).

The account of an occasion, when the dream that all of us dream becomes reality, is narrated against a background of sumptuous hedonism and decadent splendour that stands in stark contrast to the boredom and uniformity that prevailed in the bourgeois society of Gautier's own day:

> The story we are writing, and the great name of Cleopatra which figures in it, have plunged us into … reflections which displease a civilized ear. But the spectacle of the ancient world is something so overwhelming, so discouraging for imaginations that believe themselves unlicensed, and for spirits that imagine they have attained the last limits of fairy-like magnificence, that we could not refrain from registering here our complaints and regrets that we were not contemporary with Sardanapalus, with Tiglath-Pileser, with

> Cleopatra, Queen of Egypt, or even of Heliogabalus, Emperor of Rome and Priest of the Sun. (Gautier, 1933, pp. 56–57)

For Gautier the French language, "so chaste, so glacially prude", is stretched to breaking point in describing the night of excess—"this frantic outburst, this mighty, powerful debauch that was not afraid to mingle blood and wine, those two purples, and the furious transports of unsatisfied voluptuousness rushing to the impossible" (Gautier, 1933, p. 57)—in the story of Cleopatra and her lowly lover, Meïamoun. Cleopatra, before the eventful night of destiny rouses her from her habitual preoccupations, suffers from the same ailment that Gautier, Baudelaire and a host of contemporary writers would have us believe afflicted all impressionable men and women of French society living in the middle of the nineteenth century: *ennui*.

Cleopatra's life is one of uniformity, but it differs inordinately from that of the Parisian populace of Gautier's time in that what weighs upon her so heavily is the burden of omnipotence that she carries in a land of unchanging landscape and intolerable climate. All the majesty of her person, all the opulence of the East and all the grandeur of the despot are of no avail in the face of the monotony of empire. The African land is alien to her: she is, after all, a monarch of Macedonian descent. Egypt, for her, is summed up in a phrase: "Mystery and granite" (Gautier, 1933, p. 37). Cleopatra, however, is attracted to neither the mystery nor the granite: both are expressive of an attrition ascribed not to time, but to timelessness. In a country that she finds so inimical, the sphinxes serve as a constant reminder of the heaviness of the granite and the incomprehensibility of the mystery:

> Of what invisible herd are those mighty sphinxes, crouching like watch-dogs, the guardians, that they never close an eyelid and hold for ever their claws at attention? What is the matter with them, then, that they fix so obstinately their eyes of stone on eternity and infinity? What strange secret do their tightly closed lips lock in their breasts? (Ibid., p. 37)

The menace of the sphinxes identified here, as elsewhere, by their crouching posture, is a far cry from the softer, more benign, facial aspect expressed in the profound gentleness of the eyes depicted by Chassériau. The crouch, associated in Gautier's fiction with fierce animals, such as guard-dogs and lions, or with the elders in the biblical story of Susanna, is a comportment adopted in preparation for sustained or intense surveillance. This surveillance may be of the immeasurable, as in the unflinching stare of the sphinxes, or of the forbidden, as in the male espionage of the exposed female body. Because of the association with spying, Gautier's references to the crouching posture are frequently accompanied by descriptions that focus upon eyes, the stone eyes of the sphinx or, as later in the narrative, the "burning eyeball" of Meïamoun, while he watches Cleopatra bathing.

In the scene, which leads to Meïamoun's detection and which has the unexpected outcome of his spending a last night of sensual enchantment with Cleopatra before he meets his death, Gautier brings to bear several items of a repertoire encountered elsewhere in his prose: the coy euphemism of feminine "treasures"; the painterly evocation, through a simile, of the classical epiphanies of Venus and Diana; the comparison of the male voyeur with a predatory animal; and, of course, the naked female body that is the object of the gaze:

> [S]he was queen even in the bath. She came and went, diving and bringing up in her hands from the bottom handfuls of powdered gold which she threw laughing to some of her women; at other times she hung from the balustrade of the pool hiding and revealing her treasures, now letting no more than her polished, lustrous back be seen, now showing herself complete like Venus Anadyomene and varying ceaselessly the aspects of her beauty.
>
> Suddenly she uttered a cry more sharp than that of Diana surprised by Actæon; she had seen through the foliage a burning eyeball gleam, yellow and phosphorescent like the eye of a crocodile or of a lion.
>
> It was Meïamoun who, crouching on the earth, behind a tuft of leaves, more breathless then a fawn among the corn, was growing intoxicated with the dangerous good fortune of seeing the queen in her bath. (Gautier, 1933, pp. 53–54)

Meïamoun, however, is no mere lustful male. He is the divinely appointed ambassador of love, sent by Hathor to release Cleopatra briefly from her prison of monotony. The scene presented above, in which the two central characters meet for the first time, concludes dramatically. The reader's attention, initially directed towards a contemplation of Cleopatra's bathing, her "treasures" now hidden, now revealed, is diverted abruptly, by the queen's exclamation, to the sight of a gleaming eyeball, which, in similar fashion, is first hidden and then revealed. At the moment of Cleopatra's unveiling, before she entered the bath, when "the linen tunic, held only by a golden brooch, was loosened, slipped down her marble body, and lay collapsed in a white cloud at her feet like the swan at the feet of Leda" (Gautier, 1933, p. 53), the narrator had paused to ask "And Meïamoun, where was he?" The implication of the interjected question is that he was not there to witness the prospect. (The next sentence sets out to consolidate this impression: "Oh, cruelty of fate! So many insensible objects were enjoying favours that would ravish a lover with joy." (Ibid.))

The reader only becomes aware of Meïamoun's presence at the same moment as Cleopatra does. If, therefore, it is the discovery of Meïamoun, not Cleopatra, which constitutes the climax of the scene, this serves only to bring home more clearly the importance of the play of concealment and revelation that was for Gautier so essential an ingredient in his conception of ancient Egypt. It was this conception of surprise which, directly or indirectly, Gautier associated with the sphinx. The symbolism of the fabulous creature, as it appears in his writings, was sufficiently ambivalent to allow the two characters in this scene to collude with it in a secret affinity—Cleopatra as pitiless custodian of Egypt's destiny, Meïamoun crouching and animal-like in his venery—and, thus, with each other. Cleopatra rules over Egypt as *la belle dame sans merci* and Meïamoun, who "loved only the perilous or the impossible" (Gautier, 1933, p. 43) in all things, seeks her out at the risk of his life. Earlier in the tale, frustrated in his longing for Cleopatra, "he gave himself up to hunting with a redoubled fury, and tried to subdue by fatigue the heat of his blood and the tumult of his desires" (ibid., p. 44) .

Cleopatra's composite sphinx-nature is prefigured in Gautier's fiction, in *Mademoiselle de Maupin,* when the character of Madelaine de Maupin appears in the imagination of the novel's perplexed hero, d'Albert, as a Greco-Egyptian divinity. At one moment, in the tortured *profession d'amour* that d'Albert writes to the disguised heroine of the novel, he imagines her as Aphrodite "emerging from the bosom of the sea" (Gautier, 1981, p. 296); at the next, he compares her to Isis, the mysterious goddess, "wrapped in a veil which I did not dare to lift" (ibid., p. 298). Yet, since at this stage in the novel's proceedings he is uncertain as to her gender and thus her identity, he wonders whether she is Apollo or Aphrodite, confessing that she possesses "the ambiguous and terrible beauty of the sphinx" (ibid.). Earlier in this erotic novel that toys with the idea of the androgyne, Mademoiselle de Maupin, alias Théodore de Sérannes, had been cast in the role of Rosalind in a fictional production of Shakespeare's *As You Like It*. In the course of rehearsals, d'Albert, playing Orlando, had every reason to feel bewildered as to the outcome of an adventure that would allow his "dreams of tenderness" to be realised, "were they to be transformed into this treacherous sphinx, with the doubtful smile, the ambiguous voice, before whom I stood without daring to explain the enigma!" "Take away that spark from me", he adds, "and I shall be more dismal and inanimate than the mummy imprisoned in bandelets of the oldest of the Pharaohs" (ibid., p. 247). References to the mummy and the pharaoh leave the reader in no doubt that the sphinx of d'Albert's fancy is Egyptian. The adjectives "treacherous", "doubtful" and "ambiguous" are indicative of a type of enigmatic transformation that to the young hero appears severely at odds with the unchanging quality of the inanimate mummy and, indeed, the world of ancient Egypt generally, a world whose extreme antiquity he underlines, in alluding not merely to the figure of the pharaoh, but to the "oldest" of the pharaohs.

Meïamoun, in contrast, is left in no doubt whatsoever as to Cleopatra's female nature. It is rather he who is presented as composite in the matter of gender. Gautier is specific on this point. In a description that anticipates the attributes of divinity and femininity later to be discerned in the character of Lord Evandale in *The Novel of the Mummy*, he writes:

> His look had the radiance and the fixity of the sparrow-hawk's, and serene majesty sat on his brow as on a marble pedestal; a noble disdain arched his upper lip, and swelled his nostrils like those of a spirited steed; though he had almost the delicate grace of a young girl, and though Dionysus, that effeminate god, had not a more rounded or polished chest, he hid under this soft exterior nerves of steel and Herculean strength, that singular privilege of certain ancient natures of uniting the beauty of the woman with the strength of the man. (Gautier, 1933, p. 42)

If Gautier in the 1830s was exploring the hermaphroditic in human nature, it is part of his project to cast the man as androgynous in "A night with Cleopatra" to complement a similar treatment of the woman in *Mademoiselle de Maupin*. In each work, the image of the sphinx is incorporated as part of that exploration. In the description of Meïamoun's face, we find the interplay of fluidity and fixity that is characteristic of the sphinx-nature. His nostrils swell like those of a "spirited steed", but his radiant look resembles that of the sparrow-hawk in its immobility.

The sparrow-hawk (*épervier*) is classed elsewhere in the story with the sphinx and other hybrids as belonging to a "family of horrible animals and gods with scaly wings, with hooked beaks, with tearing claws, always ready to seize you and devour you, if you pass the threshold of the temple, and if you raise the corner of the veil!" (Gautier, 1933, p. 37). The inclusion of this small hawk, a natural inhabitant of Eurasia and northern Africa, then as now, in a category otherwise consisting of fabulous hybrids appears somewhat incongruous; until we realise that the sparrow-hawk is a bird with impeccable credentials. In Egyptian mythology, Isis took the form of a bird of prey, hovering over the dead body of Osiris at a moment critical in the establishment of a permanent hegemony of the gods in Egypt, resuscitating him sufficiently with the current of air that her wings generated to allow her to conceive Horus. According to one interpretation, the bird whose form Isis assumed was the sparrow-hawk (Oakes & Gahlin, 2002, p. 311). Horus, the falcon god, came to be associated with many of the raptors that inhabited ancient Egypt. In addition to the sparrow-hawk, Gautier's preference, the list included the peregrine falcon, whose eye supplied the prototype for the *wadjet* symbol (Watterson, 1996, p. 97).

The sparrow-hawk, also mentioned in the poem "Paris obelisk", is in this story a sacred bird belonging to the family of guardians of the threshold of the temple and the veil of Isis. The identification of the motif of the sparrow-hawk with both Meïamoun (as already noted) and Cleopatra, who wears for her head-dress "a kind of very light gold helmet formed by the body and wings of the sacred sparrow-hawk" (Gautier, 1933, p. 35) is yet another indication of the affinity between the two characters. The bird possesses "yellow eyes that seem to look through you with their inquisitive regards, and to see beyond you things that cannot be told" (ibid., p. 37). A common emphasis on eyes brings Meïamoun and the sparrow-hawk into the same sphere of reference as the masterful lion and eagle, the fabulous sphinx, Cleopatra (alluded to in the story as "the Eye of Heaven") and her celestial counterpart, the "red, dripping sun which stares like the eye of a Cyclops" (ibid., p. 36).

Behind all these diverse references, unifying them as a master symbol, is the mythological representation of Horus or, more specifically, the "Eye of Horus" (the *wadjet* eye), given to Osiris to nourish him in the crisis of his resurrection (Wilkinson, 1992, p. 43; Lurker, 1982, p. 93).

Repeated allusions to the eyeball (prunelle) that either sees or fails to see are employed in "A Night with Cleopatra" to call attention to the motif of hiddenness that inheres in the concept of visualisation. The narrator, remarking that "Eagles can contemplate the sun without being dazzled", asks "what eyeball of diamond can be fixed with impunity on a beautiful woman, on a beautiful queen?" (Gautier, 1933, p. 44) The sun itself is described metaphorically as an "enflamed eyeball" in a sky of bronze that "has never yet [let fall] a single tear on the desolation of the earth", a dead sky which is "dried up like the mummies it covers" (ibid., p. 36), and Meïamoun, before he is emboldened to observe the naked queen from the covert where his burning eyeball gleams "yellow and phosphorescent like the eye of a crocodile or of a lion", had "scarcely dared to raise his eyes [to her], he who did not drop them before the yellow eyeballs of the lions" (ibid., p. 50). All these allusions to eyeballs occur during the hours of daylight. The final reference to the eyeball, however, comes at night in the concluding part of the narrative, where it serves to record—and yet to leave unrecorded—the moment when Meïamoun's forbidden desire for Cleopatra's love is eventually satisfied. At "the promise of approaching felicity", the reader is told,

> The shamefast stars looked no longer, their chaste golden eyeballs could not bear such a sight; the sky itself was hid, and a dome of inflamed mist covered the hall. (Ibid., p. 60)

Concerning the consummation that follows, we are merely informed that Cleopatra returned to seat herself near Meïamoun:

> The night wore on; the last of the black hours was about to fly away; a bluish glimmer entered with perplexed step among this tumult of red lights, like a moonbeam that falls on a furnace: the high arcades grew softly blue; day was appearing. (Ibid., pp. 60–61)

Such occlusion is unusual for Gautier. He is as forthright in his descriptions of heterosexual and lesbian lovemaking, in *Mademoiselle de Maupin* for example, as he is of the naked female body generally, but at this climactic moment in the narrative he resorts to a device familiar from Greek mythology: he introduces a mist to cover the libidinous activity of the divine Cleopatra (ibid., p. 61). The mist, it would appear, even acquires a characteristic of inflammation from the golden eyeballs of the stars, which, deprived of sight, become "chaste". The transition from night to day, which occurs in a single sentence, once Cleopatra has resumed her regal status, marks the passing of narrative occlusion and leads inevitably to the ill-fated end of Meïamoun's erotic adventure. Yet, whether that end is death or reprieve remains for a moment in the balance.

The Egyptian youth, acknowledging his acceptance of what he takes to be an inevitable termination to the night of pleasure, accepts from an Ethiopian slave the proffered vase of horn that contains a brew of effervescent poison. He casts a final look upon his sovereign as he raises the fatal cup to his lips. Seeing him about to drink, Cleopatra hesitates: "she was going to say, 'Live on to love me; I desire it—', when the blast of bugles was heard" (Gautier, 1933, p. 61). The fatal fanfare, announcing the arrival of Mark Antony, signals the ascendancy of historical actuality over the potentiality of myth. Even before the Roman general has had time to make his entrance, Meïamoun drinks and Cleopatra lets a single tear fall into the emptied vessel, "to join the melted pearl" (ibid.). This unique, pearl-like tear is the price that Cleopatra pays for her part in the evening's entertainment. Meïamoun had "[thrown] his life to his mistress in a last look" and the Egyptian queen had repaid him with "a burning tear, the only one she had shed in her life" (ibid.). The adventure ends, as it began, in the eye.

In Gautier's tale, Meïamoun is identified with the night both temporally and mythically. He first appears in the narrative as the sun is setting and he dies when a ray of sunlight falls upon his lover's brow. Viewed from the perspective of history, Meïamoun belongs simply to "one of Cleopatra's nights", but, regarded from the standpoint of myth, he may be seen as an epiphany of the god Osiris, who, according to ancient Egyptian belief, unites with Ra at the midpoint of his nightly journey, at the sixth hour, in an embrace that is a pledge for the continuance of life. Gautier substitutes a sexual encounter, reminiscent of the union of Isis and Osiris in which Horus was conceived, for a cosmic one. This account, unusually for Gautier, is shrouded in darkness. Meïamoun perishes, but Cleopatra, identified with the sun in its diurnal aspect, survives to greet the Roman general, her soul renewed and reinvigorated by contact with the representative of the night.

Sorrow and surprise are constituents of Gautier's sphinx complex. These two moods are repeatedly associated with the image of the sphinx in various situations and locations, even to the extent of an incidental remark he made about two sphinxes he saw in the city of Petersburg during his travels in Russia in 1858. But what the French author also demonstrates in his more sustained treatments of the topic is that this constellation of sorrow and surprise in the figure of the sphinx was grounded in a familiarity with the latest findings of nineteenth-century Egyptology. Decidedly, and very much in keeping with the cultural interests of the period, his sphinx was primarily Egyptian, not Greek. As a consequence, the sphinx was able to retain its mysterious and enigmatic aura, remaining blissfully innocent of the complex that was later to develop in connection with Oedipus.

## References

Freud, S. (1900a). *The Interpretation of Dreams. S. E., 4, 5.* London: Hogarth.

Gautier, T. (1852). Théodore Chassériau. *La Presse*, 25 May.

Gautier, T. (1858). *Le roman de la momie*. Paris: Hachette.

Gautier, T. (1867). *Voyage en Russie*. Paris: Charpentier.

Gautier, T. (1895). *Émaux et camées*. Paris: Charpentier & Fasquelle.

Gautier, T. (1900–03) *Travels in Russia. Belgium and Holland. A Day in London. The Complete Works of Théophile Gautier*. Vol. 7. S. C. de Sumichrast (Trans. & Ed.). London: Athenaeum.

Gautier, T. (1933). "A night with Cleopatra". L. Hearn (Trans.). In: E. Rhys (Ed.), F. C. Green (Intro.), *French Short Stories of the 19th and 20th Centuries* (pp. 31–62). London: Dent.

Gautier, T. (1981). *Mademoiselle de Maupin*. J. Richardson (Trans.). Harmondsworth: Penguin.

Goux, J. -J. (1993). *Oedipus, Philosopher*. C. Porter (Trans.). Stanford: Stanford University Press.

Jung, C. G. (1934). A review of the complex theory. In *C. W., 8* (2*nd* ed.): pp. 92–104/pars. 194–219. London: Routledge & Kegan Paul, 1969.

*Le Gastronome* (1831). Un repas au désert de l'Egypte. 24 March.

Lurker, M. (1982). *An Illustrated Dictionary of the Gods and Symbols of Ancient Egypt*. B. Cummings (Trans.). London: Thames and Hudson.

Oakes, L. & L. Gahlin (2002). *Ancient Egypt*. London: Hermes House.

Praz, M. (1933). *The Romantic Agony*. Oxford: Oxford University Press.

Tennant, P. E. (1975). *Théophile Gautier*. London: Athlone.
Watterson, B. (1996). *Gods of Ancient Egypt*. Thrupp: Sutton.
Wilde, O. (2007). *Portrait of Dorian Gray*. Norton Critical Edition. M. P. Gillespie (Ed.). New York: Norton.
Wilkinson, R. H. (1992). *Reading Egyptian Art: A Hieroglyphic Guide to Ancient Egyptian Painting and Sculpture*. London: Thames and Hudson.
Yeats, W. B. (1965). *The Collected Poems*. London: Macmillan.

# PART V

## ORPHEUS AND LITERATURE

*CHAPTER ELEVEN*

# From the archaic into the aesthetic: myth and literature in the "Orphic" Goethe

*Paul Bishop*

The archaic is the primal, the primordial, or (to use a favourite German prefix) the *Ur-*, but how does Goethe use the archaic, and what does it mean for him? To put it another way, does his late poem "Primal words. Orphic" (*Urworte. Orphisch*) really belong, as its title suggests it might, to the tradition of Orphic literature? In what sense would it be true to describe Goethe as an Orphic writer?[1]

Historically speaking, the doctrine of the cult of Orpheus represented a transitional stage from the naïve polytheism of the Homeric world, whatever form that belief might actually have taken (Veyne, 1983), to the more philosophical speculation of the fourth and fifth centuries BCE (Hoffmeister, 1930, p. 174).[2] Whilst rooted in the mother-cults of the Neolithic period and in the orgiastic cult traditions of the Middle East, Orphism initiated the process of moving away from nature by reflecting on nature, a process that resulted in the flowering of pre-Socratic thought (Wipf, 1974, p. 130). The Orphic Hymns—appearing in second to third century Greece, and addressed to various divine entities—represent the last lyrical expression of ancient Greece, bridging age-old tradition and the ethical values of a new epoch.[3]

That new epoch was characterised by the destruction of paganism and the triumph of Christianity.[4] In this period, the Orphic cult disappeared, along with the suppression of the pagan sites, but its doctrines resurfaced in the teachings of the Gnostics (Eliade, 1982, p. 371). Indeed, the iconography of Orphism is still alive and well in those paintings on the walls of the catacombs where Christ is depicted as the "good shepherd", but with facial characteristics typical of representations of Orpheus (Hiebel, 1961, p. 35). This persistence of the pagan under a veneer of the Christian perhaps explains the great revival of interest in Orphism that took place in the late eighteenth and early nineteenth centuries in the circles of German Romanticism, one of whose major preoccupations was the primal, the primordial, or the archaic.

In the writings of Novalis (1772–1801),[5] for instance, it is declared that "only when the philosopher appears as Orpheus will the whole [i.e., the whole of history] order itself in regular-general and higher-educated, significant masses—in true *sciences*" (Novalis, 1960–1968, vol. 3, p. 335). Inasmuch as he perceived the content of drama as "a process of transformation, purification, and reduction" (eine Verwandlung—ein Läuterungs, Reduktionsproceß),[6] Novalis has been regarded as a predecessor of Nietzsche in *The Birth of Tragedy* (*Die Geburt der Tragödie*) (1872). Then again, Friedrich Schlegel (1772–1829), who identified poetry with mythology—"The core, the center of poetry is to be found in mythology, and in the mysteries of the ancients"[7]—, may be considered the discoverer of the "primordial Orphic past" (orphische Vorzeit). This is indeed the title of a major section in his *History of the Poetry of the Greeks and Romans* (*Geschichte der Poesie der Griechen und Römer*) of 1798 (1958–2006, vol. 1, pp. 399–428; cf. Frank, 1982, p. 93). As Schlegel's approach to Orpheus in his writings on classical antiquity suggests, the figure of Orpheus and the meaning of the Orphic cult also came to the forefront of philological concerns.

In 1810–1812 Friedrich Creuzer (1771–1858), a classical philologist in Heidelberg, published the first edition of his massive, four-volume study, *Symbols and Mythology of the Ancient Peoples* (*Symbolik und Mythologie der alten Völker*) (1810–1812; second ed., 1819–1821, expanded with two additional volumes; third ed., 1837–1842), which stimulated a major debate on the meaning of myth (Howald, 1926). Creuzer came under attack from numerous quarters: from Johann Heinrich Voss (1751–1826), who published a study entitled *Antisymbolik* (1824; repub. 1994); from Christian August Lobeck (1781–1860) in his *Aglaophamus* (1829); from the Göttingen philologist, Karl Otfried Müller (1797–1840), in two extensive reviews in the *Göttinger Gelehrte Anzeigen*, entitled "Friedrich Creuzer's

Symbolik und Mythologie" (1821) and "Symbolik und Mythologie der alten Völker besonders der Griechen, von Dr. Friedrich Creuzer" (1825) (1847–1848, vol. 2, pp. 3–20 & 25–30); and from the Leipzig philologist, Johann Gottfried Hermann (1772–1848), in *On the Nature and Treatment of Mythology: A Letter to Creuzer* (*Ueber das Wesen und die Behandlung der Mythologie: Ein Brief an Herrn Hofrat Creuzer*) (1819; extracted in Kerényi, 1967, pp. 59–61).

On Creuzer's account, myth was subordinated to the symbol, to the embodiment of thought and sense perception (Frank, 1982, p. 91). This symbolic core expanded, through time, into the diversity of myths, reflecting different cultures. Thus behind the multiplicity of myth lay "a universal natural symbolism and a mythic, poetic, and at times ecstatic religion" (Blok, 1994, p. 30; Blok, 1998, p. 77). Whereas, for Creuzer, the work of myth lay in the transposition of "what has been thought" into "what has happened" (*das Gedachte in ein Geschehen umzusetzen*) (1819–1821, vol. 1, p. 99), one of his opponents in Göttingen, Müller, argued that myth contains "what has been thought *and* what has happened" (1825, p. 70; cf. Blok, 1994, p. 39), thereby altering the pre-eminence accorded by Creuzer to the symbol. For along with that pre-eminence, so Müller (and Creuzer's other opponents) felt, went an unwarranted emphasis on the irrational, on the religious,—on the "mystical". (In fact, shortly after his appointment to Göttingen, Müller wrote in a letter to his parents that "one has to be very careful here not to be deemed a mystic, for the old bunch of Göttingen professors mixes every possible *Naturphilosophie*, romantic poetry, new theology, higher historical analysis, symbolic mythology etc. in one bowl and then pours it all right down the sink" [Letter of 21 November 1819; Müller, 1908, pp. 54–55; cited in Blok, 1994, p. 33].) Unwarranted, that is, as far as these critics were concerned: by contrast, Friedrich Wilhelm Joseph Schelling (1775–1854) welcomed Creuzer's approach to myth (Burkert, 1980, p. 163; Cassirer, 1955, p. 15).

A further disagreement on the nature of myth took place between Creuzer and Hermann, which led to the publication of their correspondence on the issue in question: the works of Hesiod and Homer (Hermann & Creuzer, 1818).[8] Yet however much Hermann may have disagreed with Creuzer, he shared his fascination with Orpheus, editing a collection of fragmentary texts relating to his cult under the title *Orphica* (Hermann, 1805; reprinted 1971). Now, Creuzer's and Hermann's *Letters*, together with a collection of treatises on classical archaeology by the Danish archaeologist Jörgen Zoega (1755–1809), translated from Latin into German by Friedrich Gottlieb Welcker (1784–1868), professor of archaeology at Göttingen (Zoega, 1817),[9] constituted Goethe's chief source for his knowledge of Orphism. He was also well aware of the controversy surrounding Creuzer, whom he met on several occasions during his visit to Heidelberg in 1815.

As the Austrian Germanist and anthroposophist Friedrich Hiebel (1903–1989) has pointed out, there exist in the popular imagination two entirely different images of Goethe (1961, p. 20). On the one hand, there is the Olympian Goethe, the "great pagan", as Heine recalled his contemporaries knew him,[10] the Apollonian Goethe, the man of the Weimar court, the state-minister, the admirer of Greco-Roman classicism. We might call this figure, if somewhat simplistically, the "classical" Goethe or (more tendentiously) the "bourgeois" Goethe. This is the image of Goethe in the engraving on the mantelpiece in the professor's house that so disturbs Harry Haller in *Steppenwolf* of 1927 (Hesse, 1965, pp. 95–99). On the other hand, another image enjoys a certain currency, in particular among anthroposophists and some analytical psychologists: this is the "mystic" Goethe, the esoteric Goethe—Goethe as Orphic magician, as alchemist, as Gnostic, as Neoplatonist, as *Naturphilosoph*, as the wise prophet. Friedrich von Müller, for example, provides an account of how the sixty-nine year old Goethe used his role as a Merlin-like figure to excuse himself from a picnic: "'Let me go, my children', he said, suddenly rising from his seat, 'let me hasten in solitude to my stones down there; for after such conversations it befits the old Merlin to re-acquaint himself with the primordial elements [*mit den Urelementen*]'"—after which Müller and his fellow picnickers "watched him for a long time, while he, robed in his light-gray coat, descended solemnly into the valley, studying this rock, or this plant, as he went, testing the former with his mineralogical hammer", until "the hills threw longer shadows, in which, like a ghostly apparition, he gradually disappeared" (Biedermann [Ed.], 1909–1911, vol. 2, p. 420).[11]

There is something to be said for both sets of images; to discern the truth, however, we have to distinguish substance from rhetoric, and genuine argumentation from techniques of self-presentation. In the end, Goethe's attitude to the Orphic cults is a complex one, and is bound up with the preoccupations of his cultural politics.[12] For the debate about ancient Greece in Germany in the eighteenth century was,[13] as it became again in the twentieth,[14] largely a means to discuss other issues of contemporary relevance. The Orphic persists as part of the collective (cultural) unconscious, so to speak, of Western thought and literature. For an interest in Orphism persists in the twentieth century among such scholars as Otto Kern (1863–1942) (1920),[15] G. R. S. Mead (1863–1933) (1896), W. K. C. Guthrie (1906–1981) (1935; revised, 1952), Walter Wili (1900–1975) (1955) and Carl Kerényi (1897–1973) (1937 & 1950), not to mention C. G. Jung (1875–1961). In his groundbreaking work, *Transformations and Symbols of the Libido* (*Wandlungen und Symbole der Libido*; published as *Psychology of the Unconscious*) (1911–1912), as well as in its subsequent revision as *Symbols of Transformation* (*Symbole der Wandlung*) (1952), Jung discerned in Mithraism, in Christianity, in the Eleusinian mysteries (particularly those elements preserved in Orphic legends), and in the Native American epic of Hiawatha (as recounted by Longfellow) a common pattern; or, to use his jargon, an archetype (1911–12; 1911–12/1952). Underlying all these accounts and traditions, Jung argued (1911–12, para. 537; cf. 1911–12/1952, para. 528), was the archetypal structure of descent and (re)birth. For instance, in the Orphic account of Iakchos (or Dionysos Liknites, i.e., the Fan-Bearer or the Winnower) recounted in the forty-sixth Orphic Hymn, Iakchos is reared in the underworld, after which he awakes in the *liknon* or winnowing-basket:

> Licknitan Bacchus, bearer of the vine,
> Thee I invoke to bless these rites divine:
> Florid and gay, of Nymphs the blossom bright,
> And of fair Venus, Goddess of delight.
> 'Tis thine mad footsteps with mad Nymphs to beat,
> Dancing thro' groves with lightly leaping feet:
> From Jove's high counsels nurst by Proserpine,
> And born the dread of all the pow'rs divine.
> Come, blessed God, regard thy suppliant's voice,
> Propitious come, and in these rites rejoice.
> (Taylor [Trans.], 1896, p. 100)

Drawing on, among other sources, the account of the Eleusinian mysteries offered around 390 CE by St Asterius, Bishop of Amasea, Plutarch's observation that the Magi offered sacrifices to Ahriman, Lucan's narrative of the descent of the magician Mithrobarzanes, and Clement of Alexandria's record of the mystic *synthema* (confession) of the

Eleusinian initiate, Jung detected an identical psycho-anthropological motif: "The plough is of well-known phallic meaning; the furrow of the field is personified … as woman. The psychology of this idea is that of a coitus, referred back to the presexual stage" (Jung, 1911–12, para. 536; cf. 1911–12/1952, para. 527). Indeed, "the descent into the earth is also the symbol of the mother's womb, and was a widespread conception under the form of cave worship" (Jung, 1911–12, para. 537; cf. 1911–12/1952, para. 528). Jung was particularly attracted to the idea in the fifty-second Orphic Hymn that Bacchus was "virginlike" (*upokholpie*, "lying in the lap" or "he who is in the vagina or womb") (Taylor [Trans.], 1896, p. 110), pointing to a continuity between, on the one hand, the cry in the Eleusinian mysteries that "the great goddess has borne a divine boy, Brimo has borne Brimos!" and the Athenian custom of holding up before celebrants of the Epoptia a mown stalk of wheat,[16] and, on the other, the Christmas message that "unto us a son is born" (Jung, 1911–12, para. 547; cf. 1911–12/1952, para. 530).[17] Jung expounded these parallels as follows: "The mystic dies, figuratively, like the seed corn, grows again and comes to the corn harvest. […] The believer descends into the grave, in order to rise from the dead with the hero. […] It is the magic charm of rebirth" (Jung, 1911–12, para. 547; cf. 1911–12/1952, para. 536).[18]

Elsewhere in this work, Jung equated his new conception of libido with Schopenhauer's notion of the will (1911–12, para. 223; cf. para. 212)—as well as with the Platonic-cum-Hesodian figure of Eros and the Orphic figure of Phanes, the "shining one", whom Jung assimilated with Priapus, with the Theban figure of Dionysos Lysios (the Liberator, Destroyer, Releaser, Purificator), and with the Indian god of love, Kâma (1911–12, para. 223; cf. 1911–12/1952, para. 198). In his *Red Book*, work on which commenced in 1913 and continued until 1928, Jung deployed—in the full knowledge of their significance, which he had explored in *Transformations and Symbols of the Libido*—a number of Orphic motifs (Stein, 2012, pp. 291–294). For instance, in an illustration completed in April 1919, Jung gives to the image of the divine child the name of ΦΑΝΗΣ (Phanes), "because he is the newly appearing god" (Jung, 2009, p. 301).[19] As the editor of *The Red Book*, Sonu Shamdasani, notes (ibid., pp. 301–302, fn. 211), Jung's *Black Books* contain a sequence of incantations, themselves reminiscent, as Murray Stein has pointed out (2012, pp. 291–292), of the sixth Orphic Hymn to Protogonus (Taylor [Trans.], 1896, pp. 18–20). Furthermore, in the *Systema munditotius*, a schematic representation in which Jung summarised his world-view from these years, the figure of Phanes appears at the top of the diagram (Jung, 2009, p. 364).

In contrast to the mystical schematisation one finds in Jung in this crucial period of his intellectual development, the background to Goethe's image of the ancient Greeks was largely informed by the rationalism of the Enlightenment. This rationalist view of the ancient Greeks—reflected in the accounts of Greek mythology by Benjamin Hederich (1675–1748) and by l'abbé Antoine Banier (1673–1741) in *Gründliches Lexikon mythologicum* (1724; revised 1770) and *Mythologie et les fables expliquées par l'histoire* (1738–1740) respectively, as well as the sceptical approach to philology found in the work of Christian Gottlob Heyne (1729–1812) and Friedrich August Wolf (1759–1824)—culminated in the major canonical text of German Enlightenment classicism, *History of the Art of Antiquity* (*Geschichte der Kunst des Altertums* (1764) by Johann Joachim Winckelmann (1717–1768).

From Winckelmann, Goethe took over the emphasis on the Homeric world of the Olympian gods, a mixture of (in Nietzsche's terms) the Apollonian and the Dionysian, "a noble simplicity and a silent grandeur" (eine edle Einfalt und eine stille Grösse). In his essay entitled "Winckelmann and his age" (1805), Goethe expressed the ideal of human being as embodied in the work of the classicist as follows: "When our nature functions soundly as a whole, when we feel that the world of which we are a part is a huge, beautiful, admirable and worthy whole, when this harmony gives us a pure and uninhibited delight, then the universe, if it were capable of emotion, would rejoice at having reached its goal and admire the crowning glory of its own evolution" (Goethe, 1986, p. 101). In turn, this line of thought poses the aesthetic question: "What purpose would those countless suns and planets and moons serve, those stars and milky ways, comets and nebulae, those created and evolving worlds"—what purpose would there be *at all*, "if a happy human being did not ultimately emerge to enjoy existence?" (ibid.).

For Goethe, "the ultimate goal of evolving nature is the beautiful human being" (das letzte Produkt der sich immer steigernden Natur ist der schöne Mensch) (Goethe, 1986, p. 103). Nietzsche would agree with this view, and speak of the *Übermensch*. The artistic representation of this ideal was the statue, made of gold and ivory for the Temple of Zeus in Olympia, by Phidias, the Athenian sculptor of the fifth century BCE. The following conviction, Goethe assures us, seized all those who saw

Phidias's statue of the Olympian Zeus: "A god had become a human being in order to make a human being into a god" (Der Gott war zum Menschen geworden, um den Menschen zum Gott zu erheben) (ibid., p. 105).

Yet Goethe, in the wake of his study of Winckelmann, and following the death of Schiller, had become aware of something he found uncomfortable in the world of the ancient Greeks. Thanks to a personal meeting with Friedrich Creuzer, Goethe encountered the new vision of the Greeks that was beginning to evolve in Romantic circles, and so, as Hiebel puts it, into the "garden" of Greek humanism, built on the foundations of Winckelmann's classicism, there now came, via recent research into myth and oriental mystery-cults, a "taste" for the "secret" meaning of ancient Greece, for its night-side, for its "Orphic, Dionysian darknesses" (die Orphischen dionysische Finsternisse), as Goethe called them in a letter to Carl Ludwig von Knebel (1744–1834) (Hiebel, 1961, p. 209). Goethe's move towards a more complex understanding of ancient Greece took yet another step forward in 1817, when Creuzer sent Goethe a copy of his recently published correspondence with Hermann.[20]

Hermann and Creuzer's co-authored book, *Letters on Homer and Hesiod, especially on his "Theogony"* (*Briefe über Homer und Hesodius vorzüglich über die Theogonie*) (1818), was concerned with the relation of the Orphic religion to mythology. At the core of their dispute lay the so-called "Homeric Hymns"—a collection of texts, traditionally attributed to Homer or to Hesiod, and dedicated (like the Orphic Hymns) to a variety of deities, although (unlike the Orphic Hymns) it is doubtful whether their function was devotional or liturgical. The question was: Were these texts evidence of a later, mystical tradition or of an ancient, primordial religion that pre-dated even Homer?[21] In turn, this question raised another: Was the ancient world a source of rational order and beauty, or should it be understood irrationally—theologically—, even mystically? In his letter to Creuzer of 1 October 1817, Goethe thanked him for, as he wrote, "having forced me to look down into a region, against which I otherwise tend nervously to be on my guard" (Goethe, 1962–1967, vol. III, p. 401).

Goethe's interest in the Orphics had been stirred. Within a week or so, he was reading Welcker's edition of Zoega's treatises (the entry in Goethe's diary for 7 October 1817 records this fact, noting Zoega's interest in "Orphic concepts") (Goethe, 1887–1919, vol. III.6, p. 119).[22] According to Zoega (who cited the authority of Necepsos, the ancient Egyptian king who invented astrology, and Ambrosius Theodosius

Macrobius (395–423 BCE), a Neoplatonic philosopher), in the Orphic tradition four "holy words" depicted the four deities that attend the birth of the individual: Δαίμων (daimon), Τύχη (tyche), Ἔρως (eros), and Ἀνάγκη (ananke). To these, Zoega noted, there should be added a fifth word, a fifth deity—Ἐλπίς (elpis).[23] This information had a direct impact on Goethe and on the composition of "Primal words. Orphic". The relevant passage from Macrobius reads as follows:

> The Egyptians also maintain that the attributes of the caduceus illustrate the generation, or "genesis" as it is called, of mankind; for they say that four deities are present to preside over a man's birth: his Genius *(daimon)*, Fortune *(tyche)*, Love *(eros)*, and Necessity *(ananke)*. By the first two they understand the sun and the moon; for the sun, as the source of the breath of life and of heat and of light, is the creator and the guardian of a man's life and is therefore believed to be the Genius, or god *(daimon)*, of a newborn child; the moon is Fortune *(tyche)*, since she has charge of the body, and the body is at the mercy of the fickleness of change; the kiss of the serpents is the symbol of Love *(eros)*; and the knot is the symbol of Necessity *(ananke)*. (Macrobius, 1969, pp. 135–136)[24]

The French intellectual historian Pierre Hadot (1922–2010) has described Macrobius's *Saturnalia*, mediated by Zoega, as nothing less than "the source of Goethe's poem" (Hadot, 2008, p. 174). For all his scepticism about the historical Orphic religion itself, Goethe found himself to have been inspired by its hymnic tradition and by its ἱερόι λόγοι, its four "holy words", which Hermann had discussed at some length in his correspondence with Creuzer, and to which Zoega had argued that a fifth should be added. The fruit of this inspiration is Goethe's late, great poem—first published in *On Morphology* (*Zur Morphologie*) in 1817[25]—entitled "Primal words. Orphic" (*Urworte. Orphisch*). This work merits citing here in its entirety:[26]

*ΔΑΙΜΩΝ, Daimon*

As on that day, when you were given to the earth,
The sun stood in salutation of the planets,
So then and ever since you have been flourishing
According to the same law from the start.
Thus you must be, yourself you can't escape,

Thus declared the sibyls, thus the prophets;
And no time and no power can destroy
Determined form that, ever living, grows.

*ΤΥΧΗ, Chance*

Around this stern limit, though, can slip
Something changing, that with and round us changes;
You don't remain alone, you seek to be sociable
And behave indeed as others do behave:
That's how it is in life: some you lose, some win,
It's all a game you've got to learn to play.
Already the circle of the years is fully formed,
The lamp awaits the flame that will ignite it.

*ΕΡΩΣ, Love*

And here it comes!—It swoops down from heaven
Whence in ancient wilderness it flew,
It sweeps along on its airy feathers
Round head and breast through springtime's day,
It seems about to leave, then back it comes again,
A pleasure turns to pain, so sweet and terrible.
Many a heart will float away into the universal,
Yet the noblest dedicates itself to the One.

*ΑΝΑΓΚΗ, Necessity*

Then there it is again, as the stars would have it:
Condition and the law; and every will
Is only willing, because we should do it,
And in front of the will mere caprice falls silent.
What most we love is pushed from the heart,
To the harsh "Must" are reconciled will and whim.
Thus we seem to be free, for after all those years
We're more up against it than we were at the start.

*ΕΛΠΙΣ, Hope*

But this limitation's, this iron wall's
Repulsive gate can still be unbolted,
However like a cliff it may well stand!

For something's moving, light and unrestricted:
From heavy clouds, and mists, and rainy showers
It lifts us, with it, giving us its wings;
You know it well enough, it streaks through every region:
A wingbeat—and behind us lie the aeons!

*DAIMON, Dämon*

Wie an dem Tag, der dich der Welt verliehen,
Die Sonne stand zum Gruße der Planeten,
Bist alsobald und fort und fort gediehen
Nach dem Gesetz, wonach du angetreten.
So mußt du sein, dir kannst du nicht entfliehen,
So sagten schon Sibyllen, so Propheten;
Und keine Zeit und keine Macht zerstückelt
Geprägte Form, die lebend sich entwickelt.

*TYCHÊ, das Zufällige*

Die strenge Grenze doch umgeht gefällig
Ein Wandelndes, das mit und um uns wandelt;
Nicht einsam bleibst du, bildest dich gesellig,
Und handelst wohl so, wie ein andrer handelt:
Im Leben ist's bald hin-, bald widerfällig,
Es ist ein Tand und wird so durchgetandelt.
Schon hat sich still der Jahre Kreis geründet,
Die Lampe harrt der Flamme, die entzündet.

*ERÔS, Liebe*

Die bleibt nicht aus!—Er stürzt vom Himmel nieder,
Wohin er sich aus alter Öde schwang,
Er schwebt heran auf luftigem Gefieder
Um Stirn und Brust den Frühlingstag entlang,
Scheint jetzt zu fliehn, vom Fliehen kehrt er wieder,
Da wird ein Wohl im Weh, so süß und bang.
Gar manches Herz verschwebt im Allgemeinen,
Doch widmet sich das edelste dem Einen.

*ANANKÊ, Nötigung*

Da ist's denn wieder, wie die Sterne wollten:
Bedingung und Gesetz; und aller Wille

Ist nur ein Wollen, weil wir eben sollten,
Und vor dem Willen schweigt die Willkür stille;
Das Liebste wird vom Herzen weggescholten,
Dem harten Muß bequemt sich Will und Grille.
So sind wir scheinfrei denn nach manchen Jahren
Nur enger dran, als wir am Anfang waren.

*ELPIS, Hoffnung*

Doch solcher Grenze, solcher ehrnen Mauer
Höchst widerwärt'ge Pforte wird entriegelt,
Sie stehe nur mit alter Felsendauer!
Ein Wesen regt sich leicht und ungezügelt:
Aus Wolkendecke, Nebel, Regenschauer
Erhebt sie uns, mit ihr, durch sie beflügelt,
Ihr kennt sie wohl, sie schwärmt durch alle Zonen;
Ein Flügelschlag—und hinter uns Äonen!

In the Orphic Hymnary, as it has come down to us, Goethe would have found hymns dedicated "To the Daimon" (daimon), "To Fortune" (tyche), and "To Love" (eros),[27] while from the Orphic-Macrobian tradition, as he had found it in Zoega, Goethe took over directly the five "holy words" that stand as the titles for the five stanzas of his poem: ΔΑΙΜΩΝ, *Dämon* ("Daimon"); ΤΥΧΗ, *das Zufällige* ("Chance"); ΕΡΩΣ, *Liebe* ("Love"); ΑΝΑΓΚΗ, *Nötigung* ("Necessity"); and ΕΛΠΙΣ, *Hoffnung* ("Hope"). Originally, when "Primal words. Orphic" was first published in *On Morphology*, the headings of the stanzas were in Greek alone. But when the text was republished in *Kunst und Althertum* in 1820,[28] Goethe transliterated the Greek, added translations, and provided a commentary (1948–1960; 1981, vol. 1, pp. 403–407).

In this commentary, Goethe tells us that his poem tried "to compress, to present in a poetic-and-compendium-like, laconic manner" what had been "handed down from old and new Orphic doctrines" (Goethe, 1948–1960; 1981, vol. I, p. 403). It offers, then, a kind of quintessence of Orphism, new and old—an exercise, in other words, in cultural memory (Schmidt, 2006, p. 27),[29] but one with existential implications. As far from being an academic exercise in historical philology as it is from being as "a masterpiece of Orphic poetry", arising out an unconscious experience of illumination,[30] the poem is intended to be an exposition of living wisdom—"primordial, magic utterances on the fate of humans",[31] a "primordial, concentrated depiction of human fate".[32] In this text he had sought, Goethe told Boisserée, to "re-quintessentialise" a "diffuse antiquity" and turn it into a "cup that refreshes the heart"; to "freshen up" these "moribund ways of speaking" with his own "living experience" (die abgestorbenen Redensarten aus eigener Erfahrungs-Lebendigkeit wieder anfrisch[en]).[33]

His own "Orphica",[34] as he referred to the poem, represents the sum of experience of an older man, whose mature age determines the perspective from which it was written (Schmidt, 2006, p. 28). This emphasis on experience—on experience gained through life—is central to Goethe's intentions. Rather than with the Orphic mysteries of ancient time, his concern is with the "mysteries and wonders" among which, he told Eckermann on 7 October 1827, we are all groping: "We all walk in mysteries. We do not know what is stirring in the atmosphere that surrounds us, nor how it is connected with our own spirit" (Eckermann, 1998, pp. 233–234). Thus, rather than offering an initiation into the Orphic ancient mysteries, his poem uncovers the mysteriousness of life itself.

A few months after completing "Primal words. Orphic", in an important letter written to Sulpiz Boisserée on 16 January 1818, Goethe was to lament how, in his view, the approach to antiquity pioneered by Winckelmann had been abandoned. This abandonment was, he believed, a matter for great regret, because "Winckelmann's path to reach the artistic concept" had been "entirely the right one" (Goethe, 1962–1967, vol. III, p. 413). Instead, so Goethe went on to complain, "contemplation turned into interpretation, and eventually lost itself in misinterpretation; whoever did not know how to look properly, began to delude himself, and so one became lost in the distances of Egypt and India, when one had the best right at hand in front of one"—in other words, in classical Greece (ibid.). Already Zoega, Goethe continued, "began to wobble", and from that point on, "one had to suffer the unholy Dionysian mysteries"; until, in turn, Creuzer and then Welcker "deprive[d] us daily more and more of the great advantages of the delightful multiplicity of the Greeks and the dignified unity of the Israelites" (ibid.). By contrast, Hermann in Leipzig was, he maintained, "our real champion" (unser eigenster Vorfechter) (ibid.); Goethe praised in particular the fifth letter in his exchange with Creuzer, and Hermann's treatise *On the Mythology of Ancient Greece* (*De mythologia Graecorum antiquissima*) (1817) (Hermann & Creuzer, 1818, pp. 56–87; Hermann, 1817).

In a sense, Goethe was uninterested in who—Creuzer or Hermann—was, historically speaking, right about Orphism. What mattered, rather, was which interpretation—Creuzer's theological, or Hermann's rationalistic approach—was, as he put it, "critically-Hellenically patriotic", and it turned out to be Hermann's, because "from his development and from his hypothesis there is so infinitely more to be learnt than I have rarely found in so few pages to be the case" (Goethe, 1962–1967, vol. III, p. 413).

So the real question was: Whose version of antiquity, Creuzer's or Hermann's, promoted the aesthetic ideal that Goethe believed to be the true one? His rejection of Creuzer can make Goethe sound all very Apollonian. Yet there is another side to Goethe's interest, too. For Goethe, it is true, realised that one had to abandon the rationalist, Enlightenment version of the ancient Greeks, as formulated by Winckelmann, which had downplayed and neglected the role of the mystery cults. But Goethe refused simply to adopt from Creuzer, and from likeminded Romantics, an interpretation of those mystery cults which made them central to their understanding of the ancient world. Rather, one must read the situation as follows: Goethe decided to go his own way, developing, in the quarter of a century or so following his study of Winckelmann and the death of Schiller, his own individual path of Orphic mysticism (Hiebel, 1961, p. 214). In Goethe's view, another researcher in this area, the poet, playwright, and architect of German classicism, Christoph Martin Wieland (1733–1813), had been right to flee "those dark secrets" of the ancient mystery cults, but he also believed Wieland to have been equally right to recognise that "precisely under these, perhaps rather strange, covers, higher concepts had been introduced for the first time to crude, sensuous human beings, and, by means of *intuitive symbols*, powerful, illuminating ideas had been awoken" (Goethe, 1887–1919, vol. I.36, p. 344).[35] Here, then, we find the fundamental significance for Goethe (as for those, such as J. J. Bachofen [1815–1887] or C. G. Jung, who followed in his wake) of the symbol as a cognitive device.

In his study of the history of the conceptualisation and representation of Nature—her allegorical personification as Isis or Artemis, and the notion of "unveiling" or discovering her "secrets"—Hadot sets up a distinction between a "Promethean" attitude to Nature and an "Orphic" attitude (Hadot, 2006, pp. 95–96). The former is characterised by a violent, intrusive, and aggressive approach, and by "audacity, boundless curiosity, the will to power, and the search for utility" (ibid., pp. 101–51; p. 96); in contrast, the latter is marked by a more thoughtful, respectful, even seductive approach (ibid., pp. 155–210). If Prometheus represents the methods of science and technology, Orpheus represents the methods of aesthetic contemplation (ibid., p. 211)—methods, moreover, which Hadot considers to be preeminent in Goethe's scientific studies.[36] That what, at first sight, appears in Goethe to be mystical might, in fact, be aesthetic, is something that the German Romantic painter and physiologist Carl Gustav Carus (1789–1869) seems to have understood. In his *Nine Letters on Landscape Painting* (*Neun Briefe über Landschaftsmalerei*) (1831), he wrote (with reference to Goethe's poem "In honour of Howard" [*Zu Howards Ehrengedächtnis*]): "Art appears as the very peak of science, it becomes—as it clearly perceives and gracefully veils the secrets of science—in the true sense *mystical* or, as Goethe also called it: *orphic*" (Carus, [no date], p. 52) .... In this precise sense, then, Goethe is indeed an Orphic writer.

## Notes

1. The immediate research context of this paper is my recent work, undertaken in collaboration with Alan Cardew of the University of Essex, on the notion of the archaic (Bishop, 2012b; Cardew, 2012) as well as my study of Goethe's late poem, "Primal words. Orphic" (*Urworte. Orphisch*) (Bishop, 2012a).
2. For further discussion of the cult of Orpheus, see Mead, 1896; Kern, 1920; Guthrie, 1935; Kerényi, 1937 & 1950; and Wili, 1955. For a general discussion of the religious background formed by ancient Greek mystery cults, see Cosmopoulos (Ed.), 2003; Larson, 2007; and Bowden, 2010. The influence of the Orphic cult on Platonic thought is discussed in Kingsley, 1995, pp. 112–132.
3. Thus the commentary in Ebener (Ed.), 1976, p. 596. For further discussion, see Athanassakis (Ed.), 1977; and West, 1983.
4. For discussion of this period, see Fox, 1986, 2006; Freeman, 2002; and Cameron, 2011.
5. See Strauss, 1971, pp. 27–49. For further discussion, see Sewell, 1961; McGahey, 1994; Dawson, 2000; Bernstock, 2006; and Wroe, 2011.
6. "Poësie", §44 ["Logologische Fragmente", II], in Novalis, 1960–1968, vol. 2, p. 535. See Hiebel, 1948.
7. *Athenäum*, III, 18, 96; cited in Strauss, 1971, p. 20.
8. Although the book was dated to 1818, it was actually published in 1817.
9. For further discussion of Zoega and Welcker, see Dietze, 1977, p. 25 n. 29.

10. See *The Romantic School*, book 1; Heine, 1976, p. 48.
11. Unkind critics have spoken of the "creation of an aura" (*Auratisierung*) of the person of Goethe (see Bürger, 1977), but for a more sympathetic presentation of the elderly Goethe, see Eduard Spranger's essay "Goethe als Greis" of 1932 (Spranger, 1967, pp. 318–349).
12. For further discussion, see Grumach, 1949; Schwinge, 1986; and Schmidt, 2002.
13. For further discussion, see Butler, 1935; and Trevelyan, 1941.
14. For further discussion, see the articles collected in Gildenhard & Ruehl (Eds.), 2003.
15. This work includes a contribution by Josef Strzygowski (1862–1941) (Kern, 1920, pp. 58–66).
16. In his *Visions* Seminars of 1930–1934, Jung related the Eleusinian mysteries to the idea that "if we do not submit to the pains of the task, we shall not reap our reward when the time of harvest is come" (Jung, 1998, vol. 1, pp. 59–60).
17. Indeed, in *Transformations and Symbols of the Libido* Jung takes this epithet, *upokholpie* to mean that "the god enters into man as if through the female genitals" (Jung, 1991, para. 547). In his seminar on Nietzsche's *Zarathustra* and in *Symbols of Transformation*, Jung returned to this idea, found in Clement of Alexandria's *Protrepticus* (or "Exhortation to the Greeks") of "the god through the lap", associated with the Mysteries of Sabazios (Jung, 1967, para. 530; Jung, 1989, vol. 2, pp. 1061–1062).
18. As well as reflecting his interest in mysticism, Jung's emphasis on rebirth seeks to reactivate an ancient philosophical tradition; for further discussion of that tradition, see Uždavinys, 2008.
19. Cf. image [113] on p. 113 of the facsimile of the original manuscript of *The Red Book*.
20. In the wake of his reading of this correspondence, Goethe drew up a schematic historical outline, under the title "Epochs of the Spirit" (*Geistes-Epochen*). This short text, published in *Über Kunst und Alterthum* (vol. 1, no. 3) in 1817, divides intellectual history into six epochs: the Primordial Age (Urzeit), the Age of Poetry, the Age of Theology, the Age of Philosophy, the Age of Prose, and finally—and pessimistically—the Age of Dissolution (Goethe, 1948–1960; 1981, vol. 12, pp. 298–300). For further discussion of this text, see Bergstraesser, 1948.
21. See Dietze, 1977, p. 24. For the texts in question, see Hesiod, 1982, pp. 285–463.
22. In his conversation with his secretary, the philologist Friedrich Wilhelm Riemer, on 10 May 1806, Goethe observed that, in earlier centuries, "the great ideas of life" had been expressed in "intuitions of fantasy", that is, "in figures, in gods"; whereas, by contrast, we (the moderns) express them in "concepts" (Biedermann [Ed.], 1909–1911, vol. 1, p. 409).

23. Georg Zoega, "ΑΓΑΘΗΙ ΤΥΧΗΙ: Tyche und Nemesis", in Zoega, 1817, pp. 32–55 (esp. pp. 34–40, 46 and 52); see Macrobius, *Saturnalia*, book 1, Chapter Nineteen, §16-§18, in Macrobius, 1969, pp. 134–136; cited in Borinski, 1910, pp. 2 and 7.
24. Macrobius, *Saturnalia*, book 1, Chapter Nineteen, §17-§18; in Macrobius, 1969, pp. 135–136. This passage is cited in Welcker's edition of Zoega's *Abhandlungen*, "ΑΓΑΘΗΙ ΤΥΧΗΙ: Tyche und Nemesis" (Zoega, 1817, pp. 39–40).
25. See *Zur Morphologie*, vol. 1, no. 2 (1820), 97–99.
26. The poem is cited here in German from Goethe, 1948–1960; 1981, vol. 1, pp. 359–60; the translation, which does not attempt to reproduce Goethe's rhyme scheme, is my own.
27. *The Mystical Hymns of Orpheus*, nos 73, 72 and 58 (Taylor [Trans.], 1896, pp. 141, 139–140 and 117–120).
28. See *Über Kunst und Alterthum*, vol. 2, no. 3 (1820), 66–78.
29. See Assmann, 1992, who in turn draws on the notion of a collective memory, proposed by the French philosopher and sociologist Maurice Halbwachs (1877–1945) (Halbwachs, 1950).
30. Thus the claim in du Bos, 1949, pp. 33 and 42–43; cited in Dietze, 1977, p. 14.
31. Letter to Sulpiz Boisserée of 21 May 1818; Goethe, 1887–1919, vol. IV.29, p. 180.
32. Letter to C. G. D. Nees von Esenbeck of 25 May 1818; Goethe, 1887–1919, vol. IV.29, p. 185.
33. Letter to Sulpiz Boisserée of 16 July 1818; Goethe, 1962–1967, vol. 3, p. 435. For further discussion, see Kunisch, 1991, p. 21. At this point in his letter, Goethe refers to a legend—deriving from an Eastern version of the Alexander romance and involving Alexander the Great and the Arabic sage, Al-Khidr—about how a dried fish is thrown into the rejuvenating pool of the water of life, and swims away happily (Goethe, 1962–1967, vol. 3, pp. 435–436), and the sentiment is summed up well in Schiller's elegiac distich: "Believe me, it is no tale, the stream of eternal youth / Really does flow; you ask—where? In the poetic art" (Glaubt mir, es ist kein Märchen, die Quelle der Jugend, sie rinnet / Wirklich und immer, ihr fragt wo? In der dichtenden Kunst) (Schiller, 2004, p. 432).
34. Letter to Boisserée, 16 July 1818; Goethe, 1962–1967, vol. 3, p. 435.
35. "Zu brüderlichem Andenken Wielands" (1813), Goethe's commemorative speech on Wieland, was delivered to members of the Anna Amalia Masonic Lodge on 18 February 1813.
36. See Chapter Eighteen, entitled "Aesthetic perception and the genesis of forms", and Chapter Twenty, entitled "Isis has no veils" (Hadot, 2006, pp. 211–229 and 247–261). Hadot finds in Nietzsche a similar (implied)

contrast between the Promethean and the Orphic in *The Gay Science*, Preface to the Second Edition, §4; and *The Birth of Tragedy*, §15 (p. 292).

## References

Assmann, J. (1992). *Das Kulturelle Gedächtnis: Schrift, Erinnerung und Politische Identität in frühen Hochkulturen*. Munich: Beck.

Athanassakis, A. N. (Ed.) (1977). *The Orphic Hymns*. [Society of Biblical Literature: Texts and Translations, 12; Graeco-Roman Religion Series, 4]. London: Scholars Press.

Bergstraesser, A. (1948). Die Geistesepochen der Geistesgechichte in Goethes Denken. *Monatshefte für deutschen Unterricht, deutsche Sprache und Literatur, 40*: 127–136.

Bernstock, J. E. (2006). *Under the Spell of Orpheus: The Persistence of a Myth in Twentieth-Century Art*. Carbondale, IL: Southern Illinois University Press.

Biedermann, F. von (Ed.) (1909–1911). *Goethes Gespräche*. 5 vols. Leipzig: Biedermann.

Bishop, P. (2012a). *Reading Goethe at Midlife: Ancient Wisdom, German Classicism, and Jung*. Texas: Spring.

Bishop, P. (Ed.) (2012b). *The Archaic: The Past in the Present*. London and New York: Routledge.

Blok, J. H. (1994). Quests for a scientific mythology: F. Creuzer and K. O. Müller on history and myth. *History and Theory, 33: 3* [Theme Issue 33: Proof and persuasion in history]: 26–52.

Blok, J. H. (1998). "Romantische Poesie, Naturphilosophie, Construktion der Geschichte": K. O. Müller's understanding of history and myth. In: W. M. Calder, III & R. Schlesier (Eds.), *Zwischen Rationalismus und Romantik: Karl Otfried Müller und die antike Kultur* (pp. 55–97). Hildesheim: Weidmann.

Borinski, K. (1910). Goethes "Urworte. Orphisch". *Philologus, 69*: 1–9.

Bos, C. Du (1949). *Der Weg zu Goethe*. C. Fischer (Trans.). Olten: Walter.

Bowden, H. (2010). *Mystery Cults in the Ancient World*. London: Thames & Hudson.

Burkert, W. (1980). Griechische Mythologie und die Geistesgeschichte der Moderne. In: O. Reverdin & B. Grange (Eds.), *Les études classiques aux XIXe et XXe siécles: Leur place dans l'histoire des idées* (pp. 159–199). Geneva: Fondation Hardt.

Bürger, C. (1977). *Der Ursprung der bürgerlichen Institution Kunst im höfischen Weimar*. Frankfurt: Suhrkamp.

Butler, E. M. (1935). *The Tyranny of Greece over Germany: A Study of the Influence exercised by Greek Art and Poetry over the Great German Writers of the*

*Eighteenth, Nineteenth and Twentieth Centuries*. Cambridge: Cambridge University Press.

Cameron, A. (2011). *The Last Pagans of Rome*. Oxford: Oxford University Press.

Cardew, A. (2012). The archaic and the sublimity of origins. In: P. Bishop (Ed.), *The Archaic: The Past in the Present* (pp. 93–146). London and New York: Routledge.

Carus, C. G. [no date]. *Neun Briefe über Landschaftsmalerei*. Villingen/Schwarzwald: Reichelt.

Cassirer, E. (1955). *The Philosophy of Symbolic Forms* [1923–1929], vol. 2, *Mythical Thought* [1925]. R. Manheim (Trans.). New Haven & London: Yale University Press.

Cosmopoulos, M. B. (Ed.) (2003). *Greek Mysteries: The Archaeology and Ritual of Ancient Greek Secret Cults*. London and New York: Routledge.

Creuzer, F. (1810–1812). *Symbolik und Mythologie der alten Völker, besonders der Griechen*, 4 vols. Leipzig: Leske; Heyer und Leske. Second edition, 4 vols. Leipzig and Darmstadt: Heyer und Leske, 1819–1821. Expanded with two additional volumes by Franz Joseph Mone. Third edition, Leipzig and Darmstadt: Leske, 1837–1842.

Dawson, T. (2000). The Orpheus complex. *Journal of Analytical Psychology, 45*: 245–66.

Dietze, W. (1977). Urworte, nicht sonderlich orphisch. *Goethe-Jahrbuch, 94*: 11–37.

Ebener, D. (Ed.) (1976). *Griechische Lyrik*. Berlin and Weimar: Aufbau-Verlag.

Eckermann, J. P. (1998). *Conversations of Goethe*. J. K. Moorhead (Ed.). J. Oxenford (Trans. [1930]). New York: Da Capo.

Eliade, M. (1982). *A History of Religious Ideas*. W. R. Trask (Trans.). Vol. 2. *From Gautama Buddha to the Triumph of Christianity*. Chicago and London: University of Chicago Press.

Fox, R. L. (1986; 2006). *Pagans and Christians*. London: Viking.

Frank, M. (1982). *Der kommende Gott: Vorlesungen über die Neue Mythologie, 1. Teil*. Frankfurt am Main: Suhrkamp.

Freeman, C. (2002). *The Closing of the Western Mind: The Rise of Faith and the Fall of Reason*. London: Heinemann.

Gildenhard, I. & Ruehl, M. (Eds.) (2003). *Out of Arcadia: Classics and Politics in Germany in the Age of Burckhardt, Nietzsche and Wilamowitz*. London: Institute of Classical Studies.

Goethe, J. W. (1887–1919). *Werke: Weimarer Ausgabe*. Ed. on behalf of Großherzogin Sophie von Sachsen. 4 parts, 133 vols in 143. Weimar: Böhlau.

Goethe, J. W. (1948–1960; 1981). *Werke: Hamburger Ausgabe*. E. Trunz (Ed.). 14 vols. Hamburg: Wegner; Munich: Beck.

Goethe, J. W. (1962–1967). *Briefe: Hamburger Ausgabe*. K. R. Mandelkow (Ed.). 4 vols. Hamburg: Wegner.

Goethe, J. W. (1986). Winckelmann and his age. In: *Essays on Art and Literature*. J. Gearey (Ed.), E. & E. H. von Nardroff & Ernest H. von Nardroff (Trans.). [Goethe Edition, vol. 3] (pp. 99–120). New York: Suhrkamp Publishers.

Grumach, E. (1949). *Goethe und die Antike*, 2 vols. Berlin: de Gruyter.

Guthrie, W. K. C. (1935). *Orpheus and Greek Religion: A Study of the Orphic Movement*. London: Methuen. Revised, 1952. Reprinted Princeton: Princeton University Press, 1993.

Hesiod (1982). *The Homeric Hymns and Homerica* (pp. 285–463). H. G. Evelyn-White (Trans.). Cambridge, MA: Harvard University Press.

Hadot, P. (2006). *The Veil of Isis: An Essay on the History of the Idea of Nature*. M. Chase (Trans.). Cambridge, MA: Belknap Press.

Hadot, P. (2008). *N'oublie pas de vivre: Goethe et la tradition des exercices spirituels*. Paris: Albin Michel.

Halbwachs, M. (1950). *La Mémoire collective*. Paris: Presses universitaires de France.

Hiebel, F. (1948). Goethe's *Maerchen* in the Light of Novalis. *Publications of the Modern Language Association*, *63*: 918–34.

Hiebel, F. (1961). *Goethe: Die Erhöhung des Menschen: Perspektiven einer morphologischen Lebensschau*. Munich and Berne: Francke.

Heine, H. (1976). *Die romantische Schule*. H. Weidmann (Ed.). Stuttgart: Reclam.

Hermann, G. (Ed.) (1805). *Orphica*. Leipzig: Fritsch. Reprinted Hildesheim: Olms, 1971.

Hermann, G. (1817). *Dissertatio de mythologia Graecorum antiquissima*, Leipzig: Staritz.

Hermann, G. (1819). *Ueber das Wesen und die Behandlung der Mythologie, ein Brief an Herrn Hofrat Creuzer*. Leipzig: Fleischer.

Hermann, G. & Creuzer, F. (1818). *Briefe über Homer und Hesodius vorzüglich über die Theogonie*. Heidelberg: Oswald.

Hesse, H. (1965). *Steppenwolf* [1927]. B. Creighton (Trans.). W. Sorrell (Revised trans.). Harmondsworth: Penguin.

Hoffmeister, J. (1930). Goethes "Urworte. Orphisch": Eine Interpretation. *Logos*, *19*: 173–212.

Howald, E. (1926). *Der Kampf um Creuzers Symbolik: Eine Auswahl von Dokumenten*. Tübingen: Mohr.

Jung, C. G. (1911–12). *Psychology of the Unconscious: A Study of the Transformations and Symbolisms of Libido: A Contribution to the History of the Evolution of Thought*. B. M. Hinkle (Trans. [1916]). London: Routledge, 1991.

Jung, C. G. (1911–12/1952). *Symbols of Transformation. C. W., 5* (2nd ed.). Princeton, NJ: Princeton University Press, 1967.

Jung, C. G. (1989). *Nietzsche's "Zarathustra": Notes of the Seminar given in 1934–1939*. J. L. Jarrett (Ed.). 2 vols. London: Routledge.

Jung, C. G. (1998). *Visions: Notes of the Seminar given in 1930–1934*. Claire Douglas (Ed.). 2 vols. London: Routledge.

Jung, C. G. (2009). *The Red Book: Liber Novus*. S. Shamdasani (Ed.). M. Kyburz, J. Peck, & S. Shamdasani (Trans.). New York & London: Norton.

Kerényi, C. (1937). Pythagoras und Orpheus. In: F. Altheim et al. *Aufsätze zur Geschichte der Antike und des Christentums* (pp. 16–51). Berlin: Die Runde.

Kerényi, C. (1950). *Pythagoras und Orpheus: Präludien zu einer zukünftigen Geschichte der Orphik und des Pythagoreismus*. Zurich: Rhein-Verlag.

Kerényi, K. (1967). *Die Eröffnung des Zugangs zum Mythos: Ein Lesebuch*. [Wege der Forschung, vol. 20]. Darmstadt: Wissenschaftliche Buchgesellschaft.

Kern, O. (1920). *Orpheus: Eine religionsgeschichtliche Untersuchung*. Berlin: Weidmann.

Kingsley, P. (1995). *Ancient Philosophy, Mystery, and Magic: Empedocles and Pythagorean Tradition*. Oxford: Clarendon Press.

Kunisch, H. (1991). Goethes Menschenbild. In: *Goethe-Studien* (pp. 9–83). Berlin: Duncker & Humblot.

Larson, J. (2007). *Ancient Greek Cults: A Guide*. New York and London: Routledge.

Lobeck, C. A. (1829). *Aglaophamus; sive, De theologiae mysticae Graecorum causis libri tres*, 2 vols. Königsberg: Bortntraeger. Republished as *Aglaophamus: Drei Bücher über die Grundlagen der Mysterienreligion der Griechen mit einer Sammlung der Fragmente der orphischen Dichter*. Darmstadt: Wissenschaftliche Buchgesellschaft, 1968.

Macrobius, (1969). *The Saturnalia*. P. V. Davies (Trans.). New York and London: Columbia University Press.

McGahey, R. (1994). *The Orphic Moment: Shaman to Poet-Thinker in Plato, Nietzsche, and Mallarmé*. Albany, NY: State University of New York Press.

Mead, G. R. S. (1896). *Orpheus*. London: Theosophical Publishing Society.

Müller, K. O. (1825). *Prolegomena zu einer wissenschaftlichen Mythologie: Mit einer antikritischen Zugabe*. Göttingen: Vandenhoeck & Ruprecht.

Müller, K. O. (1847–1848). *Kleine deutsche Schriften über Religion, Kunst, Sprache und Literatur, Leben und Geschichte des Althertums, nebst Erinnerungen aus dem Leben des Verfassers*. E. Müller (Ed.). 2 vols. Breslau: Max, 1847–1848.

Müller, C. [K.] O. (1908). *Lebensbild in Briefen an seine Eltern, mit dem Tagebuch seiner italienisch-griechischen Reise*. O. & E. Kern (Ed.). Berlin.

Novalis (1960–1968). *Schriften*. R. Samuel & P. Kluckhohn (Ed.). 5 vols. Stuttgart: Kohlhammer.

Schiller, F. (2004). *Sämtliche Gedichte und Balladen*. G. Kurscheidt (Ed.). Frankfurt am Main and Leipzig: Insel.

Schlegel, F. (1958–2006). *Kritische Friedrich-Schlegel-Ausgabe*. E. Behler [et al.] (Eds.). 15 vols. Paderborn, Munich, Vienna; Zurich: Schöningh; Thomas-Verlag.

Schmidt, J. (2002) *Metamorphosen der Antike in Goethes Werk*. [*Schriften der philosophisch-historischen Klasse der Heidelberger Akademie der Wissenschaften*, vol. 26]. Heidelberg: Winter.

Schmidt, J. (2006). *Goethes Altersgedicht "Urworte. Orphisch": Grenzerfahrung und Entgrenzung*. Heidelberg: Winter.

Schwinge, E. -R. (1986). *Goethe und die Poesie der Griechen*. [*Abhandlungen der geistes- und sozialwissenschaftlichen Klasse*, vol. 5]. Stuttgart: Steiner.

Sewell, E. (1961). *The Orphic Voice: Poetry and Natural History*. London: Routledge & Kegan Paul.

Spranger, E. (1967). *Goethe: Seine geistige Welt*. Tübingen: Wunderlich; Leins.

Stein, M. (2012). How to read *The Red Book* and why. *Journal of Analytical Psychology*, *57*: 280–298.

Strauss, W. A. (1971). *Descent and Return: The Orphic Theme in Modern Literature*. Cambridge, MA: Harvard University Press.

Taylor, T. (Trans.) (1896). *The Mystical Hymns of Orpheus: Translated from the Greek, and demonstrated to be the Invocations which were used in the Eleusinian Mysteries* [1787]. 2nd ed. London: Dobell; Reeves and Turner.

Trevelyan, H. (1941). *Goethe and the Greeks*. Cambridge: Cambridge University Press.

Uždavinys, A. (2008). *Philosophy as a Rite of Rebirth: From Ancient Egypt to Neoplatonism*. Westbury: Prometheus Trust.

Veyne, P. (1983). *Les Grecs ont-ils cru à leurs mythes?* Paris: Seuil.

Voss, J. H. (1824). *Antisymbolik*. 2 vols. Stuttgart: Metzler. Republished, 2 vols. Eschborn: Klotz, 1994.

West, M. L. (1983). *The Orphic Poems*. Oxford: Clarendon.

Wili, W. (1955). The Orphic mysteries and the Greek spirit [1944]. In: J. Campbell (Ed.). *The Mysteries* (pp. 64–92). R. Manheim (Trans.). London: Routledge & Kegan Paul.

Wipf, K. A. (1974). *Elpis: Betrachtungen zum Begriff der Hoffnung in Goethes Spätwerk*, Berne and Munich: Francke.

Wroe, A. (2011). *Orpheus: The Song of Life*. London: Cape.

Zoega, G. (1817). *Abhandlungen*. F. G. Welcker (Ed.). Göttingen: Dieterich.

CHAPTER TWELVE

# Orpheus, Eurydice, Blanchot: some thoughts on the nature of myth and literature*

*Lyndon Davies*

The myth of Orpheus and Eurydice has always been a staple of western European culture, a thematic and symbolic resource for writers, craftsmen, and artists in every age and genre. Even now, in our post-modern era, it's apparent that the tale has lost none of its fascination for creative practitioners; in fact, if anything, it's more popular than ever: poets, composers, painters, choreographers, dramatists—at the moment everyone seems to want a piece of Orpheus.

The more you look into it the more you begin to feel that maybe this particular yarn has been done to death, but then there always seems to be something more to say about it, and it always seems to have something more to say about us. As a story it covers so many of the human bases: love, joy, loss, fear, mourning, disintegration, and no doubt this is one of the reasons for its popularity. But at the same time it seems so apposite to the artist's situation, so congruent with the inner shape of the creative process, not least in its depiction of a consuming passion, a commitment potentially destructive in its intensity. At bottom you

*Some elements of this essay appeared in an earlier form as a text for collaborative presentation with artist Penny Hallas at the University of Essex Conference on "Myth, Literature, and the Unconscious", 2010, and as an article in *Poetry Wales* Vol. 47, No. 1.

could say it's a story about death, and about the search for reparation for that potentially catastrophic event. Reparation, that is, through the power of art. Orpheus loves Eurydice, who dies, so Orpheus goes down into Hades to rescue her. By the beauty of his song he charms the infernal gods into releasing her, then loses her again by defying the gods' injunction not to look back. Orpheus' search for reparation, beginning from the sense of an irreparable loss at the surface of things, echoes the human drama in a civilisation whose validating rituals have been drained of power. But it also parallels the artist's humiliating search for the true poem, the true painting, the truest song, the one that completes the chain of yearning, if only for the merest particle of a moment.

Of course, a myth is not merely an allegory, or a symbol; a myth is a kind of electron-swarm in which certain lines of force may at times become apparent, in terms of narrative or symbolic reference, different patterns in different ages and places in response to differing individual necessities. A myth is not even a myth: it's a melding of tale, countertale, strands, variants, interpretations; it's a swarm into which we read the lineaments of whom we need to be and what we need the world to be at that moment.

A myth, then, can perform the function of a diagram, delineating a pattern which we may (or may not) have intuited in the world, which without such a naming may never have been fully revealed in that form. Yet the power of myth, the hallucinatory vividness of its machinery, is such that we are often hypnotised by the insight it has granted, shackled to the perception it has interposed. You only have to think of the way Prometheus, both in his anguished and his triumphant aspects, haunted nineteenth-century western imaginations. He is there in the Romantic image of the inspired artist, the revolutionary rising up against his oppressor, the scientist challenging the divine order, the industrialist framed by satanic fire and smoke. In the twentieth century, notably, it was Oedipus, surging out from psychoanalytic insights, who held sway over whole areas of intellectual and not-so-intellectual endeavour, although this hegemony was contested from the start and ever more radically as the century developed. For instance, for Gilles Deleuze and Félix Guattari, writing in *Anti-Oedipus* (1972), the metaphor of the Oedipus complex, which supposedly delineates a psychical structure of desire and repression, itself becomes an agent of repression, as one of the categorical moulds which hierarchical systems of social control clamp over the free play of desire:

> If desire is repressed, this is not because it is desire for the mother and for the death of the father; on the contrary, desire becomes that only because it is repressed, it takes on that mask only under the reign of the repression that models the mask for it and plasters it on its face. (Deleuze & Guattari, 1972, p. 126)

This is myth as self-fulfilling prophecy, and, on the broad scale, perhaps, through a process of vulgarisation—equivalent say to the equating of existentialism with black polo-neck jumpers—as popular unexamined article of faith.

So a myth, from some angles, can be a diagram or a mould, but because in spite of ourselves we are still only superficially rational, it can also be called on when necessary to confer a shadowy kind of sacralisation on significant phenomena, including, for instance, constructed forms such as institutions, transformative social or natural events, and intrinsic drives. It simplifies us, it charms us, it encloses an aspect of ourselves that insists upon being contained, and at the same time it raises the dignifying sign of origin over what's contained, the validating odour of the authentic. For some the word "authentic", here, may mean nothing more than being saturated by centuries of use, or longing, or devotion. For others it will mean something altogether more absolute. Authenticity as a notion has as many nervous systems as it has histories, and I suspect that the same could be said of any myth: we cannot possess it except provisionally, since we cannot locate it in its original form but only ever as a retelling, a recasting of a recasting for each particular age. The idea of an originary myth, expressing some kind of pure connection with the ultimate grounds of existence, is itself, and can only ever be, a speculation or an article of faith. Myths mutate, proliferate, and the development of any one of them is contingent on a multitude of social and natural factors. Nevertheless, the pictorial energy of myth, coupled with the irresistible dream of the authentic, remains still, as it has done throughout history, one of the prime motivational drivers of human behaviour, both mischievous and sage.

Myth, then, is an endless temptation, but it is also woven into the fabric of the languages we use. Every time a poet sits down to write, a painter to paint, a musician to play, they find themselves enmeshed in a discourse that is already speaking through them and for them, nudged by an intention that relentlessly insists on the primacy of the structures of meaning that support it. It's a question of identity, belief, orientation, contract, all of which spring from a mythologising instinct. The art which succumbs to, or celebrates, these forces could be described as an art of accommodation, depending at worst for its justification on a virtuoso rearrangement of prefabricated elements, at best on a re-initiation and renewal of established forms. When the work aspires, though, under the pressure of whatever impulse, to anything but a consummation of the already accomplished, it requires at first something drastic of the practitioner, a kind of death-plunge through the interstices of the known. Orpheus, emblem of a ritualistic perfection of expression, reveals himself here as his own antagonist, plunging headlong through the surface of an intolerable familiarity to a labyrinth of uncertainty and estrangement hidden in the weave of it.

My own fascination with the myth of Orpheus and Eurydice derived from teenage readings of Rainer Maria Rilke's *Sonnets to Orpheus*, and his marvellously dramatic poem "Orpheus. Eurydice. Hermes". The hero of the sonnets is really the ex- or meta-catastrophic Orpheus: in his all-containing and transcendent song, life, death, past, future, joy, and despair are brought into a balanced and rather comforting relation. In the earlier poem, it's the moment of loss which is the crux, the moment in which Orpheus loses his beloved for the second and final time, although the dramatic moment is itself almost expunged by a shift of focus to the indifferent consciousness of a barely wakened Eurydice.

> And when, abruptly,
> the god had halted her and, with an anguished
> outcry, outspoke the words: He has turned round!—
> she took in nothing, and said softly: Who? (Rilke, 1979, p. 143)

This disturbingly blank figure out of whom all emotional relatedness has been sucked seems to chime with so many familiar childish nightmares. One might think, for instance, of the body-snatching alien, the assassin, the mother who abandons her own offspring (you). The responses to all these might be similar and contradictory: horror at a disjunction between world and self; despair at one's own powerlessness in the face of it; but also an illogical conviction that redemption might still be possible, if not in this case then in some perhaps related one, by means of audacious action: persuasion, translation, rendition from the lower place to the upper. There is something else, though, which shouldn't be forgotten, held in the gravitational field of such response-reflexes: the uncategorisable phenomena of the human moment, that species of dark matter without which awareness, development, space, and even consciousness itself would be unattainable and in fact inconceivable. On a personal note (and the personal here is very much to the point): as a writer witnessing my mother's journey into dementia, and wanting to find a way of writing about it, I was initially drawn to the time-honoured formula, with me in the role of Orpheus, and she as the Rilkean Eurydice figure. It quickly became apparent, however, that this could only ever be a provisional means of approaching a situation that cannot be generalised. Any inroads I was able to make into the subject came from determinedly writing away from the reductive syntax that this perspective seemed to impose on the productive heterogeneities of the material. But still, even this was a writing away "from". Every step into the unforeseen has to be a step from somewhere, and every human somewhere has either some kind of mythical affiliation, usually buried, or will have passed at some point through the body of a myth.

For Maurice Blanchot, the twentieth-century French literary theorist, novelist, and philosopher, myths can sometimes provide an allegorical starting point for thinking about the nature of literature. In Blanchot, these allegorical vehicles, like literature itself, like language, have to be encountered as never quite present in the utterance that encodes them, and therefore never quite fundamental or authoritative in the way myths are expected to be. A myth, like a poem, is an act occurring in language, in the here and now, although it alludes to a hypothetical origin, to a sign, also deferred, hypothesising an origin.

Through a series of intricately argued, paradox-reticulated improvisations, Blanchot pursues and enacts the maddeningly now-you-see-it now-you-don't reality of the work, the image, and the word. For him, death is central to the literary act: it's there in the way a word seems to call forth a being out of non-existence and at the same time to push it back into nothingness. The cadaver is one of his equivalents for an image—familiar and yet wholly other, uncanny, both solidly here and yet somehow elsewhere, unreachable.

In Blanchot's extraordinary essay *The Gaze of Orpheus* (Blanchot, 1981) Eurydice is the animate cadaver which Orpheus pursues by means of the self-surpassing magic of his song. Orpheus' journey beyond the song that holds everything in some kind of ecological balance is also a journey through song, to the point where it approaches an otherness that is beyond it, but also inside it. This is not a matter of choice—his grief at the loss of the beloved sends him there, that's to say the intensity of his connection with an object that is already beyond reach: Eurydice, the real, or whatever you want to call it. Eurydice is "the limit of what art can attain; concealed behind a name and covered by a veil, she is the profoundly dark point towards which art, desire, death and the night all seem to lead" (Blanchot, 1981, p. 99).

Orpheus' task as an artist is to descend to this ultimate point, to "bring it back into the daylight and in the daylight give it form, figure and reality" (Blanchot, 1981, p. 99). To create, in other words, a work. For Orpheus, however, in Blanchot's version, this is not enough: his explosive impulse of desire for the real woman in the fullness of the reality of her real death inevitably entails the wrecking of the figural work. In turning at the wrong moment, he glimpses the absolute loss of the desired one, the loss at the core of the loss he was bringing to the light in the shape of his own lament, as reparation, as harmonisation with a pre-existing system of harmony, that system of "order, rectitude, law" (ibid., p. 104), which embodies and encloses a theoretically sanctifying quality we are in the habit of referring to as the sacred, or, in another context, literature.

In fact, the impatience of the poet's turning, prefigured in the audacity of his descent to the essence of the night, is already a gaze into the destruction of the work he is so carefully leading towards the light: "It is inevitable that Orpheus defy the law forbidding him to 'turn around', because he has already violated it the moment he takes his first step towards the shadows" (Blanchot, 1981, p. 100). His impatience shatters the work, looking through it into the absolute inessentiality and futility of the form it had seemed to carry in it as sacralising essence. Blanchot refers to this moment as "the extreme moment of freedom, the moment in which he (Orpheus) frees himself of himself and—what is more important—frees the work of his concern, frees the sacred contained in the work" (ibid., p. 104). This moment of freedom is the moment of inspiration, but it is also the moment when everything is put at risk; the poem is no longer the poem intended, the sacred is released to itself, and is no longer contained by the pattern of the myth or the poem generated by the myth. It is not a question of yet another cycle of death and regeneration, of individuation or renewal of the self: it's a question of the infinite openness of the possible, the possibilities of the openness released by the negated work. The possibility of freedom, then, the continuing return to an openness inherent in language but which the mythologising drive is continually closing in on and shutting down, corralling into one normative system of understanding or another.

That notion of containment again. Of course, Orpheus, as the primal artist, is the one who sings the containers into being, but he is also the shatterer of all containers. You might think of that space into which he so recklessly hurls himself as the space the artist routinely turns away from, locked into the repetitive compulsions of voice, technique, sociality, patterns of perceiving and conceiving, whilst knowing that it's really the only space into which the releasing work, the one that's not already closed in on itself, can appear. Orpheus, in one guise, is the generator of harmony, charming and calming, that's to say colonising, the very rocks and animals and trees, not to mention the louche creatures of the underworld. But there is this other thing, this ripping open which the drive for the new vision, the new vocabulary, requires: a matter of violence, grief, and confusion, entailing the abandonment of appropriated territory. In this light Orpheus is the anguish of harmony; the suffocation of healing, individuation, and reparation; he (who could equally well be she—I am talking here about any artist) is the drive for the cleaving of what his song has already brought into balance and fruition, probably against the grain of his whole existence. He projects his longing for the harmony of reparation into the rending place where no reparation is possible. Two aspects are here, then, the Apollonian and the Dionysian, completely intertwined in the myths, symbolised after Orpheus' destruction (in some versions) by the placing of his head in a shrine to Dionysus and his lyre in a shrine to Apollo.

As Blanchot presents it, Orpheus is the artist who risks everything that's already sacred to his art, for the sake of an outcome that is beyond his own measure or comprehension. To risk the work means going to the bottom of that maddeningly familiar dream of articulated selfhood, to that loss glimpsed in the core of the bereavement which the work names and contains and repairs. Perhaps, Blanchot is saying, at this infinitely estranging and disabling moment, the artist who has had the courage to risk everything might discover a further kind of authenticity, one no longer pre-given in the mode of utterance: the song of the sacredness of the open, rather than of the sacredness of the already signed, sealed, and delivered.

Orpheus, of course, fails, but only in so far as the work itself exceeds him. The work remains in an impossible relation to the world in which he had hoped to plant and domesticate it. Eurydice is, after all, dead; she can't really enter the living world again except as an aspect of Orpheus' song. This is the meaning of the gods' injunction to Orpheus never to turn and look at Eurydice; as long as Orpheus has his attention turned to the composition which he is constructing, or at least performing, the composition in which Eurydice is present as a formal quality, he can believe in a certain kind of resurrection into the daylight realm. But his real passion for the real Eurydice, his impatience, his explosive moment of desire for the real woman in the reality of her real death, makes him turn, and at that moment his voice loses its enchanting power. The song, and the myth in the song, is invalidated: the work has taken into itself the futility and absolute inessentiality of the other death; Orpheus can no longer manipulate and maintain it by his power of enchantment. It's become a song in which Orpheus himself is entirely lost, a stranger in a strange land, defeated and torn to pieces.

It's at that moment rather than later, that he's torn to pieces, although Blanchot insists that this had already happened, at the moment he turned his face to the Underworld: "only in the song does Orpheus have power over Eurydice, but in the song Eurydice is also already lost and Orpheus himself is the scattered Orpheus, the 'infinitely dead'" (Blanchot, 1981, p. 101). His limbs are scattered to the four winds, the four corners of the earth and the cosmos, through all the elements of the periodic table. His limbs, his extremities already overlapped the boundaries of every sacred enclosure; from that point of view he was already in the most humiliating and irremediable state of dismemberment. He is torn to pieces: nothing remains of Orpheus but the head (I am straying from Blanchot here), still singing, while, as Milton so briskly puts it, in "Lycidas" (ll. 62—63), "His goary visage down the stream was sent, / Down the swift Hebrus to the Lesbian shore" (Milton, 1980, p. 42).

This ripping apart seems a pretty dire reward for Orpheus' immense and daring expenditure of effort, a terrible price to pay for a moment of vision, a moment of passionately unconcerned engagement. Artistically, however, you could argue that the point of rending symbolises the moment when the leap, the irresistible impulse of inspiration overwhelms the integrity of the willed mission, scatters the intentionality of the aesthetic commitment. In the myth, Orpheus' head just carries on singing, but this is a head which no longer has any control over where it's going or what happens to it; it's a head which has to go wherever the stream takes it, if it takes it anywhere. Perhaps the voice which still finds its locus there is a voice full of the openness of all song, and perhaps inside that openness is the new song, the releasing one, flowing down into it out of the future, the one whose existence hadn't even been suspected. Or it may be that there is nothing left in that voice but futility and hopelessness and emptiness, or some kind of agonising and disastrous challenge. That's the risk you take when you turn away from the comfortingly beckoning pavilions of the daylight world.

You could say that Blanchot's essay depicts myth not simply as the source of narratives about the world, but as a source within a source, or more accurately, as a sourcelessnes within a source. Myth here slips below the order of functionality, below the schematic and the symbolic, is encountered as an unforeseen eruption into the patternings of discourse, not as an archetype erupting, but as a potentiality disrupting even the archetypal reflex of the ordering artist, the interpreting intellect. The work of art may be one of the paths to this encounter, although it can only occur in the disintegration of the work of art and the chain of meaning. This is where the self meets itself in the moment before its ordering into systems of knowledge and sociality—the utterly personal collision with a generative estrangement hidden in the weave of its own being, but always within language, never beyond it.

Of course there is no escaping the fact that every use of myth has political and social implications. The Orpheus myths, for instance, are significantly, and from some viewpoints problematically, gendered, as likewise Blanchot's appropriation of them. It's certainly true that in the myth it's the male figure who represents the striving creative power, and the female who is the receptive and passive goal of that phallic energy. But it seems to me that the essay exceeds such a reading, by refusing to concede a space where the essentialising discourses it makes use of, as all language must, can arrive at a (theoretically) definitive configuration. It's very possible to approach it as a dramatic reading of the irresolvable (and perhaps multiple) nature of any artist—male, female or neuter—in the crisis of an abandonment to the creative act. It could be argued, in other words that, as Blanchot sees it, Orpheus and Eurydice are aspects of each other, separate and therefore guilty and ripe for punishment, but pointing out beyond that to a place where the simple binary categorisations no longer apply.

In the essay, the moment of the gaze is the moment when Eurydice abruptly ceases to be the sanctifier of Orpheus' prowess as culturally validated form-giver and phallic cause. His imaginary, colonising version of the beloved gives way before the vision which reveals the "welcoming intimacy" of the night of which she is both centre and limit (Blanchot, 1981, p. 99), and in which his wounded masculine passion is to receive its blessing and renovation, to be an untenable illusion. Orpheus is torn apart, castrated. Stripped of his physical and metaphorical regalia by this revelation, he passes under the dismantling judgment of the real and is delivered up to a destiny which is beyond the tyrannies of any form of totalising discourse, a destiny in fact in which all categories are suspended, perhaps fruitfully (though, it has to be admitted, perhaps not). This is a space and a moment towards which, it seems to me, Blanchot's use of the word "authenticity" might gesture (ibid., p. 102).

Orpheus' body has been scattered, his limbs and his organs can no longer fulfil their role as functionaries of an invasive and appropriative phallic principle; they are dispersed, subject to the vagaries of localised fluxations of energy and desire. Deleuze and Guattari spring to mind again here, in particular their notion of the "body without organs/corps-sans-organes", borrowed from the French poet, Antonin Artaud, who coined it in a 1947 script for radio—*Pour en finir avec le jugement de Dieu* (Artaud, 2003). The body without organs, as discussed in *Anti-Oedipus* (Deleuze & Guattari, 1972), might be thought of as a deterritorialised, unstratified state of existence, in which energy flows unchecked by prescriptive mapping or by the imposition, as you might say, of a controlling mythos. Ian Davidson describes it as "an idea of the body capable of providing both freedom from desire and freedom of desire" (Davidson, 2007, p. 56). It might be visible where the self-replicating system of an organism breaks down, is repudiated, or superseded; or in the stutterings and misfirings of cybernetic automatisms and structures (bodies) of knowledge. In other words it's already present in any structure or process as the condition which that structure or process strives both to negate and to realise; it is an impossible but also inescapable condition of freedom, against which an organism strives to define itself and into which it endlessly fears and desires to be consumed.

> The body without organs is not the proof of an original nothingness, nor is it what remains of a lost totality. Above all, it is not a projection; it has nothing whatsoever to do with the body itself, or with an image of the body. It is the body without an image. (Deleuze & Guattari, 1972, p. 9)

The body without organs, then, is a kind of mythless myth, a myth which is any myth and no myth. It is, anyway, a locution with which you can begin to speak about locutions, shape, image, as well as of the silences around and inside any possible locution. A kind of baseline or "recording surface" on which provisional existences enunciate themselves over and against the ceaseless, mechanistic desiring/producing processes of life.

> Something on the order of a *subject* can be discerned on the recording surface. It is a strange subject, however, with no fixed identity, wandering about over the body without organs, but always remaining peripheral to the desiring-machines, being defined by the share of the product it takes for itself, garnering here, there, and everywhere a reward in the form of a becoming or an avatar, being born of the states that it consumes and being reborn with each new state. (Deleuze & Guattari, 1972, p. 17)

In Blanchot, what we're faced with are organs without a body, but he insists, as we know, that this scattering, this disempowering, is an event which has already taken place within the destiny of the song, that's to say within the body of the work which, although the event robs it of its reparative force, remains as a nominal horizon:

> [Orpheus] loses Eurydice because he desires her beyond the measured limits of the song, and he loses himself too, but this desire, and Eurydice lost, and Orpheus scattered are necessary to the song, just as the ordeal of eternal worklessness is necessary to the work. (Blanchot, 1981, p. 101)

In the work, at the crucial juncture of Orpheus' turning, there is, for a moment, an opening up into a space of absolute freedom from (and, perhaps dangerously, of) the directional and containing forces of desire, power, history, and the work itself must pass through and subsume this if it is to move beyond its measured limits. This is an event which any true artist or writer may endure again and again in the course of a creative engagement, although the extent to which it changes the destiny of a particular song depends on the tenacity of a commitment to pre-established contracts, both aesthetic and social.

Blanchot's essay is about writing, but it's about more than that: it places the act of writing at the centre of a vital and terrible existential crux. What the essay names and dramatises is the moment when process gives way to the paradigm-overturning jolt of inspiration. The question is what do you do with that jolt of vision, assuming that you cannot turn your back on it again? And if you could turn your back, would that save you, or merely doom you at that point to an inauthentic relation to your own art? Even more so, what does the world do with that blast of disruptive energy which comes belching out at it from the mouth of the underworld?

One plausible way of being a writer is to think of oneself as protector of the myths. It's a matter of sacralising the forms of the known, reconfiguring and refining the norms of a given culture, giving the culture back to itself, renewing its vision of itself. This writer has his or her eyes turned to the utterance that is in a sense already formed, structured according to established, mythically grounded parameters: he or she lures, as Blanchot suggests, the fecundity of the depths by the perfection of this utterance, investing it in this way with significance and substance. To put it another way, he or she invokes the validation of a muse; that's to say, some form of transcendent principle. But a muse exists only as a function within an utterance, and can retain its meta-literary power only in so far as the writer persists in keeping his or her eyes averted. To turn directly to it would be to have to acknowledge that there is a void where the validating principle had seemed to be, an emptiness where the singer's magic is both absent and inapplicable, where, in a sense language is torn apart and has to begin again from scratch. Blanchot talks elsewhere of the way a word, an image, shuts out—in the act of distancing—its referent at the very point it calls it forth, or is called forth by it (1982, p. 80). We could infer from this that the referent can only be sustained within the word by a willed inattention to the obliteration which has occurred at the moment of its naming. We could think of Orpheus as the word and Eurydice as the referent the word names and seeks to integrate into itself, since, after all, Orpheus is nothing without his beloved. To turn back and look into the absence of the referent is to feel language as knowledge quivering on the edge of the unspeakable, to render what remains of language infinitely delicate and questionable and strange.

At this point another kind of writer comes into being, and, perhaps at some stage in the process of creation, every writer, however fleetingly, is that other kind of writer; every writer worthy of the name anyway. Perhaps it's just a question of what you do with the knowledge; how many or how few powerful reasons you have for forgetting, or for putting the broken pieces together again, and whether indeed you imagine such a restitution even to be possible.

Of course a work also has to be read, and a work always exceeds the context the readers bring to it, and the understanding they impose on it, before or after the fact. Criticism and scholarship are continually opening new doors into a work of art, providing new tools with which to explore it, but this in no way absolves readers from the necessity of risking their own unauthorised and undirected encounter with it.

You could perhaps think of the critic as the one who receives the gift of the work and oversees its distribution into the channels of social discourse. In *The Prodigal Sign*, an exploration of the nature of literature, language, and criticism, built around the biblical parable of the Prodigal Son, Kevin Mills writes:

> Like parable, criticism is always exchange, both because it involves dialogue and because it transports meanings between the creative, cultural or literary text and the analytical discourse: it trades its reading for writing. It is also economic in that it operates as such an exchange and in that it carries it texts to market. (Mills, 2009, p. 32)

So, in certain instances you might think that the critic socialises the work, or helps to, by controlling its integration into a system of organised exchange and valuation. There is nothing in this to prevent our thinking of the critic as a figure as heroic in his own way as Orpheus, descending into the underworld of the text with a view to wrenching some kind of transferable essence from it. Such a reader is open to the possibility of revelation but, for the critic, any revelation has to be defended against the bottomless non-referentiality of its own nature, by means of a turning away towards the goal of the critical venture. The goal is always, by fair means or foul, to draw the unruly energies of the text into something approaching resolution and stasis, even where this is understood as provisional, matter for further dialogue and exchange.

Later in *The Prodigal Sign* Mills discusses how a critical reading might differ from the kind of reading people normally engage in:

> Reading is just letting the text happen to you, while ideology, memory, imagination and genes make the words dance. A *reading*

> is the choreographic text: the construction of a score or diagram, an anatomising and a selection, a focusing and an excision. (Mills, 2009, p. 132)

He suggests that an initial approach to a text with a critical purpose in mind will probably hover between the two, with the critical score emerging out of the interplay—or more likely wrestled out of it—smoothing out the discontinuities induced by the everyday demands of existence on the reader, who is always, after all, a human being with a personal and professional life outside of the text in question.

I find this persuasive, full of fascinating implications, but it also seems to beg (or deliberately to provoke) an interesting question: namely, to what degree can we even begin to speak of a text simply "happening" to us? Can readers ever be anything less than active, over their ears in the purpose-driven business of their personal existence, both prior to and during their descent into and ascent out of the text, always actively and passionately pursuing, ordering, projecting what they need in there, or engaging with what they cannot avoid? Surely, without this there would be no "work" to happen, just an imbroglio of disconnected marks? From this angle, reading is always a kind of choreographic preparation for a future writing, for a future text which is already gathering, adjusting, remembering, giving back to the reader the experience they're in the process of undergoing. In which case a critical reading could no longer be envisioned as the active surpassing of a passivity, but more as a specialised extension of this devotional, existential struggle to possess meaning. Of course, no reader can be active without simultaneously enduring the passivity of the meaning that is lost, the passivity of the absence which drives the great motor of engagement, in the same way as Blanchot talks of how the impatience of the artist comes out of the endless patience which endures it.

So what is the work? The work is nothing less than the (ultimately ungraspable) totality of our human encounter with it. But in a critical universe founded on the primacy of hermeneutic or structural reduction, it seems to me it's vital to maintain our commitment to the irreducibly personal here-and-now of the encounter. There may be some who imagine that the truth about an artwork can only be the truth when we have put it behind us and made certain statements about it, from the outside, as if it was an object "over there", or "down there" in the past. But I'm suggesting that we can never actually get outside the immediacy of our autobiographical engagement with that object, and that it may only be temporarily useful to imagine that we can. It's there in the colour and the odour of the thing, driving our emotional responses, and after that, no doubt, the interpretative choices that we make. Removing it from our equations can only falsify those equations and the equations that come after them.

Eurydice, for instance—what or who is Eurydice? Many things, of course, both abstract and highly personal. She is the lover, yes, but she is also the assassin, the alien, the parent who abandons his or her own child. For me, as I've said, she carries in her something of the impress of the peculiarly gathering absence of my own mother. Beyond that, resemblance itself becomes non-resemblance. For Orpheus, Eurydice is not simply a lost referent for the word he speaks; she is, herself, turning into a sign without referent, a sign which is no more and no less than its own referent, whose self-enclosure implies a presence, but without containing it: the presence is elsewhere. The presence and the meaning of Eurydice, like the work itself, depends on the other going down into the shadows and bringing it back to the surface constantly: an activity repeatedly doomed to failure. A failure, certainly—Orpheus always fails, but his failure is itself a method, a reason and a shareable value.

To turn back to Blanchot again, it's obvious that however determinedly I attempt to anatomise his essay, it still remains as the undiscovered country, the unknown domain which I myself must pass through, from term to term, syllable to syllable: a work rather than just a trophy, say, or a tomb.

The essay, then, cannot be got. That's normal. It cannot ultimately be put to bed. In this it is like any other work of literature, but more starkly perhaps because it situates itself at the most originary point of origins—myth—just precisely at that point where the reader would expect to implant himself with a view to taking the measure of the work, but which reveals itself, by revealing itself, to be a point of emptiness, empty even of emptiness. For instance, what are we to do with those worryingly grand terms Blanchot flourishes in *The Gaze of Orpheus*, terms such as "inspiration", "the day", "the sacred", "authenticity", without ever really beginning to define what he means by them? We could speculate that, outside of the operative processes of the text in which they are embedded, these terms are meaningless and, in so far as they position themselves at the very root of signification, very possibly absurd, so that the text alone, in relation to other texts—especially his own—gives form to them as they give form and provisional legibility to the text. Blanchot uses these terms almost like ritual objects, which, without necessarily being magical themselves, demarcate a point of entry for powers invoked by the ritual, powers rooted in a transcendent non-relative zone of being. In the literature of "the day" (Blanchot, 1981, p. 100), the ritual objects—that's to say, words—are veiled by familiarity, the immediacy of their connection to the transcendent, their identity with it, simply taken as read, an unconscious function of signification within language. Blanchot, however, presents these objects in all the starkness of their objectivity, as well as in the mysteriousness of their ungraspable import, so that the impression of an oracular fullness is offset by the intrinsically postponed nature of a thing that exists only in relation to other things. So, finally, all we can do at the moment of our encounter with such terms is to encounter them, and in doing so we come face to face with ourselves, with our own voids and solids, face to face with our own viscera as well as our own conceptual, emotional and phantasmal paraphernalia.

Myth permeates the world and is ingrained into our culture, our gestures, our rhythms, and our very modes of feeling and perceiving. There is no hiding from the mythical transference. To attempt to do so would be like trying to step outside your own skin. Wherever the madness or peace of love is, there is myth; wherever social or artistic or political engagement is, there is myth. It's there in the everyday reification of terms such as subject and object, self and other, man and woman, citizen and state, teacher and pupil, poet and reader—reductions which are at the root of social interaction—with all the rigidifying effects of such objectifications, but also with all the possible commencements that they give rise to.

Above all, literature is stuffed with it, and Blanchot's explorations of the nature of a literary act acknowledge and enact this fact time and again by commencing from the very heart of myth. To write about writing, one must already be writing, swimming through the stuff of which writing is made. One must already be compromised, that's to say, enmeshed in the already spoken, in order to approach the unspoken, the unimagined formulation. Myth saturates and enfolds literature both as material and horizon against which literary actions can be perceived and measured, but it also persists, as Blanchot seems to imply, as a force welling up from within the act itself, breaking open the fixed forms and perhaps opening the doors to new and revivifying ones. Of course, doors do not always open into positive spaces, and not everyone will want to step through when invited, but if literature is going to carry on developing and, in fact, living, there must always be some who do, who take the risk on offer.

## References

Artaud, A. (2003). *Pour en finir avec le jugement de Dieu*. Paris: Gallimard.

Blanchot, M. (1981). *The Gaze of Orpheus and Other Literary Essays*. P. A. Sitney (Ed.). Lydia Davis (Trans.). New York: Station Hill.

Davidson, I. (2007). *Ideas of Space in Contemporary Poetry*. London: Palgrave Macmillan.

Deleuze, G. & Guattari, F. (1972). *Anti-Oedipus*. Robert Hurley, M. Seem, & H. R. Lane (Trans.). London: Continuum.

Mills, K. (2009). *The Prodigal Sign*. Eastbourne: Sussex Academic Press.

Milton, J. (1980). "Lycidas". In: *John Milton: The Complete Poems* (pp. 42–46). B. A. Wright (Ed.). London: Dent.

Rilke, R. M. (1970). *Sonnets to Orpheus*. M. D. H. Norton (Trans.). New York: Norton.

Rilke, R. M. (1979). "Orpheus. Eurydice. Hermes". In: *New Poems* (pp. 142–147). J. B. Leishman (Trans.). London: Hogarth.

# INDEX

Printed in Great Britain
by Amazon

20853379R00147